C Programmer's Library

Jack J. Purdum
Timothy C. Leslie
Alan L. Stegemoller

Que Corporation
Indianapolis

Library of Congress Catalog No.: LC 83-62490

ISBN 0-88022-048-1

88 87 86 85 84   8 7 6 5 4 3 2 1

Interpretation of the printing code: the rightmost double-digit number is the year of the book's printing; the rightmost single-digit number, the number of the book's printing. For example, a printing code of 83-4 shows that the fourth printing of the book occurred in 1983.

About the Authors

Jack J. Purdum

Dr. Purdum received his B.A. degree from Muskingum College and M.A. and Ph.D. degrees from Ohio State University. He is currently Associate Professor of Economics at Butler University, where he teaches both computer programming and economics courses. Dr. Purdum has received many teaching and research awards, including a National Science Foundation grant to study microcomputers in education. He has published a number of professional articles; a BASIC programming text; and magazine articles in *Byte, Personal Computing,* and *Interface Age.* He is also the author of the best seller, *C Programming Guide,* published by Que Corporation. Dr. Purdum is president of Ecosoft, Inc., a software house that specializes in microcomputer software.

Timothy C. Leslie

Mr. Leslie studied math and physics at Indiana University before becoming a system analyst in the U.S. Army in 1970. From 1974 to 1978 he *was* the Army's Chief Data Processing Branch in Berlin. Later, as a civilian, he was the system analyst for Ecocardiology with Microsonics, Inc., from 1981 to 1982. Currently, Mr. Leslie is Director of Software Development for Ecosoft, Inc.

Alan L. Stegemoller

Mr. Stegemoller received his B.S. degree in Electrical Engineering from Purdue University in 1975. From 1978 to 1983 he worked for Digilog Dynamics, Inc., and served as senior engineer in the field of hardware and software design for Medical Image Processing Systems. Currently, he is self-employed as a consulting engineer for Microsonics, Inc., a manufacturer of medical imaging hardware, and for Ecosoft, Inc. Mr. Stegemoller is coauthor of Ecosoft's Eco-C C compiler.

Editorial Director
David F. Noble, Ph.D.

Editors
Diane F. Brown, M.A.
Pamela Fullerton
Virginia D. Noble, M.L.S.

Managing Editor
Paul Mangin

Technical Editor
Chris DeVoney

Technical Consultants
Greg Dunn
James Fleming, Ph.D.

Dedication

In fond memory of my mother,
Janette B. Purdum.

J. J. P.

To my parents, Carl and Emily Leslie.

T. C. L.

To my parents, Henry and Ethel Stegemoller.

A. L. S.

Table of Contents

Foreword

The *C Programmer's Library* is like two books in one. The first is a textbook, making suggestions and showing examples on designing and writing functions for your personal C library. This book demonstrates several ways to analyze and attack problems that confront C programmers daily or weekly. The second book contains the functions and programs. This book represents the first effort by a publisher to include extensive and highly useful C source code in book form.

In writing this book, the authors noted two facts about the C language. The core of C is portable and can be easily implemented on a variety of processors under various operating systems. This portability of C accounts for its increasing popularity. However, the C language is incomplete without an operating system. C is I/O-less and must execute under the shell of an operating system. This requires that the "standard library" be customized for each operating system.

After witnessing the testing of the code in this book on twelve different C compilers running under CP/M®, MS-DOS, Apple® DOS, QNX™, and UNIX™ environments, I am convinced that the C standard library is not so standard, nor has the C language been fully standardized. The evident truth is that not all the functions and programs presented in this book will work on many C compilers without modifications.

To compile the functions and programs in this book, you will need a C compiler that meets or exceeds UNIX Version 7 specifications. This means that the compiler must handle int, char, long, struct, and union data types; typedef; and the ifndef preprocessor macro. The float and double data types are not used in this book, although the sorting programs presented in Chapter 2 will work with `float` and `double`.

In addition, the functions presented in Chapter 5 (ISAM) and the book cataloger program in Chapter 6 make extensive use of `setjmp()` and `longjmp()` functions. These functions must be available in your C compiler for the routines in these chapters to compile and run successfully.

Possibly, a compiler may meet these specifications and yet be unable to compile the functions and programs in this book. Causes may be insufficient RAM memory, the compiler's lack of symbol or expression table space, or nonstandard functions in the "standard library"—that is, standard library functions that do not conform to Version 7 specifications.

All functions and programs were written, tested, and validated on the Eco-C compiler. All functions and programs, except those presented in Chapter 3, were tested and validated under the Portable C Compiler (`pcc`) under the UNIX operating system.

A brief word about the programs is necessary. Chapter 2 presents three sorting functions and an example disk-sorting program. Chapter 3 provides a terminal code handler and installation program. Presented in Chapter 5 is a fully functional index sequential access manager (ISAM). Chapter 6 contains a book-cataloging program that uses the ISAM functions.

The terminal handler and installation program was designed for programs running the CP/M and MS-DOS operating systems. Some CP/M and MS-DOS computers have limited disk storage capacity. Many of these machines use floppy disks. Programmers try to minimize the number of files associated with a program so that the user can easily copy the programs from one diskette to another. For these reasons the terminal installer modifies the object code; this practice is acceptable and even desirable in the CP/M and MS-DOS worlds but loathed by the UNIX programmer.

In the UNIX world, the `termcap` and `curses` libraries for terminal handling are used. The functions and programs presented in Chapter 3 are inapplicable to the UNIX environment. This is the reason the code in Chapter 3 was not validated on `pcc`.

xii

The book cataloger in Chapter 6 required modification to compile and execute under pcc. The cataloger, which uses the terminal-handling routines in Chapter 3, was rewritten with the termcap and curses functions and was successfully compiled and validated. However, this modified version of the book cataloger is not presented in this book.

In Chapter 5 the ISAM functions have been heavily casted to minimize the potential conflicts between computers using different CPUs. This casting, unnecessary for 8-bit CPUs, was critical to ensure that the code would function properly with C compilers on 16-bit and 32-bit CPU computers.

Because of the differences among the CP/M, MS-DOS, and UNIX environments and corresponding C compilers, editor's notes appear at the beginning of several chapters to warn of the machine- or compiler-specific issues that must be addressed for the various compilers and operating systems.

Note that the data files produced by these programs are not guaranteed to be portable. This problem is CPU-specific. For example, some CPUs store integers in a low-byte, high-byte sequence, whereas other CPUs store integers in a high-byte, low-byte sequence.

Appendix E summarizes the modifications needed to make the functions and programs work in the UNIX environment.

Appendix F provides the results of the tests on the various CP/M and MS-DOS C compilers. This appendix also summarizes what modifications may be necessary to run the programs with other C compilers.

I wish to thank Greg Dunn, who tested the functions and programs on various C compilers running under Apple DOS, CP/M, and MS-DOS; and Jim Fleming, who validated the functions and programs under UNIX and provided helpful insights on portable programming.

For increased legibility, the functions, programs, examples, C keywords, and file names are set in a font called Digital. This font is reproduced below.

```
ABCDEFGHIJKLMNOPQRSTUVWXYZ
abcdefghijklmnopqrstuvwxyz
0123456789
!@#$%^&*()+~|
-=`\[]:;'<>",.?/{}
```

A ruler line is provided below to help you count the spaces in a program line.

```
         0         1         1         2         2         3         3         4         4         5         5
12345678901234567890123456789012345678901234567890
```

Chris DeVoney

Preface

There has been a growing interest in C in the past few years; we need not repeat its strong points here. This interest is evidenced by an increasing number of introductory books on C. Such books, by necessity, must use fairly simple coding examples to teach any given concept. Our experience is that the C programmers who have mastered the first level of the language view it as a high-performance race car: they know the power is there, but they haven't yet gained the driving experience to use it to its full potential. Part of this lack of experience is that relatively little published material is commercially available that presents a view of C based on more sophisticated examples and techniques designed to teach the awesome power that C offers.

This book is designed for the C programmer who is comfortable with the general structure of C but wants to tap the second level of power that C offers. The book has three primary sections. The first is designed to teach the reader to view the C data types in a more formal manner. This is crucial for understanding complex data structures. The second section draws on material in the first section to present a general methodology for library development. The third section provides coding examples to reinforce your understanding of earlier topics that complement your C library. Although numerous routines and programs are presented throughout the text, they should not be viewed as ends in themselves.

The entire source code presented in this book is available on magnetic media. Cursor functions and the ISAM library are broken into succinct modules for easier editing and implementation. Additionally, the delete function for ISAM is included. This media form of the source code, which will save the programmer hours of typing and debugging, is available directly from Que for $124.95.

Many people have contributed to this text in a variety of ways. We would especially like to recognize Chris DeVoney, who served as technical editor of the project; Kim Brand for his (often comical) comments on earlier drafts of the manuscript; Jim Fleming and Greg Dunn for testing the code under a variety of C compilers and operating system environments; about three dozen people at Que, who contributed in various ways to the book; and to Bill Burton for no particular reason.

Jack Purdum
Tim Leslie
Alan Stegemoller

Indianapolis, 1984

0

Laying the Groundwork

> Give a man a fish, and you feed him for a day. Teach a man to fish, and you feed him for a lifetime.
>
> *— Chinese Proverb*

Writing a program in C is fairly straightforward. Most programmers begin with an outline of the task to be performed. This outline is usually written in *pseudocode,* which is an imaginary, English-like language with some of the underlying syntax of C. (For a more complete discussion of pseudocode, see Chapter 3 of Que's *C Programming Guide*.) If properly done, the pseudocode outline should identify all the C functions needed in the program.

Usually, most of the C functions a program requires are already part of your standard C library. Although the word *standard* may suggest that all function libraries are the same, they are not (*C Programming Guide,* Chapter 1).

Some C compilers have a few dozen library functions, whereas others have more than a hundred. To make matters worse, each compiler implementer is free to assign different names to library functions that perform identical tasks.

Even if all libraries were identical, each new program requires the writing of one or more new functions. The number of new functions varies with the nature of the program being developed and the comprehensiveness of the function library.

When an unusual programming task arises, the standard library probably will not contain all the functions needed to complete the task. For example, the program may require sampling data from a specific instrument, manipulating the data in some way, then controlling a set of valves based on the data. No library is so complete that new functions will never need to be written. The more comprehensive your library, however, the fewer new functions you will have to write for a given program.

Two factors that affect the comprehensiveness of your library are the number and the generality of the functions. The greater the number of functions, the greater is the probability that a needed function is already available. One advantage of C is that new functions written for use in a program can be placed in the library for future use. Consequently, your library can grow along with your programming experience.

The term *generality* reflects the ability of a given library function to cope with a changing program environment. For example, suppose that you are writing a sort program. Do you write the function to handle only a given data type (for example, integers), or, more generally, to sort any data type? (Chapter 2 presents a detailed discussion of generality.)

Library functions that are not written in a generalized form suffer from one major limitation: they must be changed as the program environment changes. A generalized function, on the other hand, is written only once. The larger and more generalized your library of C functions, the easier and more efficient becomes your program development.

The Purpose of This Book

This book presents suggestions for the development of generalized library functions. Taking the time to write generalized functions is more difficult than using the "quick and dirty" approach to writing functions. Generalized functions require more thought and frequently use more complex data types and programming techniques. The time and effort invested in writing these functions, however, are definitely worthwhile.

Many function examples provided in this book will be useful additions to your library, but the book does not include all the library functions you will ever need. In fact, you could not possibly list all of the C functions you will be needing in the next few years, because software development is too dynamic for accurate forecasting of future requirements.

Although many of the functions presented in this text are helpful, they are not ends in themselves, but teaching tools. For example, most chapters conclude with a program illustrating the major points that have been made. In some cases, a less than optimal example is used because it demonstrates the points more clearly than an alternative program would. As a general rule, however, the functions in the sample program are very efficient.

To avoid overburdening the discussions, we have not included in the chapters detailed analyses of the underlying algorithms. For example, Chapter 2 contains several sorting algorithms. Since many good books are available just on sorting algorithms, this book cannot hope to do justice to the subject. In many cases, references are included to appropriate sources for further investigation by the interested reader.

The examples in this book provide a framework for discussing three aspects of library and program development: (1) analysis, (2) generalization, and (3) taking full advantage of the power of C.

Analysis

Suppose that you are teaching a beginning programming course and have just asked each member of the class to write a program that will sort 100 numbers in ascending order. Then you announce that the computer lab is open for those students who want to work on their programs. If our experience is any indication, 90 percent of the students will rush out of the class, go to the lab, and immediately start entering source code for their programs into the computers.

These students are not programming; they are *bugging*. They will spend ten minutes bugging and another hour *debugging* (that is, correcting) the mess they will make in the first ten minutes.

It is the other 10 percent of the class that makes teaching worthwhile. These students remain in the room with paper and pencil and analyze the problem for ten to fifteen minutes. They then stroll into the lab (does analysis breed confidence?) and have their programs running in another fifteen minutes. This scenario happens semester after semester.

Analysis is the first step in writing any program. Therefore, analyzing a programming problem is a discipline that must be learned, regardless of the language used. Formulating a formal statement, or definition, of the task is the most difficult aspect of analysis.

Once the task has been analyzed and formally stated, the next step is to develop an algorithm for the program. After the algorithm is specified, it should be written out in pseudocode. Once this has been done, any new functions that will be needed should become obvious. The primary purpose of analysis is *to identify any new functions that need to be written*. Analysis of a given programming problem should lead you directly to its solution.

Generalization

After a new function has been identified, a programmer is often tempted to begin immediately to write the source code for the function. At this point, the function exists as a concept in your mind, but one that still tends to be a little "fuzzy." It's almost as if you want to rush into coding the function before you forget it. If you feel this way, then you haven't thought about the function long enough.

We all have been guilty of not giving enough thought to functions once they have been identified. Often, too little time is devoted to defining the function in concrete terms. However, it is precisely here that an investment of time can pay off handsomely in the future.

Writing in C is different from writing in most other languages because of C's intensive use of library routines. To help you develop a "feel" for the concept of generalization, you must learn to think in terms of writing functions for your *library* and not for a given program. Define functions so that they are "portable" to future programming tasks. These goals can best be achieved through generalization.

Refer again to the previous classroom example. If you were to look at the code written by the anxious 90 percent of the class, you would probably find that many of the students used a loop with the terminating value of 100 coded in as a constant. The remaining 10 percent of the class probably used a symbolic constant (for example, #define MAX 100) or an input routine for the terminating value of the loop. This latter group generalized their programs so that they can be run with little or no modification for a different number of data points. These class members are the "B" students.

The "A" students carry generalization a step further. In their analysis (including the design of the algorithm and pseudocode outline), they recognize that a generalized sort routine should be able to cope with all data types, not just integers. Superior students also recognize that all sort algorithms involve a comparison and a swap of the data—both of which are data dependent. In other words, the compare and swap routines must be written for a specific data type. The actual sorting of the data, however, can be generalized to handle any data type. As a result, "A" students will write three functions: (1) a generalized sort function, (2) a data-specific compare function, and (3) a data-specific swap function.

Note that all three functions are candidates for inclusion in the library. For example, suppose that the functions are a generalized bubble sort function, an integer-compare function, and an integer-swap function. If the student now wants to sort integer data with a Shell sort, the student only needs to write a generalized Shell sort function. The existing compare and swap functions do not have to be rewritten. (See Chapter 2 for more information on Shell sorting.)

Most students, however, bury the swap and compare elements of the sort in the sort routine itself. If you ask them to write a bubble sort, a Shell sort, and a quick sort, you will usually find three distinct swap and compare routines, one pair in each sort. This method not only duplicates the code unnecessarily, but also increases the chance that the students will have to debug three separate swap and compare routines.

A related problem is that each of these sorts will be able to process only one data type. Each new data type will require a new version of the sort. These sort routines are inflexible because they have not been generalized.

Writing a generalized version of a sort has another benefit as well. Because comparing and swapping data are not unique to sorting problems, these functions can be used for other purposes. This generalized approach to writing a sort function, therefore, increases the utility of the library.

Learning to generalize takes practice because generalization is both a design philosophy and a state of mind. Generalization requires dissecting each function into its smallest parts and removing as many program-specific features as possible.

How do you identify a nongeneralized function? The first step is to look for elements in a function that are not applicable in all cases. Usually, the inflexible elements of a function are related to data types. For example, suppose you need a function that will print out an error message based on a value passed to the function. The way you write such a function reflects how well you understand C.

A beginning C programmer will place the error messages in `main()` because the programmer doesn't completely understand how functions work or how to use them properly. Once functions are understood, the second-level programmer will write something similar to the function shown in Figure 0.1.

Figure 0.1
A Common Error Message Function

```
int perror(erno)
int erno;
{

    switch(erno) {
        case 0:
            print f("Divide by zero error");
            break;
        case 1:
            print f("Machine overflow");
            break;
        case 2:
            print f("Machine underflow");
            break;
        case 3:
            print f("Undefined error");
            break;
    }

}
```

In this figure, the `perror()` function does what it is intended to do, within the confines of the program. However, because error messages are common in programs, `perror()` can be more useful if it is generalized. The first question you need to ask is this: What makes the function specific to the program at hand? Obviously, the answer is the string constants in the `printf()` functions. If you remove the string constants from the functions, `perror()` can be generalized to display any error message.

Because the string constants are specific to a given program, that is where they belong—in the specific program, *not* in the function. Figure 0.2 illustrates one possibility.

Figure 0.2
Generalized Error Message Function

```
static char *mess[4] = {
     "Divide by zero error",
     "Machine overflow",
     "Machine underflow",
     "Undefined error"
};

main()
{
     .
     /* perror() called in a variety of places */
     /* as needed by the program */
     .
}



int perror(erno)
int erno;
{

     printf(mess[erno]);

}
```

In this example, a character array (`mess[ ]`) is initialized to hold pointers to the error messages. Because `mess[ ]` is external to any function, its storage class gives `perror()` access to the contents of the array, as necessary. This function is generalized so that it can cope with any reasonable form or number of error messages. The function also gives the programmer total freedom in the wording and placement of error messages without the necessity of modifying the `perror()` library function.

This simple example shows a critical difference between a library function and a program. A program contains the specifics that the functions handle in a generalized manner. Program-specific code is the programmer's responsibility and should not be included in library functions, if at all possible.

Not all functions can be generalized. A little extra thought, however, can often reveal ways that may have seemed impossible at first for generalizing functions. If you make the effort to create generalized functions as you develop your library, the flexibility and usefulness of your library functions will be significantly improved.

Taking Full Advantage of C

Every programmer knows that source code must pass through a C compiler to generate an executable program. It is quite another thing, however, to look at a line of code and be able to *see* the different ways the same section of code may be written. Yet some C programmers can even envision how the compiler treats a given sequence of C statements! The only assertion you can make with confidence about an executable program is that it conforms to the rules of C. (And even conformity isn't guaranteed by all C compilers!) A program's successful execution does not necessarily mean that it was written in the most efficient way (that is, with faster execution, less generated code, or both).

In the pages that follow, we assume that you already know the rules and syntax of C. If you are not sure about them, review an introductory text on C before proceeding with the following chapters.

Knowing the syntax and rules of C and writing efficient code are not the same thing. Again using the classroom example, suppose you assigned to your second semester class of C programming students a program that involved the manipulation of a large set of floating-point numbers.

Even if each student turned in a working program, some programs will be more efficient than others.

Differences in program efficiency are most likely due to the use of the float rather than the double data type. Two factors should be considered when selecting one data type over the other: (1) all math operations on floating-point numbers are done in double precision, and (2) any float that is passed as a parameter to a function is first converted to a double before being passed to the function. Examine the skeletal program outline in Figure 0.3.

Figure 0.3
Skeletal Program Using an Absolute Value

```
main()
{
     float x, fabs();


          .
     fabs(x);
          .

}


float fabs(y)
float y;
{
     return (y < 0 ? -y : y);
}
```

If a student declared the relevant variables as type float, consider the conversions that the compiler must have to go through to process the data correctly. In the discussion that follows, keep in mind that any float which appears in an expression is converted to a double. Function calls and their parameters are expressions.

When the fabs() function call is executed in Figure 0.3, the compiler converts the float x to a double before calling fabs(). The passed copy of x is actually a double. When the function is entered, fabs() receives the variable y as a double. The float y; in the argument declaration is interpreted as `double` y by the C language. Once the absolute value of x has been determined, it is *then* converted back to a `float` as part of the return from `fabs()`. This conversion happens because `fabs()` was declared to return a `float`, not a `double`.

As mentioned earlier, before any arithmetic operations can be performed on x [in `main()`], it must be converted to a `double`. The result of the arithmetic operation is a `double`. If the result will be assigned to a `float`, the compiler must convert the `double` back to a `float`. Conversions cost time and increase code size.

When you see a `float` data type in a program, a bell should ring in your head telling you to examine the way the `float` is used in the program. If the `float` is involved in many math operations or function calls, the program may be improved by changing the variable to a `double`.

Knowing C vs. Knowing the Compiler

As you read this text, you will see other instances that should sound an alarm. We do *not,* however, stress "compiler-specific tricks." That is, we do not advocate coding techniques that work efficiently on just one compiler. Efficiency should come from your understanding of C, not from the quirks of the compiler.

One of the major forces behind C is its portability. An intimate knowledge of a given compiler may tempt you into using practices that work well on your compiler but fail miserably on all others. Several compilers, for example, allow you to treat an `int` as a pointer (no cast involved). Although this use may produce more efficient code for a given compiler, any gain is lost when the program is compiled on another C compiler. In fact, you will probably spend considerable time debugging the program in the future.

A programmer, however, may ask this question: If the trick works for my compiler and it's the only one I use, why should I worry about it? The answer lies in the concept of portability. Although you may be using only one compiler today, changes in hardware and software may force you to switch compilers in the future. Writing the code correctly at the time of program development (when everything is fresh in your mind) is easier than debugging the code at some later time. This argument is even more forceful for programmers who write in a commercial environment.

The rules and syntax of C are well defined, and you should not engage in compiler-specific tricks that allow you to "bend" these rules. On the other hand, we do encourage you to practice visualizing how a given line of code is treated internally by the compiler. Understanding what the compiler must do to generate the resulting code can often lead to better ways of writing the program. (One example is the question of `float` versus `double`, as mentioned earlier.)

Knowing C and *Knowing* C

In a C programming course, students who demonstrate different levels of knowledge earn different grades. Examine the program segment in Figure 0.4.

Figure 0.4

```
y = 0;
if(x == 5)
    y = 1;
```

The code in this figure sets the variable y equal to 1 if x equals 5. Otherwise, the value of y will be 0. Nothing is wrong with the code; it will execute properly. A more knowledgeable C programmer, however, will probably use the code in Figure 0.5.

Figure 0.5

```
y = (x == 5) ? 1 : 0;
```

In Figure 0.5, the programmer used the ternary operator to accomplish the same task. The difference between the two examples comes from programming experience. The second example reflects more expertise in C and generates less code.

In Figure 0.6, a third code reveals an even greater knowledge of C.

Figure 0.6

```
y = x == 5;
```

This code produces the same result as the previous two, but it relies on a good understanding of the hierarchy of C operators. Because the test for equality (==) has higher precedence than assignment (=), the comparison of x to 5 is performed first. If the test is logic True (that is, x does equal 5), then y is assigned the value of 1. If x does not equal 5, the test is logic False, and y is assigned the value of 0.

The code in Figure 0.6 does not involve any compiler-specific tricks. All C compilers should produce the same results. This code simply reflects more expertise in C and usually generates less code.

Code Readability

You may argue that the first two examples are more "readable" than that in Figure 0.6. When pressed for an operational definition of readable, you may say that the intent of the code is clearer in the first two examples. This argument, however, assumes a level of expertise on the part of the person who is reading the code. Although an inexperienced C programmer may need time to understand what the code y = x == 5; is doing, an experienced C programmer will understand the code immediately.

Indeed, the experienced C programmer probably uses the technique illustrated in this last example so often that it is more obvious than the other two forms. What is "obtuse" code to one person may be obvious to another. One goal of this book is to help you gain an understanding of C that makes the obtuse obvious.

Developing and Testing a Function

In subsequent chapters, a substantial number of functions are discussed, many of which are probably not in your library. Even though the source code to these functions is listed in this book, no attempt has been made to include the programs that test these functions. Indeed, the test code would literally double the size of this book. Although the code has been tested for accuracy, the code's purpose is to illustrate the development of functions for your library. We would like to suggest some guidelines that you may follow when developing a new function for your library.

It is probably safe to assume that most programmers write a new function only after clarifying some perceived need for it. That is, a new function is written in response to a particular program requirement. In many cases, the programmer tacks the new function onto the end of the program being developed, then uses `main()` and the rest of the program to test the function. Usually, this approach is an inefficient way to test a new function.

Most functions are like a black box that has information entering one end and different (albeit related) information coming out the other end. For example, a square root function probably is passed a `double` as input to the black box, with the square root coming out the other end.

The purpose of this function is clear: return the square root of the number. The problem with immediately making the function a part of the program is that the function is tested with data that must pass through `main()` and other functions. *The data going into the function, therefore, is constrained to what can be passed through the other segments of the program.* In assuming the function processes these constrained forms of data correctly, the programmer is lulled into an attitude of safety about the certifiability of the function. In other words, once the function processes the data in the program, the programmer feels it is safe to place the function in the library.

The problem with this approach to function development and testing is twofold. First, extreme values that may be passed to the function are probably never tested; few programs are designed to test extreme values. For example, how does the square root function handle values that are zero or negative? Second, most functions will go through several iterations before the programmer feels that each function works properly. If the function is part of the program, loading and editing a large source file must be done even to make relatively minor changes in the function. The compile and link phases are time-consuming.

A better approach is to make the function a separate source file. The edit-compile-link process is faster when only a small function is edited, compiled, and then linked into the program. In many cases, we write a little `main()` program that permits data input from the keyboard. The data is then passed to the function being tested. This eliminates any constraints that the program may impose and lets us easily pass extreme values to the function for testing. When we have finished testing the function in this manner, we can be reasonably confident that all extreme values have been tested and that the function will process those extremes in a graceful (and predictable) fashion.

Although testing functions in the manner described here may appear to be more time-consuming, the approach concisely and quickly passes the function through its acid test and to its incorporation into our library.

Data Types

What is it about C that makes the uninitiated think of it as a difficult language? The perceived difficulty in learning C does not stem from the use of reserved words in statements. C has relatively fewer keywords than do most dialects of BASIC. Nor does the difficulty come from the syntactic constructs of C (for example, the elements of a for loop). The constructs are not hard to learn. But the variety of data types, along with some of the perceived "difficult" rules, often confuse the beginning C programmer.

Unfortunately, the potentially confusing variety of data types is also one of C's many strong points. This variety of data types and the many ways in which the data types can be manipulated give the programmer flexibility and power unsurpassed by any other language.

With these advantages, however, comes the responsibility of understanding what you are doing. (This responsibility can be appreciated only after your program manages to write the alphabet into the middle of your operating system.)

It is critical that you develop a systematic methodology for viewing the variety of data types and constructs that can be used in C. Many of the functions presented in upcoming chapters draw on your understanding of data types used for generalization. Without this understanding, much of the power and flexibility of C will go unused, resulting in less efficient library and program development. Chapter 1 will help you to develop such a systematic methodology.

1

Understanding C Data Types

In the preceding chapter, the perror() function illustrated how a function can be made more useful when it is written in a generalized form. This generalization was accomplished by making the error messages available to perror() through indirection into an external character array. This change removed the specifics of the function and placed them into the program where they belong. As a bonus, perror() became smaller in the process.

What triggered the change? It was triggered by the recognition that the string constants (a particular data type) did not need to be part of the function itself. The string constants were removed from the printf()'s in perror() and indexed by using pointers to an external character array, thereby changing the data type of the constants.

Although the change was a simple one, it drew on information about C data types and how they are made available to functions. Indeed, *generalizing functions almost always requires altering the way the data is used in the function*. Consequently, you must understand the data types available in C and how they are used. Without this understanding, you will not be able to take full advantage of the many ways a given task can be written in C.

15

Data Types

Knowing how C uses data internally often suggests program changes that produce more efficient code. The C programming language provides two classifications of data types: simple and aggregate.

Simple

When declared, a *simple* data type is allocated storage space by the compiler. That is, each simple data type causes the allocation of storage for the language's use in a program. Simple data types (as listed in Table 1.1) are the fundamental building blocks for the data used in a program.

Table 1.1
Simple Data Types

char	float
int	double
unsigned	pointer
long	function
short	

Note that the int data type may have modifiers associated with it. In most expressions, C treats each modified int differently; also each int may have different storage requirements. For example, the storage requirements for long int and int are usually different, but the requirements for int and unsigned int are usually the same. Remember that modifiers affect the way the simple data type int will be treated in C.

Aggregate

An *aggregate* data type is built from a simple data type. Aggregate data types are listed in Table 1.2.

Table 1.2
Aggregate Data Types

array	structure	union

No aggregate data type can exist by itself. It cannot be used in a program unless the composition of the aggregate data type has already been defined. One example of a common aggregate data type is an *array,* such as an "array of chars" or an "array of pointers." All elements in an array are the same data type. A *structure,* however, ultimately includes one or more different simple data types (for example, char and int) as part of its definition.

A union consists of one or more members, each of which is a simple data type. The size of the union is determined by the largest member in the union. In the case of a union whose members are an int, a char, and a long int, the union will have the size of the long int. If a structure is contained within a union, the size of the union is determined by the simple data types that make up the structure.

Think of an aggregate data type as a collection of simple data types. An aggregate data type, then, allows you to work with a number of simple data types in a convenient manner.

Together, the simple and aggregate data types are the building blocks from which all C data types are formed. Table 1.3 summarizes these data types.

Data Declarations

A simple data type must be declared before it can be used in a program. The data declaration declares the attributes that are associated with a given variable.

Attributes

An *attribute* is a characteristic of a data item. The attribute specifies the context in which C uses a variable. *Context* refers to the changing environment of an expression. C has two kinds of attributes: terminating and intermediate. The importance of attributes will be shown later as we discuss building and examining attribute lists.

Terminating Attributes

The *terminating* attributes are listed in Table 1.4. Note that this list is *not* the same as the list of simple data types in Table 1.1. Simple data types refer to data items that require a particular (hardware dependent)

Table 1.3
Simple and Aggregate Data Types

	Simple	Aggregate
char	X	
int	X	
short	X	
unsigned	X	
long	X	
float	X	
double	X	
pointer	X	
function	X	
array		X
structure		X
union		X

amount of storage, including pointer and function. Terminating attributes include struct and union, but exclude pointer and function. (These differences are discussed later.)

In a proper declaration, a terminating attribute must be the final attribute of the data item. For example, in

```
char c;
```

char is the terminating attribute. It tells the program that the variable c will be used as a character. Regardless of what c actually contains, it will be used in the context of a char.

Table 1.4
Terminating Attributes

char	float
int	double
unsigned	struct
long	union
short	

Intermediate Attributes

C is different from most other languages in that it does not limit you simply to using a terminating attribute but allows you to extend this attribute to alter the context of the data. These extensions are possible through the *intermediate* attributes shown in Table 1.5.

Table 1.5
Intermediate Attributes

array	pointer	function

An intermediate attribute must be followed by either a terminating attribute or another intermediate attribute.

Intermediate attributes become clearer when you see them in use. You should think of intermediate attributes as specifying "array of," "pointer to," or "function returning," followed by a terminating attribute or another intermediate attribute.

A data item with an intermediate attribute is undefined. Only after a terminating attribute has been supplied do intermediate attributes make sense (for example, "array of" char's, "pointer to" int, or "function returning" double).

Consider the declaration used for the message array with perror() in the previous chapter (ignoring its initialization, for the moment).

The numbers in parentheses in Figure 1.1 refer to the order in which C evaluates the declaration (as dictated by the hierarchy of C operators). The declaration states that we have an "array of pointers to chars." In this example, two intermediate attributes ("array of" and "pointer to")

Figure 1.1
Using Intermediate Attributes in a Declaration

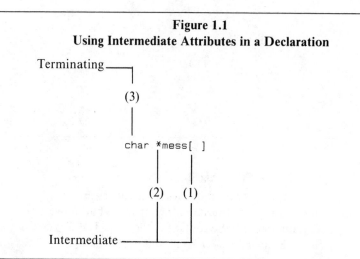

precede the terminating attribute char. You can use as many inter-mediate attributes in the declaration as you like, as long as it ends with a terminating attribute.

Note how important the context is here. Since we have declared mess[ ] as containing "pointers to chars," it is in this context that C uses *whatever* the pointers point to. If, for some reason, you try to place integer data where the char's should be, C won't care. You will get "half an int" when the pointers are referenced. You have total freedom to place whatever you want where the char's should be. However, the declaration tells C the context in which your data will be used.

Beginning programmers rarely make mistakes when they use ter-minating attributes in data declarations. The trouble occurs when intermediate attributes are introduced because they remove the one-to-one correspondence between the data type and the variable name being declared. For example, the declaration

```
int i;
```

is easy to understand because the variable i has a one-to-one correspondence between its data type and the variable name (i). On the other hand, the declaration

```
int *ptr;
```

is not so easy for the beginner because the one-to-one correspondence is lost between the variable named ptr and the actual data associated with it. The associated pointer variable has a name in the program (that is, ptr), but the integer data being pointed to does not.

The programmer is free to point (or initialize) the pointer variable anywhere. The declaration says that the programmer wants the pointer variable to point to an int. However, the pointer variable can point to a char, a double, or the middle of the operating system, if you like. The context, however, is always the same—in other words, the program will treat whatever is being pointed to as an int. The fact that what ptr is pointing to has no variable name makes things that much more difficult for the beginner.

Any time an intermediate attribute is used, C assumes that the programmer has correctly declared the context in which the data will be used. Unfortunately, it is not uncommon to have one context in mind, but to write the declaration in a totally different way. Therefore, it is critical that you understand how data declarations are properly formed.

Another complication is that intermediate attributes can be "stacked" as deep as necessary. This means that they can be followed by one or more additional intermediate attributes or by a terminating attribute. For example, you can define a variable as "an array of pointers to functions returning int." In this case, three intermediate attributes (array, pointer, and function) precede the terminating attribute int.

On the other hand, you cannot define a variable as a "pointer to function returning function." This declaration is incomplete because it does not end with a terminating attribute. Functions must return something. In this example, the compiler has no idea of what data type it is trying to use. A function must return a data item with either (1) only a terminating attribute other than a structure or union, or (2) the attribute pointer followed by a definition ending with a terminating attribute.

You could, however, have a "pointer to function returning pointer to functions returning int." This declaration is proper because it ends with a terminating attribute.

Table 1.6 shows the relationship between intermediate and terminating attributes.

Table 1.6
Intermediate and Terminating Attributes

Data item	Terminating	Intermediate
`char`	X	
`int`	X	
`short`	X	
`unsigned`	X	
`long`	X	
`float`	X	
`double`	X	
pointer		X
function		X
array		X
structure	X	
`union`	X	

Only terminating attributes can appear first in a data declaration; intermediate attributes cannot.

C allows you to create a variable with as many intermediate attributes as you want. The ultimate goal, however, is to manipulate a data item with a terminating attribute. With this freedom, how can you keep track of what is actually being declared and used in the program? Keeping track is the purpose of an attribute list.

Attribute Lists

Remember that each attribute causes the compiler to view a data item in a specific context. For example, the data types pointer and `int` are treated differently by the compiler even though they may require the same amount of physical storage. The intermediate attribute pointer will cause the compiler to allocate a certain number of bytes of storage for the pointer, which is a simple data type. The attribute pointer is not a data item by itself. A pointer is used contextually by C to "prepare a path" for indirection to some other data item.

An *attribute list* is a sequence of attributes used to locate the final simple data type for processing in a program. You might think of the attribute list as a road map that C follows to arrive at the final data item.

Defining Variables in C

We are now in a position to define what a variable, or data item, must be in a C program:

> A variable is defined by a sequential list of attributes. This list may contain an optional, arbitrary-length list of intermediate attributes followed by a terminating attribute.

With this definition in mind, examine the data declarations in Figure 1.2.

Figure 1.2
Sample Declarations

```
1)          int x;
2)          char s[MAX];
3)          char *mess[MAX];
```

In Example 1, the variable x is declared to be an integer variable; there are no intermediate attributes. Example 2 has one intermediate attribute (array) followed by the required terminating attribute (char); this example declares an "array of chars." Example 3 is more complex. It has two intermediate attributes (pointer and array) that must be processed before the terminating attribute char.

Using the *right-left* rule for parsing the declaration (see Chapter 6 in the *C Programming Guide*), we know that this example shows an "array of pointers to chars." The right-left rule does nothing more than reveal the attribute list for a variable. Figure 1.3 illustrates how these lists will appear visually.

Figure 1.3
Attribute List for Declarations in Figure 1.2

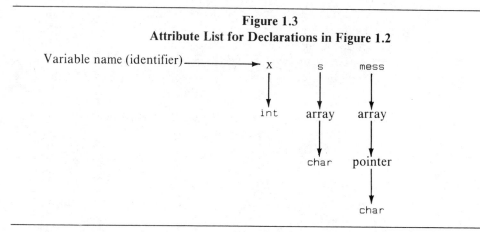

Note that all the declarations follow the rules associated with intermediate and terminating attributes for defining a variable in C. Any variable, regardless of its complexity, that conforms to the semantic and syntactic rules of C will follow these rules. But how is a variable used in a C program?

Using Variables

A variable must be declared before it can be used in a program. You have seen that the declaration of a variable creates a list of optional intermediate attributes followed by a terminating attribute. For purposes of this discussion, variable declarations with one or more intermediate attributes are called *complex* variables. If no intermediate attributes are used, the variable is a *simple* variable.

A variable can have only one "active" attribute at any particular time. For complex variables, all other attributes are inactive, except the one being acted on, or "used," by the program. For an illustration of this concept, consider the following declaration:

```
char *mess[MAX];
```

Remember how the right-left rule was used to construct the attribute list in Figure 1.3. First, you locate the name (identifier) of the variable; in this example, it is mess. Once the name has been found, you look to the right for any intermediate attributes. Here, "array of" is the intermediate attribute.

The right-left rule then instructs you to look to the left of the identifier for any further attributes. The asterisk indicates that a pointer is another intermediate attribute. (Can any intermediate attribute other than pointer be located to the left of the identifier? Hint: No.) Now you look to the right for any additional intermediate attributes (or parentheses), and you find none. The terminating attribute, therefore, must be a char. The attribute list is now complete: the variable is an "array of pointers to chars."

The attribute list for this example is visualized in Figure 1.4.

Figure 1.4
Attribute List for char *mess[MAX];

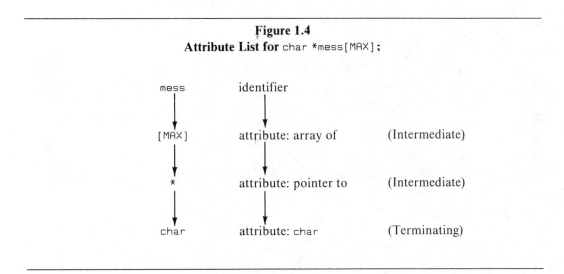

Using Variables in Context

A subtle and important point should be made here: the only way you can construct an attribute list is by using the right-left rule for parsing the declaration of the variable. The attribute list looks quite different from the data declaration and is more direct than the declaration is. The attribute list tells you how the variable is used in the program. In other words, the attribute list tells you the *context* in which the variable is being used.

C processes attributes one at a time and *only* in sequential order, from the top of the list to the bottom. The right-left rule is used to form the list. Anytime an intermediate attribute is applied to a variable, that attribute must be exhausted before the next one will become active. Each time the compiler uses the complex data item, the compiler repeats this processing of the attribute list.

Functions

When an attribute follows a function, the attribute declares the data item returned by the function. A function must return a simple data type, but with three exceptions: a function cannot return another function, structure, or union. In other words, two function attributes cannot appear sequentially in an attribute list.

This rule reinforces another rule of C: a function cannot return an array because it is not a simple data type. (Functions can, however, return *pointers to* arrays.) In fact, functions cannot return any aggregate data type (array, structure, or union).

(At the time this book was being written, another exception to this rule was gradually becoming accepted. Some compilers, principally UNIX System V™ compatible compilers, allow a structure to be passed to and returned from a function call. This feature is not universal, however. Check your compiler's documentation to see whether this exception applies to your compiler.)

Now consider the following declaration:

```
double atof();
```

This simple data declaration, according to the right-left rule, states that atof() is a "function returning double." Let's try another declaration:

```
int (*ptr[MAX])();
```

If you construct an attribute list for this declaration, you will find that it is "an array of pointers to functions returning ints." This example follows the rule that functions must return a simple data type. The final objective of this data declaration is to use the int data type.

Any sequential attribute list that follows a function attribute not only describes what the function returns, but also the context in which it will be used. Because an int is the simple data type in the previous example, whatever is returned from the function will be treated as an int. If you have ever forgotten to declare a function that returns a double in main( ), you already know that garbage can creep into the program. This happens because the double that the function is trying to return is being treated as an int in main( ).

Only by knowing the attribute list of a variable can you understand what data item is actually being used. The more complex the declaration, the more important it is to spend time thinking about the attribute list. Because C provides for complex declarations, it also provides the means to abbreviate (a typedef) or alter (a cast) complex attribute lists.

typedef's

A typedef is the shorthand notation for a previously declared attribute list. In the typedef

```
typedef char C_RAY[ ];
C_RAY *ptr_c;
```

C_RAY is established as the shorthand notation for the attribute list "array of chars." *The attribute list created by the* typedef *is appended to the attribute list of the variable being declared.*

Let's ignore the typedef for a moment. The declaration for the variable ptr_c has an intermediate pointer attribute. Because C_RAY is not on our list of terminating attributes, however, the typedef is "added on to" the attribute list for ptr_c. The correct attribute list for the variable ptr_c is "pointer to array of chars." This list forms a legal attribute list for the variable ptr_c.

Note that using a typedef does not violate the right-left rule. In the example, you find the identifier ptr_c and look to the right for an attribute. After finding nothing, you look to the left and find pointer. Again looking to the right of the identifier, you find no further attributes. With a final look to the left, you find C_RAY, which is a typedef for "array of chars." Because the typedef has an intermediate attribute (array) followed by a terminating attribute (char), the variable declaration is valid. The variable ptr_c is a "pointer to array of chars."

Generally, think of a typedef as the "tail" of a variable's attribute list. You might visualize it as the following:

Complete attribute list = variable's attributes + typedef

With the example

    pointer to array of chars = pointer to + array of chars

now use

```
C_RAY *ptr_c = *ptr_c + char C_RAY[ ]
```

The typedef is simply added to the attribute list created by the variable's declaration.

typedef's may seem difficult to the beginning programmer because they appear to create a new data type. But a typedef cannot "create" a new data type or anything else. A typedef does nothing more than provide a shorthand way of expressing a previously declared attribute list. As a result, typedef's must obey all the rules associated with constructing a proper attribute list.

Creating a Variable Declaration from an Attribute List

In our discussion of attributes, we used the right-left rule to construct a proper attribute list. This method is fine for deciphering what someone else has written (or what you have written and since forgotten). The right-left rule does not, however, directly tell you how to declare a variable from a known attribute list. What you need is a "left-right rule," the right-left rule in reverse, to create the declaration from an attribute list. The algorithm that follows will help you construct such a declaration.

The first step in constructing the declaration is to define the attribute list for the variable. Suppose you want a variable that is an "array of pointers to functions returning pointers to ints." Because the desired variable has four intermediate attributes followed by a terminating attribute, the variable declaration is syntactically correct.

The second step is to give the variable a name. Instead of selecting a specific name, let's use the generic term *identifier*. Place the identifier at the top of the attribute list. Remember that attributes are processed from top to bottom. What you have done so far is shown in Figure 1.5.

You can now proceed to construct the declaration from the attribute list. First, write the identifier in the middle of a piece of paper. Next, complete the declaration, using the following algorithm:

Figure 1.5
Attribute List for Identifier

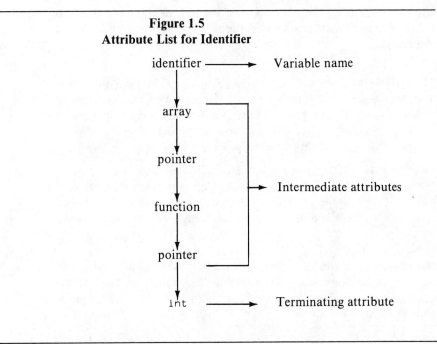

1. If the attribute is a left attribute, write it in. Pointer is the only possible left attribute because it is the only nonterminating attribute that can appear to the left of the identifier.

2. If the attribute is a right attribute (array or function only), the following applies:

   a. If there is an active left attribute (that is, a pointer attribute that was added in Step 1), place parentheses around the full declaration to this point and add the right attribute. Go on to Step 3.

   b. If there is no active pointer attribute, add the new right attribute.

3. Repeat Steps 1 and 2 for all intermediate attributes.

4. Add the simple attribute at the far left and a semicolon at the end of the declaration.

Now let's construct the declaration according to the steps outlined above. You were instructed to write the identifier first in the middle of a piece of paper:

```
identifier
```

The first intermediate attribute is `array`. Looking at Step 1, you see that it applies only to pointer; therefore, you skip this step. (You are working with an array attribute.) Step 2 first asks whether a right attribute is about to become active. Because you are going to add an array attribute, which is a right attribute, proceed to Step 2.a.

Step 2.a asks whether there is an active left attribute. If there were, "pointer to" (or an *) would appear to the left of the identifier. Because this is not the case, proceed to step 2.b. Step 2.b says that if there is no active left attribute, add the new attribute (array). You should now have

```
identifier[ ]
```

Note that array is now the active attribute because you have added it to the declaration. Refer back to the attribute list in Figure 1.5 to find the next attribute to be added, which is "pointer to." After reading Step 3, go back to Step 1.

Step 1 says that if "pointer to" is a left attribute, add it to the declaration. You should now have

```
*identifier[ ]
```

Now that you have "used up" the array attribute, the pointer attribute is the active attribute. Referring back to the attribute list, you find that the next attribute is function.

With function, Step 1 does not apply.

Step 2 asks whether you are adding a right attribute. Because you are about to add the function attribute, Step 2.a applies. Since pointer is the currently active attribute, this step says that you must place parentheses around the complete declaration to this point before you add the new attribute. After the parentheses have been added, you should have

```
(*identifier[ ])
```

Once the function attribute (a right attribute) has been added, your declaration should look like this:

```
(*identifier[ ])( )
```

Function is now the currently active attribute. Return to Step 1, which tells you to add directly any new left attribute. You should now have

```
*(*identifier[])()
```

Because there are no further intermediate attributes on the list (see Figure 1.5), proceed to Step 4 and add the terminating attribute. The final variable declaration is

```
int *(*identifier[])();
```

You can check the declaration with the right-left rule to see if the declaration produces the desired attribute list. We have declared an "array of pointers to functions returning pointers to ints." If you follow the steps correctly, the two lists will always match.

In later chapters, you will learn how to construct many complex data declarations. Some of these declarations are necessary in generalizing library functions. As you see the advantages of such complex data types, the need for constructing an attribute list will become obvious. For the moment, look at examples of source code that use complex data declarations and practice constructing the appropriate attribute list.

Expressions and Their Impact on Attribute Lists

An *expression* is a series of variables or constants that are separated by operators. As you saw earlier, variables and constants may be modified by intermediate attributes. A *statement* in C is one or more expressions followed by a semicolon (;).

The operators that may be used in expressions are listed in Table 1.7.

The *classification* of an operator is determined by its purpose in an expression. Operators can have the following classifications:

1. A *context modifier* (C) is an operator that controls the currently active attribute of a variable. Examples are the "array of" ([ ]) and "pointer to" (*) operators.

2. An *administrative* (A) operator controls the order in which subexpressions are evaluated; parentheses () are a common example. These compile-time directives assure that the attribute list is processed in the proper order.

Table 1.7
Hierarchy of Operators

Order	Operator	Class
1.	() [] -> .	C or A, C, C, C
2.	! ~ ++ -- -	All are U
	(cast) * &	All are C
	sizeof	A
3.	* / %	All are B
4.	+ -	All are B
5.	<< >>	All are B
6.	> >= <= <	All are B
7.	== !=	All are B
8.	& /* bitwise AND */	B
9.	^	B
10.	|	B
11.	&&	B
12.	||	B
13.	?: /* ternary */	T
14.	= += -= *= /= %=	All are B
	>>= <<= &= |= ^=	All are B
15.	,	A

3. A *unary* (U) operator performs an operation on a single subexpression. A unary minus (-) is an example of a unary operator.

4. A *binary* (B) operator controls two subexpressions.

5. A *ternary* (T) operator controls three subexpressions.

The following statements illustrate an expression:

```
float a;          /* declarations */
int b;
char *c;

  .
  .
  .
a = b + *c        /* the expression is here */
```

The line a = b + *c is the expression. It may also be divided into subexpressions (such as b and *c) and can be viewed as a subexpression of some larger, arbitrary expression. (Subexpressions are covered in greater detail later in this chapter.) Note that the semicolon is omitted because it is an expression, not a statement.

Resolved Data Types

The result of any subexpression must be a *resolved* data type. All data types in expressions are resolved. C has five resolved data types, as shown in Table 1.8.

Table 1.8
Resolved Data Types

int	double
unsigned	pointer
long	

Note that expressions and subexpressions can use only a resolved data type. This resolution is automatic; the programmer has no control over it.

To understand resolved data types, think of each simple data type as a record that must be played at a certain speed. A list of these hypothetical speeds appears in Table 1.9.

A data type can be understood only if it is "played" at the appropriate speed. Expressions can understand only a limited number of speeds but have the ability to recognize "gibberish" and translate one speed into another. Expressions need this capability because all elements of an expression must talk at the same speed for successful communication.

Table 1.9
Hypothetical Recording Speeds for Simple Data Types

	Simple	Speed
`char`	x	100
`int`	x	200
`short`	x	300
`unsigned`	x	400
`long`	x	500
`float`	x	600
`double`	x	700
pointer	x	800
function	x	900
array	700	1000
structure		error
`union`		error

Suppose that expressions are fluent in the following speeds: 200, 400, 500, 700, and 800. Any data item in an expression that does not work at one of these speeds must be translated to another speed. The rules for translation are strict, and the possible translations are listed in Table 1.10.

This table shows how all the data types are translated into resolved speeds for communication in an expression. In an expression involving an `int`, when a `char` or `short` is used, its speed is translated to match

Table 1.10
Hypothetical Translations for Data Types

	Simple	Speed	Resolved Speed
char	x	100	
int	x	200	200
short	x	300	
unsigned	x	400	400
long	x	500	500
float	x	600	
double	x	700	700
pointer	x	800	800
function	x	900	
array		1000	
structure		error	
union		error	

that of the int. Likewise, a float has its speed increased to that of a double. The speeds for arrays and functions are translated into the speed of a pointer. Structures and union's cannot be directly translated by an expression. Only their addresses or members can communicate through an expression.

Clearly, expressions involving mixed data types take more time and code space than expressions using only resolved data types. Obviously, such translations can be avoided if only resolved data types, such as those in Table 1.8, are used in expressions.

For example, if a `float` is a parameter in a function call, the `float` is converted to a `double` before the call because parameters are expressions. The parameter must be a resolved data type. However, the function declaration can be stated in such a way that it modifies the return value. For example, suppose that you have the following declarations in a program:

```
main()
{
        float func1(), x;
                .
                .
        x = func1(x);
                .
}


float func1(y)
float y;
{
        .

        .
        return(y);
}
```

The attribute list for this declaration indicates that x is a `float`, and `func1()` is a "function returning float." The data in Table 1.10, however, suggests that `float`'s are immediately converted to the resolved data type `double` because `float` is not a resolved data type in an expression. Therefore, when `func1()` is called, x is immediately translated to a `double` *before* its value is passed to `func1()`.

When `func1()` receives the parameter as y in the function call, the argument declaration (that is, `float y;`) says that y wants to talk at the speed of a `float` (500). But y was passed as a `double` (600). Because the parameter is already a resolved data type, C will *ignore* the `float y` declaration and maintain y as a `double` (resolved data type).

When the `return(y)` statement is executed, C *must* convert y back to a `float`, because that is the data type which the function must return. Since the function was defined as `float func1(y)`, a `float` is passed back to `main( )`. Note that the `double` must be converted to a `float` before the `return` is executed.

Once the `float` is back in `main( )`, the `float` must be reconverted again into a `double` in preparation for assignment into `x`. This reconversion must be done because assignment is an expression that can only be done as a resolved data type.

Keep the resolved data type in mind when writing libraries, because of all the data conversions that may have to take place. You can avoid these conversions by using resolved data types for parameters in function calls as well as in the functions themselves. Using these data types improves the overall performance of the function.

The list of simple data types (see Table 1.3) indicates the possible contexts in which the return values may be used. The programmer must determine if the resolved data type returned by the function is used in the proper context.

Consider one more example of passing parameters in a function call. If the variable `str` is a string array (`str[ ]`), all C programmers know that the function call

```
func2(str);
```

will not pass the string array to the function but will pass a *pointer* to the start of the string array. Again, because array is not in Table 1.8, it is converted to the resolved data type pointer. All parameters passed in a function call must be resolved data types.

Table 1.11 presents a complete list of the simple and resolved data types. In the table, the last column indicates whether a conversion is required for the simple data type in an expression.

Using resolved data types in expressions lets you avoid the code required for conversion. Resolved data types also produce programs that require less memory and execute somewhat faster than data types requiring conversions.

How Context Alters
the Currently Active Attribute

All arithmetic expressions use resolved data types. If data types are mixed (for example, if an `int` is multiplied by a `double`), the data is

Table 1.11
Simple and Resolved Data Types with Conversions Indicated

	Simple	Resolved	Conversion
char	x	int	yes
int	x	int	no
short	x	int	yes
unsigned	x	unsigned	no
long	x	long	no
float	x	double	yes
double	x	double	no
pointer	x	pointer	no
function	x	pointer	yes
array		pointer	yes
structure		error	---
union		error	---

changed to the data type of higher order (that is, int is promoted to double before the operation is performed). The result is a high-order resolved data type. (If you are unfamiliar with the rules for conversion and promotion, see Chapter 6 in the *C Programming Guide*.)

Consider the expression in Figure 1.6.

The first subexpression in the example is the variable a followed by the = operator. (Evaluation of this subexpression is postponed because of the assignment operator.) The next subexpression is the variable b followed

---

Figure 1.6
Example of an Arithmetic Expression

```
float a;      /* a -> float */
int b;        /* b -> int */
char *c;      /* c -> pointer to -> char */

.

.

a = b + *c
```

---

by the plus (+) operator. Because the plus is a nonassignment operator, the subexpression b must be resolved. Since the currently active attribute of b is int, no conversion is performed. At this point, we have the following:

```
subexpression ---->        a =              b +
                            ↓                ↓
                          float             int
```

Now we come to the subexpression of the contextually modified variable c. (Notice that the pointer operator is a context modifier operator from Table 1.7.) The initial attribute list for the variable c looks like this:

```
         c
         ↓
      pointer
         ↓
       char
```

The indirection context modifier (*) causes the currently active attribute pointer to be processed. The next attribute in the list then becomes the currently active attribute; we have used up the pointer attribute. The attribute list for the new subexpression *c is

```
       *c
        ↓
      char
```

Note that *c is *not* the same as the variable c; its context has been modified. While this subexpression is being processed, it must be converted to a resolved data type. In this case, char is converted to int because char is not a resolved data type. The current attribute list for the subexpression *c after conversion is

```
*c
 |
int
```

The three subexpressions and their currently active attribute lists look like this:

```
subexpression ---->           a =        b +      *c
                              |          |        |
                            float       int      int
```

Now the subexpression b + *c is processed because of the hierarchy rules associated with operators. Since the attributes of b and *c are both resolved data type int, no further data resolution occurs prior to processing the subexpression. Both the attributes are communicating at the same speed. (Note that if the currently active attribute of b was long rather than int, the currently active attribute of *c, which is int, would be converted to long.)

The subexpression b + *c is now processed. The resulting attribute list for the subexpression is

```
b + *c
  |
 int
```

Now we are ready to process the rest of the subexpression a =. The attributes appear as

```
  a =        b + *c
  |            |
float         int
```

The assignment operator causes the subexpression b + *c to be converted to double, resulting in

```
  a =        b + *c
  |            |
float        double
```

The conversion must be to a double rather than a float because float is not a resolved data type. Conversion is always resolved to the highest resolved data type whenever conflict arises.

The result of the subexpression b + *c is now converted to float to match the declared data type for the variable a. At this point, the subexpression's attribute list is

```
      a
      |
    float
```

Note that the subexpression b + *c has fulfilled its purpose and, therefore, has been used up. The variable a contains a float. However, the variable a is still viewed as a subexpression. Because a may be part of some larger expression, it must be resolved.

The current subexpression is converted to a resolved data type. The subexpression must be a double because float is not a resolved data type, and double is the next higher resolved data type. The attribute list now appears as

```
      a
      |
    double
```

It is important to understand that what is stored at a is a float, but that the result of the subexpression a = b + *c is a double. Only after all operators and subexpressions have been resolved can we progress from "subexpression" to "expression." Note that what is stored in variable a is a float, but that the value of the expression is a double.

We could treat the example above as a subexpression of some larger expression, such as

```
    x = (a = b + *c)
```

In this case, the expression in the earlier example becomes a parenthesized subexpression of the larger expression. The methodology used is the same, however.

When you consider the number of conversions necessary to produce a resolved data type, the expression discussed above could be written more efficiently as double's. The choice depends on the program requirements for the variables in the expression.

Casts

A *cast* allows you to convert one data type into another. If an expression is preceded by a parenthesized simple data type, the value of the expression is converted to the simple data type in the expression. Thus, a cast causes a *new* attribute list to be substituted for the currently active attribute list. This substitution can lead to conversions. For example, suppose the code in Figure 1.7 appears in a program.

Figure 1.7
Example Using a Cast

```
int   litle_num;
long big_num, func1();


func1( (long) litle_num);
```

In this example, we assume that the argument being passed to `func1()` is a `long` data type. The variable `litle_num` has an attribute list of `int`, but the function call expects to receive a `long`. The cast is used to change the `int` attribute to a `long` attribute before the function is called. The cast changes the currently active attribute list (`int`) to the attribute list of the cast (`long`).

Notice that the attribute list of the cast can be complex. For example, if `func1()` expects a pointer to a `long`, we need to change the cast to the following:

```
func1( (long *) litle_num);
```

When this line is executed, `int` is the first active attribute. The value of `litle_num` is converted to a "pointer to long," which then becomes the currently active attribute list.

In summary, a cast has only one purpose: it causes the currently active attribute list (such as `int`) to be replaced by a new one (such as "pointer to long").

Formalize Your Thinking

Thinking in terms of attribute lists will help you to understand the complex data types that appear so frequently in C programs (and in subsequent chapters). Mastery of the keywords and statements in C is not difficult. C is such a flexible language with respect to its data types, however, that they are a common source of confusion for all C programmers. An understanding of the data types is crucial for efficient programming in C.

As stated earlier, the purpose of this text is to increase the usefulness of your library functions by making them more generalized. In many cases, generalization requires the use of more complex data types than might be used in a less general library function. Complex data declarations appear often in later chapters, and their derivations draw heavily on the material presented here.

Familiarize yourself with the terms and concepts presented in this chapter. Then study several programs containing complex C code (for example, some of the programs in later chapters). Read through each program and construct an attribute list for the complex data types. Then trace through the program, seeing how the attribute list is processed as the program executes. Using this method of study, you will find that each program is actually less complex than it first appeared to be.

Editor's Note to Chapter 2

The functions and program presented in this chapter show three different algorithms for sorting. The sorting functions perform the algorithms for the sort but remain ignorant of the sorted data.

To complete the implementation of the sorting functions, the application programmer is responsible for writing the comp( ), or comparison, and swap( ), or exchange, functions. These two functions are responsible for the physical comparison and exchange of the data, and a set of these functions must be written for each type or set of data to be sorted.

For the disk sort program, the UNIX programmer should modify the creat( ) function with either the proper call to umask( ) or the correct value for pmode.

C. D. V.

2

Sorting

Sorting data is a fundamental task that is used in a variety of programming activities. This chapter covers sorting, in general, and draws on information in Chapter 1 to present three specific sorting algorithms. Recursion is also included in one of the sorting algorithms.

Generalization

You will recall from Chapter 0 that many programmers have a tendency to make library functions specific to the task at hand, instead of writing more generalized functions for their libraries. Sorting functions also suffer this fate when the programmer becomes preoccupied with the output of the program. In other words, the specific application for the sort receives all the attention, and the sorting function is narrowly written for the types of data being sorting.

For example, suppose that the task is to sort a list of customers by ZIP Code in preparation for a bulk mailing. (Let's assume that the client file already exists in some data file.) The pseudocode for the program is often similar to that presented in Figure 2.1.

Figure 2.1
Pseudocode for a Sort Program

```
main(argc, argv)
input file is command line argument
{

declare working variables;

        is there correct number of command line arguments;
                if not, issue error message and abort;
        open file;
                issue error if cannot open;

        set ZIP Code field as sort key;
        read record number and ZIP Code into array;
        sort into ascending order;
        print address labels;


}
```

After the pseudocode outline is finished, the first task facing the programmer is to identify any new functions that need to be written. In Figure 2.1, setting the ZIP Code field as the sort key for the file can be done as a function call. Reading records and assigning their values into an array can also be handled by function calls. The sort is an obvious function call, as is the printing of the labels.

Once the required new functions have been defined, the programmer must define the algorithms and pseudocode for each new function. At this point, certain design decisions must also be made.

Tradeoffs

Generally, it is easier to design a function that handles a specific set of data than one that can cope with an unspecified data set. Writing a generalized function, therefore, requires more time. On the other hand, a generalized function eliminates the need to rewrite the function in the future. How do you decide whether you should invest the time now in a generalized function or take less time by writing a function that is specific to the task at hand?

Many factors influence your decision (for example, the difficulty in writing each version of the function, program deadlines, etc.). However, one question deserves special consideration: What is the likelihood that you will use the function again? If the purpose of the function is so unique that you cannot envision a future program with similar requirements, writing a generalized function is probably a waste of your time.

Library Routines vs. Function Calls

If you cannot think of a future use for a given function, it should not be placed in your library. A library of functions should include only those that you expect to use again. Functions that are unique to a given program should be part of the program itself. In other words, push the program-specific code out of the library and into the program.

True "library" functions should be compiled and integrated into your library. These functions should be written in a general rather than specific form. Most systems have a "library manager" to facilitate library expansion.

A library function module is part of the library and is not #included in a program. A #include preprocessor directive is best reserved for the overhead code that specific programs may require (for example, stdio.h). In most cases, such files contain preprocessor directives (such as #define's for symbolic constants like TRUE, EOF, etc.) and not function modules. Remember to reserve the library for library functions.

A Word of Warning

When you write a function that will become part of your library, you are, by definition, writing for future use. As such, you will need instructions (documentation) to go with the function. Don't fool yourself into believing that you will remember the details at some later date. At the very least, you should document the parameters used in calling the function, include a description of what the function does, and explain what it returns. (All functions return something, whether it is used or not.) These items make up the minimum reference material for your library.

Our preference is to record the details about a function as part of its source code. (See Figure 2.2a.) After the function is written and documented, we integrate it into the library. The source is saved on a special disk, containing only those functions that appear in the library, and the disk is stored in a safe place.

A listing of the source code for the function is then incorporated into a binder (available at most stationery stores) designed specifically for computer printouts. This printout contains a detailed description of all library functions. The listing can be used to re-create the library, should disaster strike. If you consider the time and effort that goes into writing a library, preserving this listing is worth the investment.

Once the function has been debugged and documented, a brief description of how it is used (noting parameters, description, return value, etc.) is then incorporated into whatever documentation already exists for the library that came with your compiler. This step eliminates the need to look through the details in the source code listing of the function to see how it is used. The collection of brief function descriptions becomes your reference manual for future use. You will not often need the source listings if the brief descriptions are well written.

Although this procedure may seem to be a burden (since most programmers dislike writing documentation), we urge you to develop the habit of following the steps outlined above for each new function included in your library. The procedure can be a real time-saver in the long run.

Keeping this in mind, let's write a generalized sort function for inclusion in your library.

A Generalized Bubble Sort

Often a function can be generalized in several ways. The pseudocode in Figure 2.1 says that we want to "sort the data." The word *sort* is a general term for two reasons: (1) data can be sorted differently (for example, in ascending or descending order); and (2) a variety of sorting algorithms may be used. Of these routines, the *bubble* sort is one of the simplest. For this reason, let's begin our discussion of sorting with the bubble sort. (Two other more complex sorting algorithms are also discussed in this chapter.)

Identifying Areas of Generality

To write a general function, you must be able to identify the areas, or tasks, that can be generalized. A detailed definition or description of the proposed function is a good starting point. You should think of these tasks as common denominators in the function, regardless of the algorithm selected. That is, which tasks are common to all variations of the function that might be written?

For example, all sorts must use two sorting algorithm features: a comparison and an exchange. In our sort, rather than have a specific sorting function include the comparison and the exchange, we shall make these features separate functions that are external to the sort function. (The reason behind this decision will be clear shortly.)

Figure 2.2a shows the detailed source code listing for the bubble sort. (For a complete discussion, see Donald E. Knuth, *Sorting and Searching,* 3 vols., Addison-Wesley Publishing Company, Reading, Massachusetts, 1973, vol. 3, p. 107). Note that sort has no references to the actual data to be sorted. The reason for the omission will be explained shortly. The listing is an example of a detailed function description that is stored on the source code function disk and is printed out for inclusion in a binder. (This listing is not the reference to be incorporated into the compiler's documentation for the library.)

Figure 2.2a goes here

The comments in Figure 2.2b describe the variables used and explain how the bubble sort works. As mentioned in Chapter 0, we will not present, in the interest of brevity, the details of sorting algorithms. The interested reader should consult the reference cited in Figure 2.2a for further discussion of sorting algorithms.

Figure 2.2a
Bubble Sort

```
/************************************************************************
 *
 *      Bubble Sort
 *      as described by Knuth, p. 107
 *
 ************************************************************************
```

```
*
*        This program performs a bubble sort on n records. It is
*        independent of the record and key. This independence is
*        possible because pointers to a key-comparison function and
*        record-swapping function are passed to the sort. The function
*        calling convention is
*
*                bsort(n,comp,swap)
*
*        where
*
*                n is the number of records to sort.
*                comp is a pointer to a function that will compare
*                    two record keys and return an integer representing
*                    the logical relationship of the keys. Returns:
*
*                    < 0    if key[i] <  key[j] (ascending) or
*                           key[i] > key[j] (descending)
*                    = 0    if key[i] == key[j]
*                    > 0    if key[i] >  key[j] (ascending) or
*                           key[i] < key[j] (descending)
*
*                swap is a pointer to a function that will swap two
*                    records.
*
*        Both comp and swap are called with two parameters that are
*        indices to records, with the first record being 0 and the last
*        record being n - 1.
*
***************************************************************************
*
*        This program illustrates the use of pointers to functions.
*        In this program the pointers to functions are used to allow
*        the sort algorithm to function independently of the data record.
*
***************************************************************************/
```

```
#define void int

void bsort(n,comp,swap)                                    /* 0001 */
unsigned n;                                                /* 0002 */
int (*comp)();                                             /* 0003 */
int (*swap)();                                             /* 0004 */
{

        unsigned t;                                        /* 0006 */
        unsigned j;                                        /* 0007 */

        do {                                               /* 0008 */
              t = 0;                                       /* 0009 */
              for(j = 0; j < n - 1; ++j)                   /* 0010 */
                    if((*comp)(j, j + 1) > 0) {            /* 0011 */
                          (*swap)(j, j + 1);               /* 0012 */
                          t = 1;                           /* 0013 */
                    }                                      /* 0014 */
        } while(t);                                        /* 0015 */

}


/*********************** end of function **********************************/
```

Figure 2.2b
Program Comments for Bubble Sort

Line 0001   Main entry point for the bubble sort. Three parameters are passed.

Line 0002   The number of records to be sorted is the first parameter, which is an
               unsigned value.

Line 0003

The second parameter is a pointer to a function that compares all keys of two records and returns an integer that expresses the following relationships for an ascending-order sort.

`r[i]-r[j]` such that:

```
if (r[i] > r[j])
        return (1);
if (r[i] == r[j])
        return (0);
if (r[i] < r[j])
        return (-1);
```

In fact, if the two keys were integers, the code can be

```
return(r[i]-r[j]);
```

`bsort()` will adjust the pointers i and j so that they are relative base 0.

Line 0004

The third parameter is a pointer to a function that swaps two records.

`bsort()` will adjust the pointers i and j so that they are relative base 0.

Line 0006

`t` is a variable used to determine if a swap has occurred.

Line 0007

`j` is a variable used to index records.

Line 0008

This function assumes that at least two records exist for sorting. Therefore, at least one comparison is to be made.

Line 0009

The swap flag is initially set to FALSE (0).

Line 0010

The record numbers vary from 0 to n-1. Since the `for` loop consists of a single statement, braces are not required.

Line 0011

The compare function is called with the two record counts as parameters. The parentheses are required around the `*comp` because of the hierarchy of C. (Function calls have higher precedence than indirection.)

Line 0012

If a swap is required, based on the results of the compare, the swap is executed here.

Line 0013

Since a swap occurred, set the swap flag to TRUE (1).

Line 0015

Continue sort until no swaps occur.

Line 0011 reflects that the compare function is called with two parameters: the two record keys to be compared. The comp() function returns an integer value that is determined by the result of the comparison. Because the bubble sort always looks at two adjacent records, the keys are key[j] and key[j + 1]. It is up to the comp() function to determine which field within the record is used for the comparison.

The integer value returned by comp() determines whether swap() is called. If the comparison shows key[j] is greater than key[j + 1], the return value from comp() is greater than 0. A return value greater than 0 indicates that the two records must be swapped. The if statement (line 0011) causes the swap() to be called only when comp() returns a value greater than 0. If key[j] is equal to or less than key[j + 1], no swap is needed, and swap() is not called.

The way the return values from comp() are set determines whether you are doing a sort in ascending or descending order. For an ascending sort, simply return a value of less than 0 when key[i] is less than key[j]. For a descending sort, change the return value to something greater than 0 when key[i] < key[j].

The important thing is that the code in the bsort() library function does not have to be changed if you want to change the sort order. These considerations have been pushed out of the sorting algorithm itself and into the hands of the programmer, who must write the comp() and swap() functions. The programmer makes the decision, not the library function, which is inflexible.

The flag variable t can have an important impact on the performance of the bubble sort. Because of the way the bubble sort works, t can remain 0 (by the assignment in line 0009) only if the list is in sorted order. Therefore, if t is zero after a pass through the loop, no call to swap() is produced. If the swap() function is never called on a pass through the do-while loop, the list must be in sorted order.

For example, if the last half of the list is already in order and the t flag is not used, the sort will still process the last (sorted) part of the list. The t flag allows you to terminate the do-while loop if a pass through the list does not call the swap() function. If swap() is not called (line 0012), the t flag remains zero, which terminates the do-while loop. This termination occurs only if the list has already been sorted.

The sort is fairly simple and should contain no real surprises. Pushing the `comp()` and `swap()` functions out of the sort adds one element of generality to the function. However, there is a very specific reason for the way `comp()` and `swap()` are used. The technique is described in the following section.

Why Use a Pointer to Function?

The most important thing to learn from the example of a bubble sort is why a pointer to function is used rather than a simple function call. To illustrate, we'll suppose that you need a program to perform two bubble sorts. The first sort is on a series of integer values, and the second is on a series of `long` data types.

Let's also assume that the library contains a bubble sort function in which the `comp()` and `swap()` features are external function calls that are called by *name,* not with pointers. In this case, the calls in Figure 2.2a would appear as those in Figure 2.3.

Figure 2.3
Function Call by Name within `bsort()`

```
        .
        .
if ( comp(j, j+1) > 0) {        /* 0011 */
        swap(j, j+1);           /* 0012 */
        .
```

You now begin to write the first sort for the integer data type and code the `comp()` and `swap()` functions to handle the integer values. If we omit the details for the moment, `comp()` and `swap()` may look like those in Figure 2.4.

Because the `i` and `j` parameters passed to `comp()` are indexes to the integer array (`int_data[]`), the values in the array can be subtracted directly to return the appropriate value (an `int`) for use by `swap()`. So far, so good. Turning to the second half of the program to sort the `long` data type, you realize that new compare and swap functions must be written (as shown in Figure 2.5).

Figure 2.4
Integer comp( ) **and** swap( )

```
int comp(i, j)
unsigned i, j;
{
        return(intdata[i] - intdata[j] );
}


int swap(i, j)
unsigned i, j;
{

    .
    .

}
```

Figure 2.5
long comp( ) **and** swap( )

```
int comp(i, j)
unsigned i, j;
{

        return(data[i] - data[j] > 0 ? 1 : data[i] - data[j] ? -1
: 0);

}


int swap(i, j)
unsigned i, j;
{

    .
    .

}
```

Now you have a real problem. The comp() and swap() functions are called by name in the bubble sort routine (lines 0011 and 0012 in Figure 2.3), but the data that must be compared and swapped by these functions varies according to the data type being sorted. That is, the first call to comp() requires the processing of int data types (int_data[ ]), whereas the second call involves long data types (data[ ]).

Think about what you've tried to do. If the call in bsort() is by function name (as in Figure 2.3), you are trying to use the same function names for two *different* sets of functions that must perform different tasks. One set of comp() and swap() works on int data types, whereas the other works on long data types. Clearly, your first approach is not going to work.

What you need is a way of passing the two different comp() and swap() functions to the sort, instead of having the sort call them by name. First, recall that every function is an external data type which has a pointer associated with its function name. If you pass the pointer associated with the function to the sort function, the function receiving the pointer remains ignorant of the names of the comparison and exchange functions. By not embedding the comparison and exchange function names in the sort function, you make the sort function more general and useful.

Now let's see what happens when you use a pointer to function. Figure 2.6 shows a skeletal outline of the entire program. We have assumed that the data array to be sorted (data[ ]) has been declared before main() and is an extern.

Notice what happens when pointers are used in the function call to the bubble sort [bsort()] routine. To understand what is happening, suppose that the functions are located at the memory addresses given in Figure 2.7.

When the sort on the integer data is needed (line 0020 in Figure 2.6), bsort() is called with the following parameters:

```
bsort(n, int_comp, int_swap);
```

To the compiler, this line appears as

```
bsort(n, 50000, 51000);
```

Figure 2.6
Skeletal Outline of Sort with Pointer to Function

```
main()                                      /* 0001 */
{

        int int_comp(), int_swap(), n;      /* 0002 */
        int lg_comp(), lg_swap();           /* 0003 */


            .
            .
        bsort(n, int_comp, int_swap);       /* 0020 */
            .
        bsort(n, lg_comp, lg_swap);         /* 0040 */
            .

}


int int_comp(i, j)                          /* 0100 */
unsigned i, j;                              /* 0101 */
{

        return(int_data[i] - int_data[j]);  /* 0102 */

}


int iswap(i, j)                             /* 0150 */
unsigned i, j;                              /* 0151 */
{

            .
            .

}
```

```
int lg_comp(i, j)                            /* 0200 */
unsigned i, j;                               /* 0201 */
{

        if(data[i] - data[j] > 0)            /* 0202 */
                return 1;                    /* 0203 */
        else                                 /* 0204 */
                if(data[i] - data[j])        /* 0205 */
                        return - 1;          /* 0206 */
                else                         /* 0207 */
                        return 0;            /* 0208 */

}


int lswap(i, j)                              /* 0250 */
long i, j;                                   /* 0251 */
{
        .
        .

}
```

Figure 2.7
Assumed Memory Addresses of Functions

int_comp()	--	50,000
int_swap()	--	51,000
lg_comp()	--	60,000
lg_swap()	--	61,000

which causes bsort() to use the integer compare and swap functions. The call to bsort() works this way because we *used the function name* in calling bsort(). Because C references all functions by pointers, using only the function name (that is, with no parentheses or parameters after the function name) causes the address of the named function to be passed as a parameter during the call; the function is *not* invoked.

Referencing functions by pointers also means that the declarations of the functions within bsort() (lines 0003 and 0004) must be (*comp)() and (*swap)(). In terms of an attribute list, both declarations are "pointer to function returning int." [What would happen to the intended declaration if the parentheses were left out? What is the attribute list for *comp()?]

To call bsort() for use with the long data type, you use the following call:

```
bsort(n, lg_comp, lg_swap);
```

This call makes the compiler use

```
bsort(n, 60000, 61000);
```

which ends up passing the address of the lg_comp() and lg_swap() functions for the long data type.

When a pointer to a function is used in the function call, bsort() doesn't have to know anything about comp() and swap(). Because bsort() receives only the *address* of the function, bsort() doesn't care about the function *name*. Indeed, bsort() has no idea of the function name, only its address. *By using pointers to functions for* comp() *and* swap() *in the* bsort() *function, the programmer is free to call any function from* bsort() *simply by passing to it the appropriate address.* The bsort() function is generalized in such a way that it can sort any data type.

You should be able to see that if function names are used in bsort(), only one comp() and one swap() function can exist in a program. It also follows that using function names in bsort() allows you to sort only one data type in a program without complicating the comp() and swap() functions. By using pointers to functions in bsort(), the programmer is free to write a different comp() and swap() function for each data type or array of data to be sorted.

Other Design Considerations

Considering the way the bubble sort is written, we see that other design decisions are implicit. First, because comp() is not part of bsort(), the programmer can determine how the compares work. The programmer can also code the comp() function for an ascending or descending sort.

The bubble sort is always called in the same manner; it functions independently of whether the sort is ascending or descending. A descending sort, for example, simply reverses the values returned by comp().

Second, the programmer can write different error-handling routines into the various comp() and swap() functions as these routines are needed. For example, error conditions on a sort of integer data can be treated differently from those for a sort of long data, even though both use the bsort() function.

Removing the comp() and swap() functions from bsort() creates a more flexible bubble sort than one in which these functions are integrated directly into bsort(). This step is the first one in generalization. Making comp() and swap() pointers to functions, however, adds another dimension of flexibility to bsort(). Keep this pointer-to-function concept in mind whenever you write new functions for your library. The concept will help you develop a more versatile function library.

A Shell Sort

Although the bubble sort is the simplest sort, it is usually not the most efficient. The main reason for this inefficiency is that the bubble sort, on each pass through the loop, compares each value in the list to all other elements. For a random list of n values, the bubble sort approaches n^2 comparisons. Clearly, the performance of the bubble sort deteriorates rapidly as n becomes larger.

The Shell sort (named for Donald Lewis Shell) is a common alternative to the bubble sort. A Shell sort divides a list of n items into smaller subgroups for comparison. (See Donald E. Knuth, vol. 3, p. 85, for discussion.) Figure 2.8a illustrates the source code for the Shell sort algorithm; program comments are in Figure 2.8b.

Notice that the comp() and swap() functions are called in the same way that they were in the bubble sort. The consistency of the calling convention also enhances the value of library functions. Again, the Shell sort works independently of the sorting of the data type because pointers to functions are used for the compares and swaps.

Given the way the sorting functions [that is, the sorts, comp()'s and swap()'s] are written, the programmer can select which sort to use "on

Figure 2.8a
Shell Sort

```
/*************************************************************************
 *
 *    Shell Sort modified for determining intervals (See Knuth, p. 85)
 *
 *************************************************************************/

#define void int

void ssort(n, comp, swap)                    /* 0001 */
unsigned n;                                   /* 0002 */
int (*comp)();                                /* 0003 */
int (*swap)();                                /* 0004 */
{

        int m;                                /* 0006 */
        int h, i, j, k;                       /* 0007 */

        m = n;                                /* 0008 */

        while(m /= 2) {                       /* 0009 */
              k = n - m;                      /* 0010 */
              j = 1;                          /* 0011 */

              do {                            /* 0012 */
                  i = j;                      /* 0013 */

                  do {                        /* 0014 */
                      h = i + m;              /* 0015 */
                      if((*comp)(i - 1, h - 1)
                              > 0) {          /* 0016 */
                          (*swap)(i - 1, h - 1);  /* 0017 */
                          i -= m;             /* 0018 */
                      } else                  /* 0019 */
                              break;          /* 0020 */
                  } while(i >= 1);            /* 0021 */
```

```
    j += 1;                                    /* 0022 */
    } while(j <= k);                           /* 0023 */


  }                                            /* 0024 */


}
```

```
/*********************** end of function ********************************/
```

Figure 2.8b
Program Comments for Shell Sort

Line 0001	Main entry point for Shell sort. Three parameters are passed to the function.
Line 0002	Number of records to be sorted
Line 0003	Pointer to function that compares two record keys, k[i] and k[j]. Compares are done by subtraction. The returned value from the function is greater than 0 if k[i] > k[j], equal to 0 if k[i] == k[j], or less than 0 if k[i] < k[j].
Line 0004	Pointer to function that swaps two records
Line 0006	Interval indicator
Line 0007	Internal counters
Line 0008	Set initial value for interval.
Line 0009	While an interval exists, data left for sorting. When m /= 2 equals zero, sort is finished.
Line 0010	Initialize k.
Line 0011	Initialize j.
Line 0012	do-while for setting lower segment boundary
Line 0013	Initialize i.
Line 0014	do-while for setting middle segment boundary and doing compare-swap

Line 0015	Set middle boundary.
Line 0016	Pointer to compare function
Line 0017	Pointer to swap is called after comparison.
Line 0018	Set i if swap made.
Line 0019	If no swap needed ...
Line 0020	break out of do-while.
Line 0021	Test i for another pass through do-while if swap was made.
Line 0022	Increment j for next set of compares.
Line 0023	Test j for other elements in list.
Line 0024	Close of outer while loop.
Line 0025	End of function

the fly." For example, the Shell sort is usually faster than the bubble sort, but not always. The bubble sort may be faster if a list has almost been sorted, which is often the case when a new item is being added to a previously sorted list. With generalized sorting functions, the programmer can call either sort based on the expected degree of order in the list. The task of sorting is much more difficult if the sort functions are not generalized.

A Quick Sort

Although the bubble and Shell sort algorithms are sufficient for most sorting problems, the *quick* sort can be faster. But performance is not the major reason why the quick sort is included here. (In fact, a quick sort on a list of data that is already in order is not quite as fast as a bubble sort on an unordered list of data.) We use the quick sort, however, to illustrate how a recursive function call can be used.

Recursive Function Calls

A *recursive function* is one that can call itself. The most common example of recursion is one that calculates factorials. To illustrate, 5 factorial (written as 5!) is 120 and is calculated through the following procedure:

$$5! = 5 * 4 * 3 * 2 * 1 = 120$$

Although many writers use the factorial example because it is fairly easy to understand, it is not a very good candidate for a recursive function call for two reasons. First, a factorial is, by definition, a sequential-processing problem. That is, it begins with the number to be factored (n) and multiplies the number by n-1. The intermediate result is stored, then multiplied by n-2. This sequence is repeated until n equals 1. When this happens, the intermediate result is the factorial. This kind of sequential-processing problem can be more easily (and clearly) written with an iterative loop.

A second reason for not using recursion with a factorial is that a recursive function call typically uses more memory than its iterative equivalent. Certain administrative data is generated by the compiler to process each function call. The data is duplicated each time the function is called recursively. Each recursive call also generates new copies of any auto variables contained in the function. As a result, a recursive function tends to be more "memory intensive" than its nonrecursive counterpart.

If the task of the function is an easily defined, sequential process (such as a factorial), it should not use a recursive function call. If the sequential process is sufficiently complex that its logic cannot be easily followed (for example, Fibonnacci numbers), recursion may be the only feasible solution.

A candidate for a recursive function call will often have the following characteristics:

1. The algorithm requires that a loop be performed in the function.

2. Variables in the loop use intermediate values that were determined on the previous pass through the loop.

3. The values are indeterminate prior to the execution of the function.

A factorial function has the first two characteristics but not the third. This means that we can determine the values of the variables before executing the loop because of the sequential nature of a factorial. On the other hand, a binary search on a sort list is a candidate for a recursive function because segmenting the list depends on comparisons of the unknown values in it. (The upper and lower boundaries are set from a comparison of two unknown values.)

To understand how recursion works, try running the program in Figure 2.9. (The function here is a modification of the printd() function described by Brian W. Kernighan and Dennis M. Ritchie in their book *The C Programming Language,* Prentice-Hall, Inc., Englewood Cliffs, New Jersey, 1978, p. 85.) In this program, the function should take an integer value and print it out in ASCII. The problem is that we must print out the value "backwards"; the hundreds-digit must be printed before the tens-digit, and the tens-digit before the units-digit.

Figure 2.9
Program to Illustrate Recursion

```
main()                                               /* 0001 */
{                                                    /* 0002 */

        int n;                                       /* 0003 */

        n = 12345;                                   /* 0004 */
        printf("Entering the recursive call: \n");   /* 0005 */
        printd(n);                                   /* 0006 */
        printf("\n");                                /* 0007 */

}                                                    /* 0008 */


int printd(num)                                      /* 0009 */
int num;                                             /* 0010 */
{                                                    /* 0011 */

        int j;                                       /* 0012 */

        printf("\nnum = %d", num / 10);              /* 0013 */

        if(num < 0) {                                /* 0014 */
                putchar('-');                        /* 0015 */
                num = -num;                          /* 0016 */
        }                                            /* 0017 */
```

```
if (j = num/10)                              /* 0018 */
        printd(j);                           /* 0019 */

else                                         /* 0020 */
    printf("\n\nReturning from recursion \n"); /* 0021 */

printf("\nnum (mod 10) = %01d", num % 10);   /* 0022 */

}                                            /* 0023 */
```

The Stack

Keep in mind that a recursive function call in C causes a new set of variables to be produced each time the function is called. The old values are pushed onto a stack. The *stack* is a place in memory that operates like a LIFO (Last In, First Out) buffer.

A LIFO buffer is like the plate dispenser at a salad bar. As freshly washed dishes are placed on the spring-loaded dispenser, the last plate on the stack is the first taken off. (Does anyone really like a hot salad plate?) The original plates on the stack get pushed farther down as more plates are added.

The stack managed by the compiler operates much the same way, except that data is pushed on the stack. The value of the integer to be printed in Figure 2.9 is 12345. Because the number has five digits, printd() should call itself four times. [The first call is from main().] However, because automatic storage class variables typically reside on the stack during a function call, the compiler has five values on the stack. Figure 2.10 illustrates the stack during the recursive calls (line 0019 in Figure 2.9) and shows the value of j each time the call is performed. (We've drawn the stack to coincide with the salad bar analogy.)

The first time we enter the function, the value of num is 12345. The check for the negative sign fails, causing us to fall into the recursive call to printd() in line 0019. Because num is an integer that is divided by 10 in line 0018, the answer (1234.5) is truncated to 1234 and pushed on the stack (column 1 in Figure 2.10). The parameter in the first recursive call to printd() becomes 1234.

Figure 2.10
Stack Picture on Recursive Calls
for Variable j from **Figure 2.9**

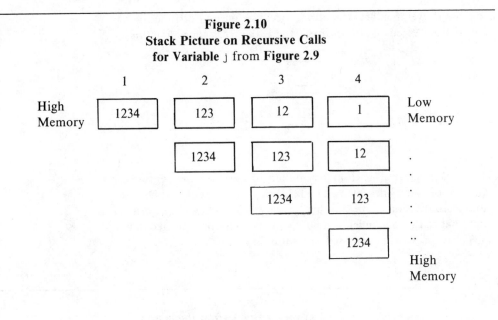

When you enter printd(), num becomes 1234 because of the first recursive call. After line 0018 has been executed the second time, j equals 123 because of the division by 10 (that is, 123.4 becomes 123). Once again, j is pushed on the stack, producing the stack picture in column 2 of Figure 2.10. Then the next recursive call to printd() is made, using 123 as the parameter.

The recursive calls continue until the expression num/10 in line 0018 has a value of zero. When this occurs, the value of num is 1. (Look at the stack in column 4 of Figure 2.10.) No further recursive calls to printd() are made. The printf() in Line 0023 (see Figure 2.9) uses the parameter n%10. Because modulo division yields the remainder of the division, a 1 is printed on the screen.

After the 1 is printed, the end of the function is reached *for the first time*. The return tells the compiler to start clearing off the stack. The stack picture in column 4 shows how the values will be "popped" off the stack, from top (lower memory) to bottom. Because one end-of-function has already been executed after printing the 1, the stack looks like this:

The stack is cleared as though a bunch of `return` statements were squeezed between lines 0022 and 0023. Each `return`, coupled with the modulo 10 division of the number on the stack, causes the rightmost digit (that is, the remainder of modulo 10 division) to be printed in line 0023. This process is illustrated in Figure 2.11.

Figure 2.11
Clearing the Stack from Recursion

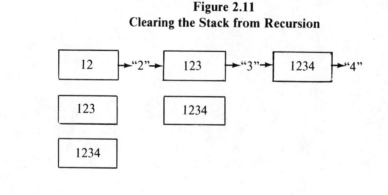

After the stack has been cleared, the 5 is printed from the first invocation of `printd()`, and the final end-of-function causes a return to `main()`.

The actual `printd()` function, of course, does not contain `printf()`'s. Run the program in Figure 2.9 without modification first, then change line 0023 to use a `putchar()`, and remove the remaining `printf()`'s. Although `printd()` can be written without recursion (see Kernighan and Ritchie, p. 85), the recursive version is much more diréct and understandable. To try your hand at a recursive function, write a function that outputs the binary representation of a number. The algorithm is similar to that of printd( ).

A Quick Sort and Recursion

The quick sort can be written as a recursive function because it has all three characteristics implicit in the algorithm. Simply stated, the algorithm partitions the list into two parts and performs left-right and right-left scans of the data. The sequence of exchanges, however, is not known from the algorithm. (For a complete discussion, see Knuth, vol. 3, p. 116; see also W. H. Burge, *Recursive Programming Techniques,* Addison-Wesley Publishing Company, Inc., Reading, Massachusetts, 1975, pp. 229-230). Figure 2.12a is an example of a quick sort; program comments are in Figure 2.12b.

Figure 2.12a
Quick Sort

```
/***********************************************************************
 *
 *      Quick Sort as described by Knuth, p. 116
 *
 ***********************************************************************
 *
 *      This program performs a quick sort on n records. It is
 *      independent of the record and key. This independence is
 *      possible because pointers to a key-comparison function and
 *      record-swapping function are passed to the sort. The function
 *      calling convention is
 *
 *              qsort(n,comp,swap)
 *
```

```
*       where
*
*               n is the number of records to sort.
*               comp is a pointer to a function that will compare
*                   two record keys and return an integer representing
*                   the logical relationship of the keys. Returns:
*
*                   < 0    if key[i] <  key[j] (ascending) or
*                          key[i] > key[j] (descending)
*                   = 0    if key[i] == key[j]
*                   > 0    if key[i] >  key[j] (ascending) or
*                          key[i] < key[j] (descending)
*
*               swap is a pointer to a function that will swap two
*                   records.
*
*       Both comp and swap are called with two parameters that are
*       indices to records, with the first record being 0 and the last
*       record being n - 1.
*
***************************************************************************
*
*       This program illustrates the use of pointers to functions.
*       In the program the pointers to functions are used to allow
*       the sort algorithm to function independently of the data record.
*       Additionally, the quick sort illustrates a recursive function.
*       Recursion is used to allow partitioning of the records into
*       smaller subgroups for sorting purposes.
*
*       Note that unsigned variables are used for counters and indices.
*       An unsigned integer not only has twice the range for indices
*       as an integer does, but also will allow for more efficient
*       code on most processors. Most processors inherently do unsigned
*       arithmetic, allowing for fast adds and subtracts. However, few
*       will do signed arithmetic, thereby forcing the generation of more
*       code to properly handle the sign of the number.
*
***************************************************************************/
```

```
#define void int

static int (*_comp)(), (*_swap)();                              /* 0001 */



void qsort(n,comp,swap)                                         /* 0002 */
unsigned n;                                                     /* 0003 */
int (*comp)();                                                  /* 0004 */
int (*swap)();                                                  /* 0005 */
{                                                               /* 0006 */

        _comp = comp;                                           /* 0007 */
        _swap = swap;                                           /* 0008 */
        _quick(0, n - 1);                                       /* 0009 */

}

/*********************** end of function *********************************/

static void _quick(lb, ub)                                      /* 0011 */
unsigned lb, ub;                                                /* 0012 */
{

        unsigned j;
        unsigned _rearr();

        if(lb < ub) {
                if(j = _rearr(lb, ub))
                        _quick(lb, j - 1);                      /* 0017 */
                _quick(j + 1, ub);                              /* 0018 */
        }

}

/*********************** end of function *********************************/
```

```
static unsigned _rearr(lb, ub)                              /* 0021 */
unsigned lb, ub;                                            /* 0022 */
{

        do {
                while(ub > lb && (*_comp)(ub, lb) >= 0)     /* 0025 */
                        ub-;
                if(ub != lb) {                              /* 0027 */
                        (*_swap)(ub, lb);                   /* 0028 */
                        while(lb < ub && (*_comp)(lb, ub) <= 0) /* 0029 */
                                lb++;                       /* 0030 */
                        if(lb != ub)                        /* 0031 */
                                (*_swap)(lb, ub);           /* 0032 */
                }                                           /* 0033 */
        } while(lb != ub);
        return lb;

}                                                           /* 0036 */


/*********************** end of function ********************************/
```

Figure 2.12b
Program Comments for Quick Sort

Line 0001   Two static variables are used for storage of the pointers to functions in order to decrease the number of parameters passed to the recursive functions in the quick sort.

Line 0002   Main entry point for the quick sort. Three parameters are passed.

Line 0003   The number of records to be sorted is the first parameter, which is an unsigned value.

Line 0004   The second parameter is a pointer to a function that compares all keys of two records and returns an integer that expresses the following relationships for an ascending-order sort.

r[i]-r[j] such that:

```
if (r[i] > r[j])
        return (1);
if (r[i] == r[j])
        return (0);
if (r[i] < r[j])
        return (-1);
```

In fact, if the two keys were integers, the code can be

```
return(r[i]-r[j]);
```

qsort() will adjust the pointers i and j so that they are relative base 0.

Line 0005   The third parameter is a pointer to a function that swaps two records.

qsort() will adjust the pointers i and j so that they are relative base 0.

Line 0007   The static variable comp is set to the parameter comp.

Line 0008   The static variable swap is set to the parameter swap.

Line 0009   The recursive static function quick is executed with a lower bound of 0 and an upper bound of n-1.

Notice the use of static variables in Figure 2.12a. For example, comp( ) and swap( ) are referenced through two pointer variables (line 0001). Because these static variables are declared outside any function, they have an external static storage class. Since the scope of external static variables is limited to the file in which they are created, we have established permanent (yet private) storage for these two variables. In other words, we do not have to pass these values as parameters in the recursive function _quick( ) and thereby waste stack space; parameter names also will not "collide" with those used in another file (for example, the program file). (See lines 0017 and 0018.)

You will also notice that unsigned variables are used for the indexes related to the lower (lb) and upper (ub) bounds of the search. (See lines 0012 and 0022.) These unsigned variables extend the range of numbers that can be used in the function.

A less obvious reason for using the unsigned data type is that most processors are designed for unsigned arithmetic, which results in faster adds and subtracts. Using integers forces the generation of code to process properly the sign of the number. The int data type, therefore, will degrade the performance of the sort and increase code size unnecessarily. Most variables used to control loops in C can be unsigned data types and should generate more efficient code.

The qsort( ) function does little more than assign pointers to the statics created in line 0001 and call _quick( ). The parameters passed to _quick( ) are the lower and upper bounds used in the sort. These are set initially to the first (0) and last (n-1) elements in the list to be sorted.

The quick sort algorithm uses the _rearr( ) function to place the sorted data back into the list. (Notice how the parameters switch positions in lines 0028 and 0032.) Depending on the lower-bound value returned from _rearr( ) in line 0036, _quick( ) may be recursively called in both lines 0017 and 0018.

The comparisons and swaps are performed as part of the _rearr( ) function (lines 0028 and 0032). The comp( ) function alters the upper and lower bounds used during the sort (lines 0025 and 0029). The swaps are made based on the relationship between these two boundaries (lines 0027 and 0031). Because the comp( ) and swap( ) functions are provided by the programmer and are external to the sort, any data type can be sorted.

A Sample Sort Program

Since the algorithms used in the Shell and quick sorts are not obvious, this chapter concludes with a program that integrates into a disk sort program examples of the comp( ) and swap( ) functions and all the sorts that have been discussed.

Figure 2.13
Disk Sort

```
/*****************************************************************************
 *
 * Application for Sorts
 *
 * Generalized Disk-Sort Program (fixed record length)
 *
 *****************************************************************************
 *
 * This program will sort a file consisting of fixed length records
 * and create an output file that is sorted in the desired order.
 * Up to ten fields may be specified for the sort criteria.
 * The input file will first be copied and then sorted in place
 * using system I/O calls for disk random access.
 *
 *****************************************************************************/

#include "stdio.h"

#define void int              /* used for function returns */
#define READ 0                /* used for open() */
#define WRITE 1               /* used for open() */
#define RW 2                  /* used for open() */
```

```
unsigned off[10];                       /* offset arrary -1 is end */
unsigned length[10];                    /* length of sort field */
int trans[10];                          /* TRUE if upper to lower */
int order[10];                          /* ASCEND or DESCEND */
int reclen;                             /* record length */
int stype;                              /* type of sort */
int infd, wfd, outfd;                   /* file descriptors */
char infile[15], outfile[15];           /* file names */
char *reci, *recj;                      /* pointers to records */
unsigned xreci, xrecj;                  /* record numbers */


/************************************************************************
 *
 * This function compares the key fields of records i and j.
 * It returns 0 if they are equal, < 0 if j > i and ascending order,
 * and > 0 if j < i and ascending order.
 *
 ***********************************************************************/

int comp(i, j)                          /* general compare function */
unsigned i, j;                          /* record indicies */
{

        int len;                        /* working counter */

        rec_read(i, j);                 /* read records i and j */
```

```
for( len = 0; off[len] != -1 &&
        len < 10; len++) {                  /* for each key */

        char *i, *j;                        /* pointers for keys */
        int k;                              /* counter */
        int ii, jj;                         /* translated chars */

        i = reci + off[len];                /* address of i key[len] */
        j = recj + off[len];                /* address of j key[len] */

        for(k = 0; k < length[len]; k++) {
                                            /* for each char in key */

            ii = trans[len] ? toupper(i[k]) : i[k];
                                /* ii=trans */
            jj = trans[len] ? toupper(j[k]) : j[k];
                                /* jj=trans */

            if( ii == jj)           /* if equal continue k loop */
                    continue;
            else
                    return ( order[len] ? ii - jj : jj - ii);
                                /* else return diff based
                                   on order */

        } /* end for(k = 0 */
    } /* end for(len = 0 */

    return (0);                             /* all keys equal */

} /* end comp() */
```

```
/**************************************************************************
 *
 * This function swaps records i and j
 *
 **************************************************************************/

int swap(i, j)                              /* swap two records */
unsigned i, j;                              /* record indicies */
{

        unsigned k;                         /* working index */

        k = xreci;                          /* swap xreci and xrecj */
        xreci = xrecj;
        xrecj = k;

        /* place file outfd at record xreci */

        lseek(outfd, (long)xreci * (long)(unsigned)reclen, 0);

        /* write record xreci */

        if(write(outfd, reci, reclen) != reclen)
                error(2);                   /* put write error */

        /* place file outfd at record xrecj */

        lseek(outfd, (long)xrecj * (long)(unsigned)reclen, 0);

        /* write record xrecj */

        if(write(outfd, recj, reclen) != reclen)
                error(2);                   /* put write error */

} /* end swap() */
```

```
/**************************************************************************
 *
 * This function reads records i and j into reci and recj if they are
 * not already there.
 *
 **************************************************************************/

void rec_read(i, j)                          /* read records */
unsigned i, j;                               /* record indicies */
{

        if(xreci != i) {                     /* if i not in memory */

                /* read record i */

                lseek(outfd, (long)i * (long)(unsigned)reclen, 0);
                if(read(outfd, reci, reclen) != reclen)
                        error(1);            /* put read error */
                xreci = i;                   /* set global to i */

        } /* end if(xreci != i */

        if(xrecj != j) {                     /* if j not in memory */

                /* read record j */

                lseek(outfd, (long)j * (long)(unsigned)reclen, 0);
                if(read(outfd, recj, reclen) != reclen)
                        error(1);            /* put read error */
                xrecj = j;                   /* set global to j */

        } /* end if(xrecj != j */

} /* end rec_read() */
```

```
/**************************************************************************
 *
 * Main line code starts here
 *
 **************************************************************************/

void main(argc, argv)
int argc;
char *argv[];
{

        int i, j, k, m;
        int nrecs;
        char *buff;
        char *l;
        char *calloc();

        printf("\nSort Version 1.00\n");
        if(argc < 2) {
                printf("Sort Parameter File Name Misssing.\n");
                exit();
        }
        if((wfd = open(argv[1], READ)) == -1) {
                printf("Error in opening file: %s\n", argv[1]);
                exit();
        }

        printf("\nReading parameter file: %s\n", argv[1]);
        if(!(buff = calloc(1024, 1)) ) {
                printf("Not enough memory to read parameter file.\n");
                exit();
        }

        if(!(i = read(wfd, buff, 1024)) ) {
                printf("Error in reading parameter file.\n");
                exit();
        }
```

```
for(j = 0; infile[j] = buff[j]; j++)
        ;                                    /* read input file name */
for(j++, k = 0; outfile[k] = buff[j]; k++, j++)
        ;                                    /* read output file name */

stype = buff[++j];                           /* read type of sort */

k = 0;
l = &reclen;
while(k < sizeof(int))
        l[k++] = buff[++j];                  /* read record length */
l = &nrecs;
k = 0;
while(k < sizeof(int))
        l[k++] = buff[++j];                  /* read number of records */
for(m = 0; m < 10; m++) {

        k = 0;
        l = &off[m];
        while(k < sizeof(unsigned))
                l[k++] = buff[++j];          /* read offset */
        if(off[m] == -1)                     /* if last offset break */
                break;

        k = 0;
        l = &length[m];
        while(k < sizeof(unsigned))
                l[k++] = buff[++j];          /* read length */
        k = 0;
        l = &trans[m];
        while(k < sizeof(int))
                l[k++] = buff[++j];          /* read tranlation */
        k = 0;
        l = &order[m];
        while(k < sizeof(int))
                l[k++] = buff[++j];          /* read order */
} /* end for(m = 0 */
```

```
close(wfd);                               /* close parm file */

free(buff);                               /* free parm buffer */

reci = calloc(reclen, 1);                 /* allocate reci space */
recj = calloc(reclen, 1);                 /* allocate recj space */
if(!reci || !recj) {
        printf("Error: insufficient memory for two records.");
        exit();
}

if(strcmp(infile, outfile)) {
                                /* if input file not output file */

        if((infd = open(infile, READ)) == -1) {
                printf("Error in opening input file: %s\n", infile);
                exit();
        }


        if((outfd = creat(outfile, WRITE)) == -1) {
                printf("Error in creatine output file: %s\n", outfile);
                exit();
        }

        for(k = reclen, m = 1; (unsigned)k > 1024; m++,
                (unsigned)k / 2)
                ;
        for(j = 0; j < 1024; j += k)
                ;
        j -= k;
        for(i = 50; i; -i)
        if(buff = calloc(j, i))
                break;

        i = (unsigned)j * i / (unsigned)reclen;
```

```
        if(!i) {
                buff = reci;
                i = 1;
        }


        printf("Copying file %s to file %s\n", infile, outfile);

        do {
                j = read(infd, buff, reclen * i);
                if(!j || j == -1)
                        break;
                i = write(outfd, buff, j);
                if(i != j) {
                        printf("Error in copying to output file: %s\n"
                                , outfile);
                        exit();
                }
        } while( j);

        if(j == -1) {
                printf("Error in reading input file: %s\n", infile);
                exit();
        }

        close(infd);

        if(buff != reci)
                free(buff);
                close(outfd);
                printf("Copy complete.\n");
}

outfd = open(outfile, RW);
```

```
read(outfd, reci, reclen);
read(outfd, recj, reclen);
xreci = 0;
xrecj = 1;

printf("Sort Started: ");
if(tolower(stype) == 'q') {
        printf("Quick Sort.\n");
        qsort(nrecs, comp, swap);
} else if(tolower(stype) == 's') {
        printf("Shell-Metzner Sort.\n");
        ssort(nrecs, comp, swap);
} else {
        printf("Bubble Sort.\n");
        bsort(nrecs, comp, swap);
}
lseek(outfd, 0l, 2);
close(outfd);
printf("Sort of file: %s completed\n", outfile);

}
```

```
/**********************************************************************
 *
 * This funtion prints error messages
 *
 *********************************************************************/

void error(i)
int i;
{

        switch(i) {
                case 1:
                        printf("\nError on read.\n");
                        break;

                case 2:
                        printf("\nError on write.\n");

        }
        exit();

}

/*********************** end of function ********************************/
```

Reading the Parameter File

The disk sort program is designed to read a parameter file that contains the information needed to perform the sort. (The details for a program that writes this parameter file are covered in the next chapter.) You can visualize the contents of the parameter file as shown in Figure 2.14.

The first two variables in the file are the file names used in the sort. Each file name is treated as a null-terminated string. If the input file is named data.num and the output file is named sdata.num, they appear in the file as

        data.num\0sdata.num\0

where '\0' is the null terminator for strings.

Figure 2.14
Contents of Parameter File

Var 1	Var 2	Var 3	Var 4	Var 5	Var 6	Var 7	Var 8	Var 9

where:

Var: (Program variable)

1 = Input file name   `infile[]`
2 = Output file name   `outfile[]`
3 = Type of sort   `stype`
4 = Record length   `reclen`
5 = Number of records   `nrecs`
6 = Offset to sort field   `off[]`
7 = Length of sort field   `length[]`
8 = Uppercase/lowercase translation   `trans[]`
9 = Ascending/descending order   `order[]`

The type of sort is stored as a single character, with the following interpretations:

'`s`' = Shell sort
'`b`' = bubble sort
'`q`' = quick sort

The variable `stype` determines which sort routine is called during program execution.

The variable `reclen` determines the length of each record in the file. Because no delimiter has been used to separate the records, the disk sort assumes a fixed-length record file. The variable `nrecs` tells you how many fixed-length records are in the file.

The variable `off[]` is an array that indicates the starting position of the field within the record to be sorted. For example, suppose that you want to sort by ZIP Code a file with 200 name and address records. Each record is 100 bytes long, and the ZIP Code starts with byte number `92`.

The contents of the first element in the off[] array will be 92. (You should be able to see why reclen = 100 and nrecs = 200.)

The disk sort allows the sorting of up to ten fields. The off[] array, therefore, contains the starting position for each field to be used in the sort. For example, to use two sort fields with the byte locations 92 and 50, the off[] array contains the following:

off[0] = 92   off[1] = 50   off[2] = -1

Notice that the -1 indicates that there are no more fields to be sorted. If only one sort field were used, off[1] would equal -1. Thus, the number of sorts to be done is equal to the number of nonnegative elements used in the off[] array.

The length of the sort field must also be provided. The length is contained in the length[] array. If a ZIP Code sort is being done on field position 92 and the ZIP Code is five digits long, off[0] equals 92, and length[0] equals 5. The nonzero elements in length[] match the nonnegative elements in off[]. (The length[] array is automatically initialized to zero because it was declared as a global variable.)

The trans[] array simply indicates whether you want the file to have uppercase translation prior to comparison. A nonzero value is used to request translation.

The order[] array indicates whether the sort is to be in ascending or descending order. A nonzero value indicates ascending.

Finally, note that the variables off[], length[], trans[], and order[] are repeated in the parameter file for each field to be sorted. A value of -1 in the off[] array indicates that all sort fields have been determined and the contents of the parameter file have been exhausted.

Using a parameter file to pass information simplifies the sort program. Consider what would happen to program size if all the information in the parameter file were requested each time disk sort was run. Another advantage in using a parameter file is that you can repeat the sort without reentering the same information a second time. That is, you can save a parameter file for each type of sort if you use a different parameter file name. If two types of sorts must be performed at the end of each day, the user has to supply only the parameter file name and does not have to answer all the questions for each sort.

A Look at the Disk Sort Program

The program begins with several preprocessor directives (such as #include's and #define's) and declarations for the global variables used in the program. Then three functions—comp( ), swap( ), and rec_read( )—are defined before the start of main( ). (The functions are discussed in the order in which they are called during program execution.)

Line 0011 checks whether the name of the parameter file was supplied at the time program execution began. If it was not, an error message is given (line 0012), and the program aborts (line 0013). The program then tries to open the parameter file (line 0015) and aborts if it cannot read the file (lines 0016 and 0017). If the parameter file is opened successfully, its file descriptor is assigned to wfd.

Some lines in this program have been split. In these cases, the line count is maintained at an increment of one, even though there may appear to be two lines. Line splitting is done to simplify printing the text. In your own version of the program, a split line will usually fit on one line.

Line 0020 does a call to calloc( ), requesting 1,024 bytes of storage. If the request is filled, buff points to the start of the 1,024-byte buffer. If the request for storage cannot be filled, calloc( ) returns a pointer with a value of zero. This action will cause the error message (line 0021) to be issued and the program to abort.

If all goes well, the parameter file is read (line 0024) and placed into the buffer pointed to by buff. Note that the variable i contains the number of bytes that were actually read into the buffer.

Lines 0028 and 0029 transfer the input file name from the buffer to the infile[ ] array. Lines 0030 and 0031 do the same thing for the output file array (outfile[ ]). Because buff is a "pointer to chars" (declared in 0007), the j++ in line 0028 marches through the buffer until the NULL is encountered at the end of the input file name. Since NULL equates to logic False, the for loop terminates.

The j++ at the start of line 0030 makes the sort read over the NULL after the file name. Then the output file name is placed in outfile[ ]. The j++ at the end of line 0030 keeps us moving through the buffer. The NULL after the file name terminates the for loop.

The preincrement on j in line 0032 again makes the sort read over the NULL after the file name. Then the character associated with the type of sort to be performed is assigned to stype.

Line 0033 prepares us for getting the record length. The variable l is a "pointer to char," and line 0034 points l to the address where the record length will be stored. Keep in mind that the program which created the parameter file wrote the record length as an integer number to the file. However, because the size of an integer can be hardware dependent, line 0035 determines the size of the integer in each hardware environment and reads the appropriate number of bytes into the integer pointed to by l. (See line 0036.)

If sizeof(int) in line 0035 had been replaced by the constant 2, the sort would probably still work on most machines. The way the line is written here, however, allows the sort to function regardless of the actual length of an int. The same reasoning applies to the expressions in lines 0039, 0044, 0050, 0054, and 0058.

The for loop created by lines 0041 through 0060 is used for assigning the appropriate values for the multiple sort arrays (for example, off[ ], length[ ], trans[ ], and order[ ]) from the contents of the buffer (buff). You will recall that a -1 in the off[ ] array means that we have finished reading the contents of the parameter file. This action is reflected in lines 0046 and 0047.

Because we have finished using the parameter file, it is closed (line 0061), and the space allocated to the buffer is freed (line 0062).

Lines 0063 and 0064 request enough storage to read two records from the file to be sorted. The variables reci and recj are pointers to that storage. Line 0065 says that if either storage request cannot be fulfilled (that is, a pointer of zero is returned), an error message will be given and the program will abort (lines 0066 and 0067).

Line 0069 tests whether the input and output files are the same. If they are, the file does not need to be copied, and the statements controlled by the if (lines 0069 through 0111) are not executed.

If the input and output files are not the same, line 0070 attempts to open the input file and assign the file descriptor to infd. Line 0074 tries to create the output file and assign its descriptor to outfd. Both lines contain error checking to ensure that the program will abort if something goes wrong.

Starting with line 0083, the code has been written to obtain the largest amount of buffer space possible in preparation for reading the file. The code attempts to allocate enough memory to hold 50 records. For example, if the record length is 100 bytes, the first request to `calloc()` is for 50,000 bytes of storage (that is, 1000x50). Many microcomputers have only 64K to begin with, so `buff` probably receives a value of zero for the pointer. Since the pointer returned by `calloc()` is logic False, the `break` is not executed, and the `for` loop tries again.

On the second pass, `calloc()` tries for 49,000 bytes of storage, since `i` is decremented in line 0083. Although a large system may satisfy the request on the first call to `calloc()`, smaller systems will sit in the `for` loop until the request is satisfied. If the request is fulfilled, `buff` has a nonzero value, and the `break` transfers us out of the loop. The result is an amount of free storage that will hold the largest multiple of a record length in 1,000 byte blocks.

Line 0088 causes a buffer equal to one record length to be allocated for the input buffer if the request for storage cannot be fulfilled. (We know at least one record can be read in because of line 0063.) This activity occurs if `i` is zero. Otherwise, lines 0088 and 0089 are ignored.

The `do-while` formed by lines 0092 through 0101 does the actual file copy. Error checking is provided for both reads (lines 0094-0095 and lines 0102-0105) and writes (lines 0097-0100), and the program aborts if something is amiss. If the copy is successful, line 0106 closes the file. Line 0108 frees the buffer space for `buff` if `buff` was not used for the file copy. The output file is then closed (line 0109), and the copy segment is finished.

Line 0112 opens the file to be sorted. The variable `outfile` is the file to be sorted. The file is then opened, and its file descriptor is assigned to `outfd`. Lines 0113 through 0116 causes two records to be read into the `reci` and `recj` buffers and assigns the record indices to be initialized with `0` and `1`.

Lines 0118 through 0127 simply cause the appropriate sort to be selected. (The choice was determined when the parameter file was established.) The `lseek()` (line 0128) positions the file in preparation for the closing of the file (0129), and the program terminates (lines 0130-0131).

Compares and Swaps

You have already seen how the comp() and swap() functions work with sorts, and most of the code in the functions needs no further elaboration. Two statements, however, may require clarification. First, consider the following statement from the comp() function:

```
ii = trans[len] ? toupper(i[k]) : i[k];
```

The value of the variable len is determined by the sort key in use. If you are working with the first sort key, len will have a value of 0. If you are using case translation, trans[0] will evaluate to logic True, the toupper(i[k]) expression will be performed, and the result of the expression will be assigned to the variable ii. Otherwise, no translation is performed. The same logic is used with the ternary operator that determines the return value from the comp() function.

Second, consider the following statement that similarly appears in both the swap() and rec_read() functions:

```
lseek(outfd, (long) i * (long) (unsigned) reclen, 0);
```

Why are there so many casts in the offset for lseek()? You will recall that the variable reclen is an integer, but the offset in lseek() must be a long. The variable reclen is first cast to an unsigned, then to a long. This process assures us that the resulting long from the expression will always be positive, even if a negative record length is entered. The rest of the disk sort program is straightforward.

A number of improvements can be made to this program. For example, a simple one is to change error() to incorporate the ideas discussed in Chapter 1 regarding the perror() function. Another change involves removing from main() the code for reading the parameter file and putting it into a function.

A more ambitious change is to add some form of memory management technique to increase the overall performance of the program. For example, the program will always read in a new record, even if the one it is looking for is currently in memory. As it stands now, the sort is rather slow. (In other words, run it on a modest-sized file just before going out to lunch.) But the sort has the redeeming feature that it does work and is not limited to a file that fits in memory. Try some of these changes and see what happens.

Editor's Note to Chapter 3

The functions and programs presented in this chapter offer a method for terminal handling. Several functions are presented for incorporation in your library. The installation program in this chapter modifies the disk-resident object code.

The installation program was written under and targeted for systems running under the CP/M operating system. The same installation program may be used in the MS-DOS environment provided the programmer has made certain that offset is at its proper value and the object code program is a .COM, not .EXE, file.

If the object code file is a relocatable executable file (.EXE), this technique of altering the disk-resident file is almost impossible. To use the terminal handler, the programmer should compile the rcur.c file and link it into the program instead.

The terminal-handling functions and installation program presented in this chapter are inapplicable to the UNIX environment, in which termcap and curses would be used in place of the code in this chapter. Intermediate UNIX programmers are nevertheless invited to read this chapter for some of the techniques used in this code.

The installation program presented in this chapter assumes that getchar() and putchar() must be unbuffered, allowing the program to communicate directly with the terminal one character at a time. If your C compiler's standard library does not follow this convention, new functions must be written to handle getchar() and putchar(), and the source code to the installation program must be modified to reflect these new functions.

The program also assumes that read() and write() from and to the terminal are possible with your compiler. It is also assumed that fd = 0 is the standard unbuffered input device and that `fd = 1` is the standard unbuffered output device. Check your compiler documentation to ensure that this assumption is correct and make changes to the installation program, if necessary.

The `atol()` (ASCII-to-long) function is also used in this chapter. Many of the CP/M compilers do not have this function. Appendix F contains an `atol()` function that may be incorporated into most libraries.

C. D. V.

3

The General Terminal Library

This book examines various techniques that can make life easier for the programmer. But what about the user, the person who will ultimately be running the program? What are we doing to make life easier for the user? We may get so bogged down in coding the program that we forget that someone totally unfamiliar with the program must be able to run it.

Computer journals are filled with such terms as "machine-human interface," "user friendly," and many others. These concepts seem to raise the question: How easy is it for the inexperienced user to run the program? And from the programmer's point of view, another question arises: How easy is it for the user to supply information to the program without making a mistake? Furthermore, does the program handle a mistake gracefully if one is made?

The only assumption you can make is that the user has a terminal at which information is entered. The terminal (an input device) is the communications link between the program and the user. Let's look at some command features that will enable you to take full advantage of the terminal as a means of communication between the program and the user.

Terminal Commands

Most terminals support a number of commands that cause specific actions to take place on the CRT. These commands can be used to make the user's data entry more understandable and less error-prone. For example, the *clear screen code* blanks the screen and usually places the cursor in the upper left-hand corner of the screen (the *home* position). This command gets rid of any "clutter" on the screen and focuses the attention of the user on the input question at hand.

Direct cursor addressing is another terminal feature that allows you to place the cursor at a specific row-column coordinate on the screen. This feature is especially useful when large amounts of information must be entered by the user. For example, suppose that the user must enter the information from a printed form into the computer. The programmer can display a duplicate of the form on the screen and use direct cursor addressing to place the cursor in the blank spaces on the form. The user then "fills in the blanks" on the screen. Because there is a direct correspondence between the printed form and the form displayed on the screen, entry error is less likely to occur.

There is a related advantage of direct cursor addressing: if the user does make an error, the program can place the cursor back at the beginning of the blank space and request that the information be reentered. Other error-handling techniques, which add consistency to error recovery, can also be implemented with direct cursor addressing. (One example is printing an error message in the same place on the screen).

Unfortunately, all terminals are not the same. The codes that clear the screen on one terminal may simply produce weird-looking squiggles on another. Although there is a standard (ANSI) for such codes, not all manufacturers have adopted it. As a result, the programmer must somehow cope with the differences of terminals to take full advantage of the terminal in general.

This chapter presents one method of writing a generalized "screen handler." In this approach, the user enters the codes for certain terminal commands and tests each command as it is entered. Once the codes have been entered correctly, they are written directly into the program that will use them. In other words, the installation program defines the codes for the terminal commands and writes the codes directly into the appropriate program(s).

Note that this approach assumes that the programmer knows the location of the code and data segments in a compiled program. If this is not the case, a second choice is to write the terminal command codes to a data file and read that file into the appropriate variables at the beginning of the program.

In many of the coding examples in this chapter, the figures refer to a segment within a given file. If, for example, we discuss a function called menu( ), which is the first function defined in a file named install1.com, the subheading for the figure is the following:

(Segment 1 of Program File install1.com**)**

This method is used because the order in which functions appear in some files is important. If the appropriate order is not followed, the compiler will not find certain information it needs and will generate an error message.

Note also that some files are called *program* files, and others are called *library* files. Program files are part of the terminal installation program discussed in this chapter but are *not* part of the library. Library files, however, should be added to your standard C library.

The Terminal Command Installation Program

To understand how this program works, let's first look at the program itself before we discuss the functions used in it. In this example, we build from a "minimal terminal" (that is, one with only a few terminal commands), simulating the missing commands with those that are supported. The only required terminal command is direct cursor addressing.

When the terminal command codes are used in a program, certain overhead variables must be present in contiguous form. These variables are defined in the file called scrdat.c, as shown in Figure 3.1. The contents of this file are part of any program in the library that uses terminal command processing.

Figure 3.2 shows part of the program that builds and tests the terminal commands.

Figure 3.1
scrdat.c **Library File**

```
/***************************************************************************
 *
 *      Global declarations for the general terminal library
 *
 ***************************************************************************
 *
 *      This file contains the data declarations necessary for the
 *      use of the terminal library functions.
 *
 *      This module must be the first file included in the program or
 *      must be separately compiled and be the first file linked.
 *
 *      If this procedure is not followed, the programmer must adjust
 *      the offset in array of structures called files in install2.c
 *      and recompile the install program.
 *
 ***************************************************************************/

char _ _cur1[9];              /* cursor addressing lead-in string */
char _ _cur2[9];              /* cursor addressing separator string */
char _ _ctr[9];               /* cursor addressing trailer string */
char _ _eolb[9];              /* erase-to-end-of-line string */
char _ _hite[9];              /* set high-intensity string */
char _ _lite[9];              /* set low-intensity string */
char _ _clsc[9];              /* clear screen string */
char _ _home[9];              /* home cursor string */
char _ _eopb[9];              /* erase-to-end-of-page string */
int _ _char;                  /* characters per line on terminal */
int _ _line;                  /* number of lines on terminal */
int _ _asci;                  /* flag for ascii conversion */
                              /* flag for cursor addressing */
int _ _rowo;                  /* offset added to row for cursor addressing */
int _ _colo;                  /* offset added to column */
                              /* offset for cursor addressing */
int _ _cb4r;                  /* column before row flag */
```

Figure 3.2
Program to Install Terminal Codes
(Segment 1 of install.c **File)**

```
#include "stdio.h"

#define void int

#ifndef TRUE

        #define TRUE 1
        #define FALSE 0

#endif

/* global definitions for terminal library     */

char __cur1[9];
char __cur2[9];
char __ctr[9];
char __eolb[9];
char __hite[9];
char __lite[9];
char __clsc[9];
char __home[9];
char __eopb[9];
int __char;
int __line;
int __asci;
int __rowo;
int __colo;
int __cb4r;

/* end of terminal library definitions          */

char *signon =
        "\tGeneral Purpose Terminal Installation Package Version 1.00\n";

char *el = "\n\tEnter character %1d: ";
```

```c
char buff[40];
char term[128];
int k;
int i, j;

extern char **msg[], *ctrl[];

/* end of global defs */

main()
{

        for(i = 0; i < 100; i++)
                putchar('\n');
        printf(signon);

        if(k = menu()) {

                setwidth();
                setlength();

                for(i = 0; i < __line; i++)
                        putchar('\n');

                do
                        setcur();
                while(tstcur());

                do
                        setclr();
                while(tstclr());

                do
                        seteol();
                while(tsteol());
```

```
       do
               seteop();
       while(tsteop());

       do
               sethome();
       while(tsthome());

       do
               sethigh();
       while(tsthigh());

       getterm();
       clrscr();
       cursor(10, 20);
       printf("Add Terminal: %s to Install Menu ? ", term);
       if(tolower(getchar()) == 'y')
               if(!add_one(k)) {
                       clrscr();
                       cursor(10, 30);
                       printf("Addition Not Successful");
                       cursor(22, 0);
                       printf("Hit any key to continue");
                       getchar();
               }
       }

       summary();
       clrscr();                               /* prepare for installs */
       doins();

}

/*********************** end of function ********************************/
```

An #include stdio.h is the first element of the program because we will be using file input/output (I/O).

Next, the program declares the variables that will be used globally throughout the program. The #define void int (before the global declarations) may seem strange at first, but makes sense when you think about it.

You will recall that all functions return something. In many cases, the only reason for the function call is the value it returns. Sometimes the return value is not even specified. If a function "falls off the end" (that is, if there is no return in the function), nothing useful is returned from it. These functions are flagged as returning a void to the program. For example, if a function named setlength() returns nothing useful from the function call, the declaration may be

```
void setlength()
```

The #define void int simply causes the word void to be replaced with int during the preprocessor pass. Otherwise, the declaration is marked as an error because the syntactic parser has no idea what void means. Using void in the function declaration should make you stop and think twice before using the function in an assignment [for example, x = setlength()].

The #ifndef TRUE is used to check whether TRUE is currently defined. If TRUE is not defined, then both TRUE and FALSE are defined.

The variable signon is used to print out a heading for the program when execution begins. It is a "pointer to char" and is initialized with a sign-on message.

Note the extern char **msg[] declaration. It indicates that we have an "array of pointers to pointers to chars." This declaration is an extern because the actual messages are stored in another file. This is also True for the declaration of the variable *ctrl[]; it is an "array of pointers to chars." (This variable holds the nonprinting ASCII codes.) The contents of the message file are presented in Figure 3.3.

Notice how the msg[] array is initialized. Because msg[] is declared to be an "array of pointers to pointers to chars," the first variable in the initializer list (m0) is a pointer. The attribute list will look like this:

Figure 3.3
Contents of Message File
(`msgins.c` **Program File**)

```
char *m0[] = {
        "\n\n",
        "\tEnter the number of characters on a line for your terminal: ",
        0
};

char *m1[] = {
        "\n\n",
        "\tEnter the number of lines on your terminal: ",
        0
};

char *m2[] = {
        "\n\n",
        "\tMost terminals require a specific set of codes to be sent\n",
        "\tprior to the cursor positions. The cursor lead-in string\n",
        "\tis this string. For example, the TeleVideo lead-in string\n",
        "\tis ESC =. This string consists of 2 characters, namely ESC\n",
        "\t(0x1b) followed by '='. The replies to the following questions\n",
        "\twould be 2 ESC =.\n\n",
        "\tEnter how many characters are in the terminal lead-in code: ",
        0
};

char *m3[] = {
        "\n\n",
        "\tSome terminals require characters be sent between the row\n",
        "\tand column cursor positions. For example, the ANSI standard\n",
        "\tterminals require a ',' sent between row and column. If your\n",
        "\tterminal does not require a row-column delimiter, enter '0'.\n\n",
        "\tEnter the number of characters delimiting row and column: ",
        0
};
```

```
char *m4[] = {
        "\n\n",
        "\tA trailing code is required to be sent following the cursor\n",
        "\tpositions, by some terminals. If your terminal does not need\n",
        "\ta trailing code, enter '0'.\n\n",
        "\tEnter the number of characters to follow the cursor position: ",
        0
};

char *m5[] = {
        "\n\n",
        "\tSome terminals require the column (character position) to be\n",
        "\tsent before the row (line). Others require reverse order.\n",
        "\tDoes your terminal require column sent before row (y/n): ",
        0
};

char *m6[] = {
        "\n\n",
        "\tIn some cases the cursor positions are sent to the terminal\n",
        "\tafter an offset is added to them. For example, the TeleVideo\n",
        "\trequires a 32-decimal offset to be added to both row and column\n",
        "\tprior to the coordinates being sent to the terminal. The upper\n",
        "\tleft character position on the terminal is coordinate 0,0.\n\n",
        "\tHow much decimal offset is to be added to the row (line): ",
        0
};

char *m7[] = {
        "\tHow much decimal offset is to be added to the column (char): ",
        0
};
```

```
char *m8[] = {
        "\n\n",
        "\tMany terminals support a code that will cause them to clear the\n",
        "\tscreen and home the cursor. If your terminal does not support\n",
        "\tthis code, enter '0' for the number of characters in the code,\n",
        "\tand this feature will be simulated by calls to erase to end\n",
        "\tof page.\n\n",
        "\tEnter the number of characters in the clear-screen code: ",
        0
};

char *m9[] = {
        "\n\n",
        "\tMost terminals support an erase-to-end-of-line code. This code\n",
        "\twill speed the erase-to-end-of-line function on your terminal\n",
        "\tif it is supported. This code will also assist in an erase-to-\n",
        "\tend-of-page if your terminal does not support this feature. If\n",
        "\tyour terminal does not support the erase-to-end-of-line code,\n",
        "\tenter a 0, and the erase-to-end-of-line will be simulated.\n\n",
        "\tEnter the number of characters in the erase-to-end-of-line code: ",
        0
};

char *m10[] = {
        "\n\n",
        "\tAn erase-to-end-of-page code may be sent to many terminals in\n",
        "\torder to facilitate clearing the screen from certain positions.\n",
        "\tIf your terminal does not support this feature, enter 0 and the\n",
        "\terase-to-end-of-page will be simulated by calls to erase-to-end-\n",
        "\tof-line calls.\n\n",
        "\tEnter the number of characters in the erase-to-end-of-page code: ",
        0
};
```

```
char *m11[] = {
        "\n\n",
        "\tAlmost all terminals support a code that will place the cursor\n",
        "\tat the top left position on the screen. This position is called\n",
        "\tHOME. If your terminal does not support this code, enter 0 and\n",
        "\tthe feature will be simulated by a cursor position of 0,0.\n\n",
        "\tEnter the number of characters in the home cursor code: ",
        0
};

char *m12[] = {
        "\n\n",
        "\tAttributes are used to highlight information on the screen of\n",
        "\tsome terminals. In some cases this attribute is half-intensity\n",
        "\tand in others inverse-video. Your terminal manual will contain\n",
        "\ta code for start half-intensity (inverse-video) and another for\n",
        "\tfull-intensity (normal-video).  Half-intensity is also sometimes\n",
        "\treferred to as protect mode. If your terminal does not support\n",
        "\tthis feature, enter a 0. This feature cannot be simulated by the\n",
        "\tgeneral purpose terminal routines.\n\n",
        "\tEnter the number of characters in the half-intensity start code: ",
        0
};

char *m13[] = {
        "\n\n",
        "\tEnter the number of characters in the full-intensity start code: ",
        0
};

char *m14[] = {
        "\n\n",
        "\tEnter the type of terminal you have: ",
        0
};
```

```
char *m15[] = {
        "\n\n",
        "\t\tDo you wish a summary of your codes (y/n): ",
        0
};

char *m16[] = {
        "\n\n",
        "\tTerminals that support the ANSI standard (VT 100) require that\n",
        "\tthe cursor addresses be sent as ASCII strings (i.e., '0' not 0).\n",
        "\n",
        "\tDoes your terminal require ASCII Conversion of coordinates (y/n) ",
        0
};

char **msg[] = {
        m0,
        m1,
        m2,
        m3,
        m4,
        m5,
        m6,
        m7,
        m8,
        m9,
        m10,
        m11,
        m12,
        m13,
        m14,
        m15,
        m16
};
```

```
char *ctrl[] = {
        "NUL",
        "SOH",
        "STX",
        "ETX",
        "EOT",
        "ENQ",
        "ACK",
        "BEL",
        "BS",
        "HT",
        "LF",
        "VT",
        "FF",
        "CR",
        "SO",
        "SI",
        "DLE",
        "DC1",
        "DC2",
        "DC3",
        "DC4",
        "NAK",
        "SYN",
        "ETB",
        "CAN",
        "EM",
        "SUB",
        "ESC",
        "FS",
        "GS",
        "RS",
        "US",
        "SPACE"
};
```

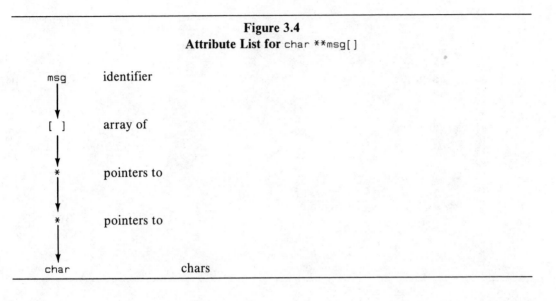

Figure 3.4
Attribute List for `char **msg[ ]`

`msg`	identifier
`[ ]`	array of
`*`	pointers to
`*`	pointers to
`char`	chars

We can see that the contents of the `msg[ ]` array are the variables `m0` through `m16`. The declaration of the `msg[ ]` array must follow the declarations of the messages themselves because the variables `m0` through `m16` must be declared before they can be used in initialization. We also know from the declaration that these 17 variables are all "pointers to pointers to char."

Now look at the declaration for `m0`. It is declared as an "array of pointers to chars." The ASCII characters that appear in the initializer list are the `char`'s being pointed to. In other words, `m0` is an array of pointers whose rvalue is the address of the characters seen in the initializer list. (You will recall that the rvalue of a pointer is the address of the object being pointed to.)

If you substitute actual names into the attribute list in Figure 3.4, you can see how the two declarations relate to each other in Figure 3.5.

Because each message ends with a `NULL` (that is, a zero) as part of the initializer list, the messages can be treated as normal strings in the program.

The obvious question is this: Why all the indirection when I can just place the messages in `main( )`? One advantage is that all the messages are

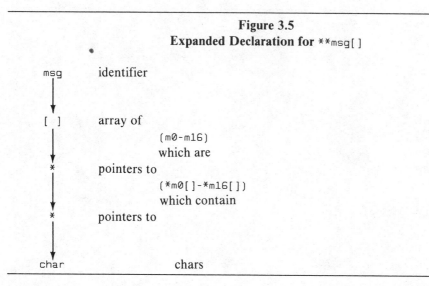

Figure 3.5
Expanded Declaration for `**msg[ ]`

```
msg          identifier


[  ]         array of
                  (m0-m16)
                  which are
 *           pointers to
                  (*m0[ ]-*m16[ ])
                  which contain
 *           pointers to


char                       chars
```

consolidated in one place (a file), which facilitates editing the messages (or adding new ones). And if a program has many long ASCII strings, memory limitations may prevent a single program with all the strings present from being compiled. Breaking out the messages allows you to edit and recompile them, then link them into the program. The technique also can be used in similar instances, such as in the `perror()` function, mentioned in Chapter 0.

The rest of the data declarations that precede `main()` in Figure 3.2 are simple and need no explanation.

Now we enter `main()`, where the first action is the sending out of 100 newlines. This is a "cheap" way of clearing the screen in preparation for the sign-on message. Once the message is given, the `menu()` function is called, which is actually another separate file linked into the program. The contents of this file are shown in Figure 3.6a.

The contents of the included file `inststr.h` will be discussed later in this chapter.

Because everything in Figure 3.6a is contained in a separate file, several `extern` data declarations are necessary. They allow the variables in this file to use the variables declared in the file containing `main()`.

Figure 3.6a
menu() **and Related Declarations**
(Segment 1 of install1.c **File)**

```
#include "inststr.c"

#ifndef TRUE

        #define TRUE    1
        #define FALSE   0

#endif

#define void int

#define BASE 0x100
#define NAME "install.com"

extern int prompt();
extern char term[];
extern char __cur1[], __cur2[], __ctr[], __eolb[], __hite[],
            __lite[], __clsc[], __home[], __eopb[];
extern int __char, __line, __asci, __rowo, __colo, __cb4r;
extern char *ctrl[];

struct __menu m_menu[10] = {                        /* open aggregate */
            {                                       /* open structure */
                    {2, 0x1b, 'Y'},
                    {0},
                    {0},
                    {2, 0x1b, 'K'},
                    {3, 0x1b, '0', 'P'},
                    {3, 0x1b, '0', '.'},
                    {0},
                    {0},
                    {0},
                    80, 24, 0, 32, 32, 0,
                    "Adds Regent"
            },                                      /* close structure */
```

```
    {                                    /* open structure */
        {2, 0x1b, 'Y'},
        {0},
        {0},
        {2, 0x1b, 'K'},
        {1, 0xf},
        {4, 0x1b, '0', 'A', 0xe},
        {1, 0xc},
        {0},
        {2, 0x1b, 'k'},
        80, 24, 0, 32, 32, 0,
        "Adds Viewpoint"
    },                                   /* close structure */
    {                                    /* open structure */
        {2, 0x1b, '='},
        {0},
        {0},
        {2, 0x1b, 'T'},
        {2, 0x1b, '('},
        {2, 0x1b, ')'},
        {2, 0x1b, '*'},
        {1, 0x1e},
        {2, 0x1b, 'Y'},
        80, 24, 0, 32, 32, 0,
        "TeleVideo 920C"
    }                                    /* close structure */
};                                       /* close aggregate */
```

```
int menu()
{

        int i, j;
        extern char buff[];

        while(TRUE) {

                printf("\n\n\t\t\tMain Menu\n\n");
                for(i = 0; m_menu[i]._spmt[0]; i++)
                        printf("\n  %2d. %s", i + 1, m_menu[i]._spmt);
                printf("\n  %2d. Not Listed", i + 1);
                printf("\n\n\t\tEnter Selection: ");
                j = atoi(gets(buff)) - 1;
                if(j > i) {
                        printf("\n\n\t\tNot a valid selection\n\n");
                        continue;
                }
                if(j == i)
                        return(i);
                move(__cur1, &m_menu[j]);
                strcpy(term, m_menu[j]._spmt);
                return(FALSE);

        }

}


/*********************** end of function ********************************/
```

Figure 3.6b

instrh.h **File**

```
struct _ _menu{
        char    _sc1[9],_sc2[9],_sc3[9];
        char    _seol[9],_shite[9],_slite[9];
        char    _sclr[9],_shome[9],_seop[9];
        int     _schar,_sline,_sasci;
        int     _srow,_scol,_scb4r;
        char    _spmt[40];
};
```

The definition of a structure, using the structure tag of _ _menu, follows the extern data declarations. (For a complete definition of struct _ _menu, see Figure 3.6b.) This creates a "mold" from which other structures can be created with the same attributes as _ _menu. Such a structure holds the variables needed to store the terminal command codes. The structure holds ten character arrays and six integer variables. (The names are not as obtuse as they appear. The variable _ _cb4r means to send "column before row." These names will become more meaningful as the discussion progresses.)

The structure declaration

```
struct _ _menu m_menu[10]
```

says to create an array of ten structures named m_menu. Each (structure) element in the m_menu[] array is "molded" from the structure tag _ _menu. The first three elements of the m_menu[] array have been initialized with the appropriate terminal command codes. (The name of the terminal that uses the codes is the last member of each structure.)

Now that all the variables have been established, we finally come to the menu() function. Some automatic variables are declared (why is buff[] an extern?), and the while loop is executed. The call to printf() displays a message, and the for loop is then executed.

In the for loop

```
for(i = 0; m_menu[i]._spmt[0]; i++)
```

notice what controls the loop. If the name of the terminal is in the structure (that is, member _spmt[] of m_menu[]), the printf() controlled by the for loop prints out the name of the terminal. This process continues until all "filled in" spmt[] members of the m_menu[] structure array are printed. Given the way the structure was initialized, you will see the following displayed on the screen:

```
1. Adds Regent
2. Adds Viewpoint
3. TeleVideo 920C
4. Not Listed

   Enter Selection:
```

Then you will be asked for the appropriate response.

If we assume that one of the numbers 1 through 4 is entered, the variable j is assigned the value entered minus 1. If j == i, we know that the user is not installing a terminal with known terminal command codes. In that case, i is returned to the calling function.

If the user's terminal is on the list (that is, if j is less than i), the move() function is called, as shown in Figure 3.7.

Figure 3.7
move() **Function**
(**Segment 3 of** install1.c **File**)

```
void move(dest, src)
char *dest, *src;
{

        int i = sizeof(m_menu[0]) - sizeof(m_menu[0]._spmt);

        do
                *dest++ = *src++;
        while(-i);

}
```

The move() function moves the contents of the selected m_menu[ ] structure into working variables. The variable i is initialized to the size of the m_menu[ ] structure minus the size of a structure member's terminal name. For example, if the structure has a total of 133 bytes and 40 are allocated to the name of the terminal, i is initialized to 93. This method avoids problems that might be caused by data sizes which vary in different hardware environments. However, the method also provides a faster way of copying the contents of a structure than straight assignments provide.

Finally, the call to strcpy() (Figure 3.6a) moves the name of the selected terminal into a character array named term[ ]. The function returns a value of FALSE, which tells the calling function that a "preinstalled" terminal was selected from the menu.

If FALSE is returned from the menu() function, the if statement in main() is not executed. Only the calls to summary(), clrscr(), and doins() are called. (We shall proceed under the assumption that a preinstalled terminal was not selected.)

The first function called after the if test in main() is setwidth(), as illustrated in Figure 3.8.

Figure 3.8
setwidth() **Function**
(Segment 3 of install.c **File)**

```
void setwidth()
{

        prompt(0);
        _ _char = atoi(gets(buff));

}

/********************* end of function ********************************/
```

This function calls the prompt() function, with zero as its argument. The prompt() function appears in Figure 3.9.

Figure 3.9
prompt() **Function**
(Segment 2 of install.c **File)**

```
prompt(index)
int index;
{

        int i = 0;

        while(msg[index][i])
                printf(msg[index][i++]);


}


/*********************** end of function *********************************/
```

The integer index is used to find the appropriate message held in the msg[ ] array. As you will recall, the attribute list for msg[ ] was "array of pointers to pointers to chars." The actual contents of the msg[ ] array are stored in a separate file—hence, the extern declaration in Figure 3.2. The following example repeats part of the contents of a file that holds the message prompts:

```
char *m0[] = {
        "\n\n",
        "\tEnter the number of characters on a line for your terminal: ",
        0
};

char *m1[] = {
        "\n\n",
        "\tEnter the number of lines on your terminal: ",
        0
};
```

```
char **msg[] = {
        m0,
        m1,
        m2,
        m3,
        m4,
        m5,
        m6,
        m7,
        m8,
        m9,
        m10,
        m11,
        m12,
        m13,
        m14,
        m15,
        m16
};
```

The declaration of msg[ ] allocates 17 pointers, each pointing to another array of pointers. Therefore, the first variable in msg[ ] is a pointer whose rvalue points to m0[ ]. But m0[ ] is an array of three pointers that have been initialized to contain two strings and a NULL. That is, the first pointer in m0[ ] has an rvalue that points to two newlines ("\n\n").

Now refer back to Figure 3.9 and notice how the message is printed out. Because prompt( ) receives an index of 0, the first pointer in the msg[ ] array (m0) is selected. [The variable i is set to zero in prompt( ).] The call to printf( ) prints whatever is being pointed to: a newline. Variable i is postincremented to get the next character string. This process continues until the NULL is encountered in the m0[ ] array, which terminates the while loop and returns from prompt( ).

The advantage of using "pointer to pointers" is that the rows of the indirected array do not have to be of uniform length. You can then alter the contents of the messages without having to be concerned about symmetry in the arrays. Be sure to familiarize yourself with this useful C construct.

Once the prompt() is printed, setwidth() uses a call to gets() to place the user's response into the buff[] character array. The call to atoi() converts this response to an integer, which is assigned to (the global variable) _ _char. This integer variable now contains the number of characters that can fit on one line of the CRT.

In Figure 3.10, the program next calls setlength(), which functions virtually the same as setwidth().

Figure 3.10
setlength() **Function**
(**Segment 4 of** install.c **File)**

```
void setlength()
{


        prompt(1);
        _ _line = atoi(gets(buff));
}


/*********************** end of function *********************************/
```

The call to prompt() selects the second message character array and gets the number of lines on the terminal from the user. This response is then assigned to _ _line. The program uses a for loop to print out _ _line newlines to the terminal, thereby clearing the screen. This action can also be achieved with the following:

```
i = _ _line;
while(i--)
        putchar('\n');
```

Some people find the for loop clearer, whereas others think the while construct is more direct. Code size should be similar in both cases, and either method can be used. We cannot directly decrement _ _line, however, because its original value is used in subsequent sections of the program.

Cursor Addressing

Direct cursor addressing is the most fundamental terminal command. Indeed, it is the only command required by our terminal handler. With support from the terminal, direct cursor addressing can simulate most of the other commands.

A do-while loop defines direct cursor addressing for the terminal. This loop is performed until the status of the function called by while becomes False. The call to setcur() gets the cursor addressing codes from the user. This function is illustrated in Figure 3.11.

Figure 3.11
setcur() **Function**
(Segment 5 of install.c **File)**

```
void setcur()
{

      do
              prompt(2);
      while(!isdigit(j = getchar()));

      putchar('\n');
      j -= '0';
      _ _cur1[0] = j;

      for(i = _ _cur1[0]; i; i-) {
              printf(e1, j - i + 1);
              _ _cur1[j - i + 1] = getchar();
      }


      do
              prompt(3);
      while(!isdigit(j = getchar()));
      _cur2[0] = j - '0';

      for(i = _cur2[0]; i ; i-) {
              printf(e1, _cur2[0] - i + 1);
              _cur2[_cur2[0] - i] = getchar();
      }
```

```
do
        prompt(4);
while(!isdigit(j = getchar()));
_ _ctr[0] = j - '0';

for(i = _ _ctr[0]; i; i-) {
        printf(e1, _ _ctr[0] - i + 1);
        _ _ctr[_ _ctr[0] - i] = getchar();
}

while(1) {
        prompt(5);
        i = tolower(getchar());
        if(i != 'y' && i != 'n') {
                printf("\n\tPlease reply 'Y' or 'N'");
                continue;
        }
        _ _cb4r = i == 'y';
        break;
}

while(1) {
        prompt(16);
        i = tolower(getchar());
        if(i != 'y' && i != 'n') {
                printf("\n\tPlease reply 'Y' or 'N'");
                continue;
        }
        _ _asci = i =='y';
        break;
}

prompt(6);
_ _rowo = atoi(gets(buff));
prompt(7);
_ _colo = atoi(gets(buff));

}

/*********************** end of function ********************************/
```

As you read through the code in Figure 3.11, you will find that messages m3 through m7 are used. These are explained in Figure 3.12 to help you understand what the setcur( ) function is doing.

Figure 3.12
Message Prompts Used in setcur( )
(Excerpted from Figure 3.3)

```
char *m3[ ] = {
        "\n\n",
        "\tSome terminals require characters be sent between the row\n",
        "\tand column cursor positions. For example, the ANSI standard\n",
        "\tterminals require a ',' sent between row and column. If your\n",
        "\tterminal does not require a row-column delimiter, enter '0'.\n\n",
        "\tEnter the number of characters delimiting row and column: ",
        0
};

char *m4[ ] = {
        "\n\n",
        "\tA trailing code is required to be sent following the cursor\n",
        "\tpositions, by some terminals. If your terminal does not need\n",
        "\ta trailing code, enter '0'.\n\n",
        "\tEnter the number of characters to follow the cursor position: ",
        0
};

char *m5[ ] = {
        "\n\n",
        "\tSome terminals require the column (character position) to be\n",
        "\tsent before the row (line). Others require reverse order.\n",
        "\tDoes your terminal require column sent before row (y/n): ",
        0
};
```

```
char *m6[] = {
        "\n\n",
        "\tIn some cases the cursor positions are sent to the terminal\n",
        "\tafter an offset is added to them. For example, the TeleVideo\n",
        "\trequires a 32-decimal offset to be added to both row and column\n",
        "\tprior to the coordinates being sent to the terminal. The upper\n",
        "\tleft character position on the terminal is coordinate 0,0.\n\n",
        "\tHow much decimal offset is to be added to the row (line): ",
        0
};

char *m7[] = {
        "\tHow much decimal offset is to be added to the column (char): ",
        0
};
```

The first `while` loop displays the required message through a call to `prompt()`. The `if` statement asks the user to enter the number of lead-in characters for cursor positioning. Because no terminal (that we are aware of) requires more than nine lead-in characters, the `j -= '0'` (Figure 3.11) converts the ASCII digit entered into an integer and assigns it to `j`. A valid digit terminates the controlling `while` loop.

The value of `j` is then assigned to the first element of the `curl[]` array for later use. A `for` loop asks the user to enter the characters that form the lead-in string for cursor addressing. Notice that `e1` is an external message array declared prior to the start of `main()`. Because this prompt appears frequently in the program, using the prompt as an external character array in the call to `printf()` is easier than rewriting the prompt as a string constant each time you want to use it. You also can change the prompt more easily, if necessary.

As the lead-in characters are entered, they are placed in the `curl[]` array. The rest of the `setcur()` function is literally a repeat of the first part of the function. Notice how the variable _ _cb4r [that is, the column-before-row variable that uses `prompt(5)`] is set. If the user answers Y, the logic test `i == 'Y'` is True. A 1 is assigned to `i`, which is then assigned into _ _cb4r. (Here is a "real world" example of readable versus obtuse code, which was discussed in Chapter 0.)

After the return from setcur(), a call to tstcur() is made. The function tstcur() tests the terminal command codes entered thus far. In doing the test, tstcur() calls several other functions. Figure 3.13 shows the tstcur() function as well as the functions it contains.

Figure 3.13
tstcur() **Function**
(**Segment 6 of** install.c **File**)

```
int tstcur()
{
        clrscr();
        printf("The screen should now have been cleared.\n");
        cursor(22, 40);
        printf("Hit any character to continue.");
        getchar();
        clrscr();
        printf("Orientation Test.");
        cursor(5, 10);
        printf("The next line should erase one character for each space hit");
        cursor(6, 10);
        printf("abcdef");
        for(j = 15; j >= 10; j-) {
                cursor(6, j);
                getchar();
        }
        eraeol(22, 0);
        printf("Was this test successful? ");
        return(tolower(getchar()) != 'y');

}

/*********************** end of function ********************************/
```

The first thing tstcur() does is call the clrscr() function. The code for
the clrscr() function appears in Figure 3.14.

Figure 3.14
clrscr() **Function**
(clrscr.c **Library File)**

```
/*****************************************************************************
 *
 *      Function clrscr() within the general terminal library
 *
 *****************************************************************************
 *
 *              void clrscr()
 *
 *      This function will clear a screen for a general purpose
 *      terminal that has as a minimum the direct cursor addressing
 *      feature installed. The program that calls this function
 *      must contain
 *
 *              #include "scrdat.c"
 *
 *      and have the fields properly initialized or installed by using
 *      the install program.
 *
 *      If a clear-screen code is present, it will be used. Otherwise,
 *      an erase-to-end-of-page will be executed. (See eraeop.c)
 *
 *****************************************************************************/
```

```
#define void int                                    /* 0001 */

extern char _ _clsc[];                              /* 0002 */
extern int eraeop();                                /* 0003 */
extern void _ _send();                              /* 0004 */

void clrscr()                                       /* 0005 */
{

        if(_ _clsc[0])                              /* 0007 */
                _ _send(_ _clsc);                   /* 0008 */
        else
                eraeop(0,0);                        /* 0010 */

}                                                   /* 0011 */

/********************** end of function ********************************/
```

Because the clrscr() function was written as a separate file, extern declarations are necessary. The first extern declaration refers to the array that was declared in the primary install program. The next two extern declarations refer to functions from two other files. Figures 3.15 and 3.16 show these two functions.

Figure 3.15
eraeop() **Function**
(eraeop.c **Library File**)

```
#define void int

extern char _ _eopb[];
extern int _ _line;


/*****************************************************************************
 *
 *        This function will erase to end of page from the cursor position
 *        supplied. If an erase-to-end-of-page command is not supported,
 *        erase-to-end-of-line will be called until the last line of the
 *        terminal is encountered.
 *
 *****************************************************************************/
```

```
int eraeop(x, y)
int x, y;
{

        if(cursor(x, y))
                return(-1);
        if(_ _eopb[0])
                _ _send(_ _eopb);
        else {

                int i;

                i = x;
                if(y){
                        eraeol(x, y);
                        if(++i > _ _line - 1)
                                return;
                }
                while(i <= _ _line - 1)
                        eraeol(i++, 0);
                cursor(x, y);
        }
        return(0);

}

/*********************** end of function *********************************/
```

Figure 3.16
_ _send( ) **Function**
(send.c **Library File**)

```
#define void int


/*************************************************************************
 *
 *      This function is used to send the actual string out to the
 *      terminal.
 *************************************************************************/


void _ _send(ary)
char ary[];
{

        int i;
        int j = 1;

        for(i = ary[0]; i-; j++)
                write(1, &ary[j], 1);


}


/********************** end of function ********************************/
```

Figure 3.16 goes here

Finally, because the eraeop( ) function uses another function called cursor( ), this function is illustrated in Figure 3.17.

As mentioned before, tstcur( ) first calls the clrscr( ) function (Figure 3.14). The if statement in clrscr( ) checks whether the clear-screen code for the terminal has been defined. Because it has not been defined at this time, the else is executed, causing the eraeop( ) function to be called (Figure 3.15). This function then calls the cursor( ) function (Figure 3.17).

Figure 3.17
cursor() **Function**
(cursor.c **Library File)**

```
/***************************************************************************
 *
 *        Function cursor() within the general terminal library
 *
 ***************************************************************************
 *
 *                int cursor(x, y)
 *                int x, y;
 *
 *        This function is the only one required to work and still support
 *        all standard terminal features with the exception of attributes.
 *        It returns a 0 on success and -1 if an addressing error was
 *        sensed. It assumes that the x coordinate is 0 in the top left of
 *        the screen and increases down the screen. The y coordinate is
 *        assumed to be 0 at the top left of the screen and increases
 *        to the right.
 *
 ***************************************************************************/

#define void int

extern  char __cur1[], __cur2[], __ctr[];
extern  int __rowo, __colo, __cb4r, __asci;
extern  int __line, __char;
extern  void __send();
```

```
int cursor(x, y)
int x, y;
{

        if(x > _ _line-1 || y > _ _char-1 || x < 0 || y < 0)
                return(-1);
        _ _send(_ _cur1);
        _ _cb4r ? addr(y + _ _colo) : addr(x + _ _rowo);
        _ _send(_ _cur2);
        _ _cb4r ? addr(x + _ _rowo) : addr(y + _ _colo);
        _ _send(_ _ctr);
        return(0);

}
```

/*********************** end of function ********************************/

```
static void addr(coord)
int coord;
{

        char buf[10];
        int i = 0;

        if(_ _asci) {
                itoa(buf, coord);
                while(buf[i])
                        write(1, &buf[i++], 1);
        } else
                write(1, &coord, 1);

}
```

/*********************** end of function ********************************/

The cursor() function checks to see that valid coordinates have been passed. Because we assume that the upper left-hand corner of the screen is row 0, column 0, these coordinates are valid. The return(-1) controlled by the if is not executed, and the _ _send() function is called (Figure 3.16).

The argument in the _ _send() function call is the address of the _ _curl[] array. The first character in this array contains the number of characters in the lead-in for cursor addressing. If the lead-in requires two characters, i is initialized to equal 2 as part of the for loop. The variable j is used to keep track of where we are in the _ _curl[] array.

The write() function call controlled by the for loop writes one character at a time to the fd defined as equal to 1. This is usually the fd defined as stdout. Although fd = 1 is associated with stdout, this relationship is not carved in stone. Check your system or compiler documentation to determine where you will be writing before you run this program (for example, check whether stdout's fd is 1).

After the lead-in has been written to stdout, _ _cb4r is checked to see whether the column coordinate must be sent before the row coordinate. The call to addr() is used to write the coordinates, which are determined by adding the row-column offsets. (The variable _ _asci is undefined at this point.) After both row-column coordinates have been sent, any trailing string is sent by the send() function call. The cursor() function then returns a 0 to the calling function eraeop(). The first if in eraeop() is not executed because the return value is zero.

Because _ _eopb[] has also not been defined at this point, the second if in eraeop() is not executed, and the program falls into the else statement. After i has been declared and assigned the value of x (which is equal to 0), the if(y) test in Figure 3.15 is performed. Because y also equals 0, we fall into the while statement in eraeop(). Since i equals 0 but _ _line has been defined, we call the eraeol() function, as presented in Figure 3.18.

The eraeol() function is almost identical to eraeop(). The call to cursor() places the cursor in the upper left-hand corner of the screen. Because _ _eolb[] is still undefined, we fall into the else part of the if statement. Variable i is set to the number of characters that will fit on one line (which has been defined)—usually 80. The write() function call then writes out 80-1-0, or 79 blank characters and a newline to the screen. The call ends, and we return to eraeop().

Figure 3.18
eraeol() **Function**
(eraeol.c **Library File)**

```
#define void int

extern char _ _eolb[];
extern int _ _char;


/*****************************************************************************
 *
 *      This function will erase from the specified cursor position
 *      through the end of the line. If this command is not supported
 *      by the terminal, spaces will be set.
 *
 *****************************************************************************/

int eraeol(x, y)
int x, y;
{

        if(cursor(x, y))
                return(-1);
        if(_ _eolb[0])
                _ _send(_ _eolb);
        else {

                int i;

                i = _ _char - 1 - y;
                while(i-)
                        write(1, " ", 1);
                write(1, "\n", 1);
                cursor(x, y);
        }
        return(0);

}


/********************** end of function ********************************/
```

The call to eraeol() is repeated _ _line times for a total of 24 calls. The newline at the end of each call, however, causes the next call to eraeol() to start at the beginning of the next line. After all the lines have been "erased" in this fashion, we call cursor(0, 0) one more time to bring the cursor back to the home position in the upper left-hand corner of the screen. In other words, the call to eraeop() using the arguments 0,0 does nothing more than clear the screen and home the cursor.

The call to eraeop() is now complete, and we return to clrscr(). Looking at the clrscr() function (Figure 3.14), we find that it is also complete, which returns us to tstcur(). Note that we cleared the screen simply by using the cursor addressing terminal command codes.

The rest of tstcur() should be self-explanatory. Cursor positioning is tested by placing the cursor at certain locations on the screen, then attempting to erase the prompts. In the install program, the return value from tstcur() is used to control execution of the do-while. If the user does not enter a y response to the tstcur() positioning test, the do-while remains TRUE, and setcur() is called again for the user to reenter the cursor addressing codes. The user is forced to stay in the do-while loop until all the tests have been passed.

The same logic is applied to the clear-screen function [setclr()], erase-to-end-of-line [seteol()], erase-to-end-of-page [seteop()], home-the-cursor [sethome()], and full- and half-intensity [sethigh()]. These functions and their related tests are illustrated in Figure 3.19.

After all the terminal command codes have been entered and tested, the program does a call to getterm(). The code for this function is presented in Figure 3.20.

The getterm() function stores the name of the terminal in the term[] buffer. After the name of the terminal has been entered, the screen is cleared, and the user is asked whether he wants to install the terminal in the menu. (You will recall that our structure will allow the installation of up to ten terminals.) If the user responds with a y, the add_one() function is called. The source code for this function is shown in Figure 3.21.

The add_one() function is called with k as the parameter. (This parameter was the option chosen by the user when the menu was first presented.) Because there are three examples in the program, k equals 4.

Figure 3.19
setclr(), seteol(), seteop(), sethome(), sethigh() **and Tests**
(Segment 7 of install.c **File)**

```c
void setclr()
{

        do {
                eraeop(0,0);
                prompt(8);
        } while(!isdigit(j = getchar()));
        __clsc[0] = j - '0';

        for(j = 1; j <= __clsc[0]; j++){
                printf(e1, j);
                __clsc[j] = getchar();
        }

}

/*********************** end of function *********************************/

int tstclr()
{

        clrscr();
        printf("The screen should have cleared.");
        cursor(23, 0);
        printf("Was this test successful? ");
        return(tolower(getchar()) != 'y');

}

/*********************** end of function *********************************/
```

```
void seteol()
{

        do {
                clrscr();
                prompt(9);
        } while(!isdigit(j = getchar()));
        _ _eolb[0] = j - '0';

        for(j = 1; j <= _ _eolb[0]; j++){
                printf(el, j);
                _ _eolb[j] = getchar();
        }


}

/*********************** end of function *********************************/


int tsteol()
{

        clrscr();
        cursor(5, 0);
        printf("This is a line at 5, 0.");
        cursor(22, 0);
        printf("Hit any key to erase 'line at 5, 0.'");
        getchar();
        eraeol(5, 9);
        eraeol(22, 0);
        printf("Was this test successful ? ");
        return(tolower(getchar()) != 'y');

}

/*********************** end of function *********************************/
```

```
void seteop()
{

        do {
                clrscr();
                prompt(10);
        } while(!isdigit(j = getchar()));
        _ _eopb[0] = j - '0';

        for(j = 1; j <= _ _eopb[0]; j++){
                printf(e1, j);
                _ _eopb[j] = getchar();
        }

}
```

/*********************** end of function *********************************/

```
int tsteop()
{

        clrscr();
        cursor(5, 0);
        printf("This is a line at 5, 0");
        cursor(10, 10);
        printf("This is a line at 10, 0");
        cursor(22, 0);
        printf("Hit any key to test erase to end of page ");
        getchar();
        eraeop(5, 9);
        cursor(0, 0);
        printf("Everything past 'This is a' on line 5,0 should have been\
erased.");
        cursor(1, 0);
        printf("Was this test successful ? ");
        return(tolower(getchar()) != 'y');

}
```

/*********************** end of function *********************************/

```
void sethome()
{

        do {
                clrscr();
                prompt(11);
        } while(!isdigit(j = getchar()));
        _ _home[0] = j - '0';

        for(j = 1; j <= _ _home[0]; j++){
                printf(el, j);
                _ _home[j] = getchar();
        }


}

/*********************** end of function **********************************/

int tsthome()
{

        clrscr();
        cursor(22, 0);
        printf("Is the cursor now at the top left of the screen ? ");
        home();
        return(tolower(getchar()) != 'y');


}

/*********************** end of function **********************************/
```

```
void sethigh()
{

        do {
                clrscr();
                prompt(12);
        } while(!isdigit(j = getchar()));
        __lite[0] = j - '0';

        for(j = 1; j<= __lite[0]; j++) {
                printf(el, j);
                __lite[j] = getchar();
        }

        do {
                prompt(13);
        } while(!isdigit(j = getchar()));
        __hite[0] = j - '0';

        for(j = 1; j <= __hite[0]; j++) {
                printf(el, j);
                __hite[j] = getchar();
        }

}

/*********************** end of function *********************************/
```

```
int tsthigh()
{

        clrscr();
        printf("This message should be in normal intensity.");
        cursor(5, 0);
        l_int();
        printf("This message should be in half-intensity/inverse-video.");
        h_int();
        cursor(21, 0);
        printf("This should be in normal intensity.");
        cursor(10, 0);
        printf("This should be in normal ");
        l_int();
        printf("half ");
        h_int();
        printf("intensity.");
        cursor(22, 0);
        printf("Was this test successful ? ");
        return(tolower(getchar()) != 'y');

}

/*********************** end of function *********************************/
```

Figure 3.20
getterm() **Function**
(**Segment 8 of** install.c **File**)

```
void getterm()
{

        while(!term[0]) {
                clrscr();
                prompt(14);
                gets(term);
        }

}

/*********************** end of function *********************************/
```

Figure 3.21
addone() **Function**
(Segment 2 of install1.c **File)**

```
int      add_one(i)
int      i;
{

        char *addr;
        int fd;
        long offset;

        addr = &m_menu[i];
        offset = addr - BASE;
        if((fd = open(NAME, 2)) >= 0) {
                lseek(fd, offset, 0);
                write(fd, __curl, sizeof(m_menu[0]) - sizeof(m_menu[0]._spmt));
                write(fd, term, sizeof(m_menu[0]._spmt));
                close(fd);
                return(TRUE);
        } else
                return(FALSE);

}

/*********************** end of function ********************************/
```

The char pointer addr is initialized to point to the address of m_menu[4], and offset is set to equal this address minus BASE (as defined in Figure 3.6). BASE depends on the operating system. For CP/M and MS-DOS, BASE is the equivalent of 100 (hex).

Next, we try to open the NAME program (see Figure 3.6a), which is the program we are working with (cleverly named install.com). We then use the (random access file) function lseek() to move to the position in the file that corresponds to m_menu[4] (in Figure 3.21). A second call to write() adds the name of the terminal being installed to the menu. We then close the file and return TRUE to show that all went well.

If you run the install program again, the terminal just installed will appear as the fourth option in the menu. To install a terminal not in the menu, you select the fifth option (that is, k will now equal 5).

If the installation is successful, summary( ) is called. Figure 3.22 shows the contents of this function.

Figure 3.22
summary( ) **Function**
(Segment 4 of install1.c **File)**

```
void summary()
{

        clrscr();
        prompt(15);
        if(tolower(getchar()) != 'y')
                return;
        clrscr();
        cursor(0, 20);
        l_int();
        printf("Terminal: ");
        h_int();
        printf("%s", term);
        cursor(1, 25);
        printf("Cursor Controls");
        cursor(3, 0);
        l_int();
        printf("Cursor Lead-in Code: ");
        sumcod(_ _cur1);
        cursor(4, 0);
        l_int();
        printf("Cursor Middle Code: ");
        sumcod(_ _cur2);
        cursor(5, 0);
        l_int();
        printf("Cursor Trailer Code: ");
        sumcod(_ _ctr);
```

```
cursor(3, 40);
l_int();
printf("Column Before Row: ");
h_int();
printf(__cb4r ? "Yes" : "No");
cursor(4, 40);
l_int();
printf("Column offset: ");
h_int();
printf("%2d", __colo);
cursor(5, 40);
l_int();
printf("Row offset: ");
h_int();
printf("%2d", __rowo);
cursor(6, 0);
l_int();
printf("ASCII Conversion: ");
h_int();
printf(__asci ? "Yes" : "No");
cursor(8, 25);
printf("Erase Codes");
cursor(10, 0);
l_int();
printf("Erase to End of Line: ");
sumcod(__eolb);
cursor(10, 40);
l_int();
printf("Erase to End of Page: ");
sumcod(__eopb);
cursor(11, 0);
l_int();
printf("Clear Screen and Home Cursor: ");
sumcod(__clsc);
cursor(11, 40);
l_int();
printf("Home Cursor: ");
sumcod(__home);
```

```
        cursor(13, 25);
        printf("Attribute Codes");
        cursor(15, 0);
        l_int();
        printf("Start Half-Intensity: ");
        sumcod(_ _lite);
        cursor(15, 40);
        l_int();
        printf("Start Full-Intensity: ");
        sumcod(_ _hite);
        cursor(17, 25);
        printf("Terminal Dimensions");
        cursor(19, 0);
        l_int();
        printf("Characters per Line: ");
        h_int();
        printf("%3d", _ _char);
        cursor(19, 40);
        l_int();
        printf("Lines per Page: ");
        h_int();
        printf("%3d", _ _line);
        cursor(22, 0);
        printf("Hit any Key to Continue.");
        home();
        getchar();

}


/*********************** end of function *********************************/
```

```
void sumcod(ptr)
char *ptr;
{

        int i, j;

        h_int();
        if(ptr[0]) {
                for(i = ptr[0], j = 1; i; j++) {
                        if(iscntrl(ptr[j]) || ptr[j] == ' ')
                                printf(ctrl[ptr[j]]);
                        else
                                printf("%c", ptr[j]);
                        if(-i)
                                printf(" ");
                }
        } else {
                printf("Not Used");
        }

}

/*********************** end of function *********************************/
```

The summary() function displays all the terminal command codes for the terminal that was just installed. (This is a great "gee whiz" display that can be used to impress friends who don't know much about computers!) After you have seen the summary, you must press a key to clear the screen in preparation for the installation of a terminal into another program.

Figure 3.23a defines the normal intensity terminal command code. This is the standard display intensity. Figure 3.23b, on the other hand, contains the terminal command codes for low (or half) intensity. The home() function in Figure 3.24 simply places the cursor in the upper left corner of the screen.

Figure 3.23a
h_int() **Function**
(hint.c **Library File)**

```
extern char _ _hite[];

/******************************************************************************
 *
 *      This function will send out the start high-intensity command.
 *      It will return either FALSE if supported or TRUE if not.
 *
 ******************************************************************************/


int h_int()
{

        _ _send(_ _hite);
        return(!_ _hite[0]);

}


/*********************** end of function ********************************/
```

Figure 3.23b
l‗int() **Function**
(lint.c **Library File)**

```
#define void int

extern char _ _lite[];

/**************************************************************************
 *
 *      This function sends the start low-intensity command.
 *      It returns FALSE if supported else TRUE.
 *
 **************************************************************************/

int l_int()
{

        _ _send(_ _lite);
        return(!_ _lite[0]);

}

/********************** end of function ****************************/
```

Figure 3.24
home( ) **Function**
(home.c **Library File)**

```
#define void int

extern char _ _home[];

/****************************************************************************
 *
 *      This function will home the cursor.
 *
 ****************************************************************************/

void home()
{

        if(_ _home[0])
                _ _send(_ _home);
        else
                cursor(0,0);

}

/*********************** end of function ********************************/
```

Figure 3.25 shows the library function that reads the terminal information from a data file and fills in the scrdat data. A pointer to the name of the data file is passed to the r_cur() function.

Figure 3.25
Read Cursor Information from Data File
(rcur.c **Library File**)

```
#include "inststr.c"


extern char __cl1[];


/************************************************************************
 *
 *      This function will read the cursor data into the global data
 *      defined in scrdat.c from file "name".
 *
 ***********************************************************************/

int r_cur(name)
char *name;
{

        int fd;
        struct __menu  i;

        if((fd = open(name, 0)) <0 )
                return(-1);
        read(fd, __cl1, sizeof(i) - sizeof(i._spmt));
        return(0);

}


/******************** end of function ********************************/
```

The Installation Function

Now that all the terminal command codes have been defined, the programmer must chose from a number of installation options. The doins() function ("do installation"), which is part of the file INSTALL2.C, is one possibility. The contents of this file are shown in Figure 3.26.

Because doins() is in a separate file (mainly for ease of editing), most of the preprocessor directives (such as #define's) are duplicates of those seen earlier in this chapter. The ins_mnu[] array holds the options for installation. Its attribute list is "array of pointers to chars," which allows us to print the options if we need them.

The structure variable files[] needs some explanation. This variable is an array of structures, each containing a "pointer to char" (variable f) and a long variable (offset). Note that one element in this structure array has been initialized with the contents of genparm.com and an offset value of 3l. (The letter *el* after the 3 establishes the value 3 as a long data type.)

The file genparm.com is simply a sample data file in which the terminal command codes are directly installed. Those familiar with the CP/M operating system will notice that BASE has been defined as the start of the CP/M Transient Program Area (TPA). BASE is identical to MS-DOS' starting address for program execution. Given the way the development compiler, assembler, and linker work, we know that the data area in any program begins at 0x103. Therefore, we can go directly into a file (for example, genparm.com) and write the terminal command codes, starting at the base address of the data area (0x103).

(*The option of directly installing the terminal command codes into a program file is both operating system specific and compiler specific.* If you are not using the Ecosoft C compiler with the Microsoft assembler (M80) and linker (L80), the constants will probably have to be changed. The same is true if you are using MS-DOS. Consult your compiler, assembler, and linker documentation for the appropriate values.)

Figure 3.26
Contents of install2.c

```
#include "inststr.c"

#ifndef TRUE

        #define TRUE    1
        #define FALSE   0

#endif

#define void int

#define BASE 0x100
#define NAME "install.com"

extern int prompt();
extern char term[];
extern char __cur1[], __cur2[], __ctr[], __eolb[], __hite[],
              __lite[], __clsc[], __home[], __eopb[];
extern int __char, __line, __asci, __rowo, __colo, __cb4r;
extern char *ctrl[];

extern struct __menu m_menu[];

static _file = FALSE;
static long offs = 0x103 - BASE;
static char *ins_mnu[4] = {
                    "Change Mode",
                    "Change Offset",
                    "Install File",
                    "Done"
};
```

```
struct {
        char *f;
        long offset;
} files[] = {
/*              {"hello.com",31},        */
                {0}};


long atol();


void doins()
{

        int i, j;
        int fd;

        extern char buff[];

        if(files[0].f) {
                for(i = 0; files[i].f; i++) {
                        if((fd = open(files[i].f, 2)) < 0 ) {
                                clrscr();
                                printf("Install Error on file: %s",
                                        files[i].f);
                                cursor(22, 0);
                                return;
                        }
                        lseek(fd, files[i].offset, 0);
                        write(fd,_ _cur1, sizeof(m_menu[0]) -
                                sizeof(m_menu[0]._spmt));
                        close(fd);
                }
                return;
        }
        clrscr();
        header();
        i = 0;
        for(j = 0; j < 4; j++)
                edit(j);
```

```
while(TRUE) {
      edit(i);
      cursor(2, i * 20);
      while(tolower(getchar()) != 's') {
            edit(i++);
            if(i == 4)
                    i = 0;
            cursor(2, i * 20);
      }
      edit(i);
      switch(i) {
            case 0:
                    _file = !_file;
                    header();
                    break;

            case 1:
                    eraeol(6, 10);
                    printf("Enter new offset: ");
                    offs = atol(gets(buff));
                    header();
                    eraeol(6, 0);
                    break;

            case 2:
                    buff[0] = '1';
                    while(buff[0]) {

                            int fd;

                            eraeol(6, 10);
                            printf("Enter File Name: ");
                            gets(buff);
                            if(!buff[0])
                                    break;
```

```
                                if(_file) {
                                        if((fd = creat(buff,2)) < 0) {
                                                cursor(8, 0);
                                                printf("File %s cannot\

be created", buff);

                                                continue;
                                        }
                                } else {
                                        if((fd = open(buff, 2)) >= 0)
                                                lseek(fd, offs, 0);
                                        else {
                                                cursor(8, 10);
                                                printf("File %s cannot\

be installed", buff);

                                                continue;
                                        }
                                }
                                write(fd, _ _cur1, sizeof(m_menu[0]) -
                                        sizeof(m_menu[0]._spmt));
                                close(fd);

                        }
                        eraeop(6, 0);
                        break;

                case 3:
                        clrscr();
                        return;


                }
        }

}

/*********************** end of function *********************************/
```

```
void edit(i)
int i;
{

        cursor(2,i*20);
        putchar(ins_mnu[i][0]);
        l_int();
        printf("%s", &ins_mnu[i][1]);
        h_int();

}


/*********************** end of function *********************************/


void header()
{

        eraeol(0, 5);
        l_int();
        printf("Mode: ");
        h_int();
        if(_file)
                printf("Create Data File");
        else {
                printf("Modify Executable File");
                cursor(0, 45);
                l_int();
                printf("Offset: ");
                h_int();
                printf("%04x", offs);
        }
        eraeol(1, 0);
}


/*********************** end of function *********************************/
```

The doins() *Function*

Several working variables are declared inside the doins() function. The buff[] character array is an extern data type because it refers to the buffer established in the primary install program. The statement

```
if (files[0].f)
```

checks whether the f member of the first element of the files[] structure array has been initialized. (If files[0] is "empty," a logic False is returned, and we skip over the contents of the if statement block.) However, because the f member of files[] has been initialized to point to genparm.com, we fall into the if statement block.

The for statement causes each f member of files[] to be checked for a file name. If a file name is found, the subsequent if statement opens the file pointed to by f in the read/write mode and assigns the file descriptor to the variable fd. If the program senses an error while trying to open the file, the screen is cleared, an error message is given, and we return from doins().

If no error is detected, the random access function call to lseek() is made. Because the offset structure member in files[] equals 3 (that is, files[1].offset = 3), the write operation (using our sample data file) begins with the third byte in genparm.com. The write() function call simply copies the terminal command codes into genparm.com, using the same technique discussed in the move() function. The terminal codes are now permanently stored in the genparm.com file.

Note what this means to the programmer. Suppose you have a commercial application that requires terminal command codes. Three program files make up the application package (for example, input.com, process.com, and output.com). Your files[] structure, in this case, will look like that in Figure 3.27.

The application package consists of four files: the terminal installation program (install.com) and three program files. The user first runs the terminal installation package, which includes the files[] structure array initialized in Figure 3.27. When install.com has finished, the user's terminal command codes will be permanently installed in all three program files. Because install.com tests each terminal code before the files[] structure is used, the programmer can also be fairly confident that the correct codes will be installed the first time.

Figure 3.27
Sample Application Installation

```
struct {
    char *f;
    long offset;
} files[] = {
                {"input.com", 31},
                {"process.com", 31},
                {"output.com", 31},
        {0}
    };
```

Once the terminal codes have been installed by doins(), the file is closed. After all files pointed to by the f member of files[] have been installed, the return is executed, and the terminal installation is complete.

What happens if there are no initialized members in files[]? The first if statement is False, and we fall into the rest of doins(). The screen is cleared [clrscr() call], then header() is called. Because _file is set to FALSE, the else part of the if statement is executed, which prints several messages on the screen. The variable offs is set to equal 0x103 minus BASE, yielding a 3 (long), which is the proper offset in this case. (This may have to be changed for different compilers and operating systems.)

After the return from header(), a for loop is used to call edit(). This function uses the j parameter to position the cursor and print out the appropriate prompt from the ins_mnu[] array. Because ins_mnu[] has the attribute list "array of pointers to chars," ins_mnu[] can be viewed as a two-dimensional array.

For example, on the first call to edit(), j equals zero. The call to putchar() causes ins_mnu[0][0] (that is, the letter "C" in "Change Mode") to be printed in normal intensity. Because l_int() sends out the terminal command code for low intensity, the argument to printf() is displayed in low intensity. After the argument is printed, the call to h_int() restores the terminal to high intensity.

What does printf() display on the first call to edit()? Note that the *address* of ins_mnu[0][1] is the argument to printf(). This means that "Change Mode" is printed in low intensity. By using the attribute list "array of pointers to chars" for ins_mnu[], we can "double index" into that array in a consistent and logical manner.

Since the call to edit() is done with a for loop, all four messages are displayed in the manner described above.

The doins() function then falls into a while loop and calls edit(), using the value of i as the parameter. Then edit() performs the same function described above, except that the value i is used. The cursor is then positioned to the appropriate location by a call to cursor().

We now encounter a second while loop, which retains control as long as the letter *s* is not returned by the call to getchar(). In other words, if you press any letter other than *s,* the cursor will bounce between the four options contained in ins_mnu[]. When the user decides which option he wants, the user presses the letter *s* to *s*elect the option. Variable i holds the value associated with the option selected.

The call to edit() uses i to repeat the selected option. The program then falls into a switch statement. If i equals 0, _file is complemented (that is, FALSE becomes TRUE), and header() is called. "Change Mode" is presented, and header() displays "Create Data File." The break statement breaks us out of the switch, but not out of the controlling while(TRUE). Then the first part of the while is repeated.

If the user selects the second option ("Change Offset" with i equal to 1), the case 1 statement is executed. The user then enters the new offset for the associated file. The break throws us out of the switch, and the process is repeated.

When the third option is selected ("Install File" with i equal to 2), case 2 is executed. The first element in buff[] is set to 1, and a while loop is entered. The file name is then requested from the user through a call to gets(). If a file name is entered, the first if statement is skipped, and we fall into the next if statement [if (_file)]. Depending on the previously set value of _file, we either try to create a new file or open an existing one.

If we open an existing file, the lseek() call positions us at the appropriate offset in preparation for writing the terminal command codes into the file. If a new file is created, there is no call to lseek(); we are at the beginning of a newly created file. In both cases, we end up at the write() function call:

```
write (fd, _ _curl, sizeof(m_menu[0]
        - sizeof(m_menu[0]._spmt));
```

As you saw earlier, this function copies the terminal command codes into the file associated with fd.

What may be less apparent is that two entirely different methods are established for using terminal command codes. If a newly created file was written, we now have a file containing nothing more than the terminal command codes. This file can be read in at the beginning of a program to initialize the terminal command codes by assignment at run time. This file allows you to use the terminal command codes even if you don't know where the appropriate data segment is located for your compiler and operating system.

If lseek() is called before write(), the terminal command codes are written directly into the file using the appropriate offset. In this way, you can run the install program on files that are not already part of the files[] structure array discussed earlier.

The entire process described above can be repeated as often as required during a run. When the user finally selects the fourth option ("Done," with i equal to 3), we return from the doins() function, and the install program is terminated.

An Example Using the Terminal Command Codes

In Figure 3.28, the terminal command codes are used to input data into a program. The data is subsequently written to a data file as specified by the user. As you will recall, this data file controls the disk sort program in Chapter 2. You will find that tracing through the logic of the program (Figure 3.28) is worthwhile.

Figure 3.28
Program to Create a Sort-Parameter File
(genparm.c **File)**

```c
#include "stdio.h"

#ifndef TRUE

        #define TRUE 1
        #define FALSE 0

#endif

#define void int

FILE *fd;
char buff[50];
int i, j;
char *m, *n;

void main()
{

        clrscr();
        cursor(0, 30);
        printf("Genparm version 1.0");
        while(TRUE) {
                lprompt(2, 0, "Enter Sort File Name: ");
                gets(buff);
                eraeol(22, 0);
                if((fd = fopen(buff, "wb")) < 0) {
                        cursor(22, 0);
                        printf("Error in creating sort file: %s", buff);
                        continue;
                }
                break;
        }
        lprompt(3, 0, "Enter input file name: ");
        gets(buff);
        m = buff;
```

```
do {
        putc(*m, fd);
} while(*m++);

lprompt(4, 0, "Enter output file name: ");
gets(buff);
m = buff;
do {
        putc(*m, fd);
} while(*m++);

lprompt(6, 0, "Enter type of sort (Q)uick (S)hell (B)ubble: ");
putc(getchar(), fd);
lprompt(8, 0, "Enter record length: ");
i = atoi(gets(buff));
putw(i, fd);
lprompt(8, 40, "Enter number of records: ");
i = atoi(gets(buff));
putw(i, fd);
lprompt(10, 0, "Sort field offset");
lprompt(10, 20, "Sort field length");
lprompt(10, 40, "Case Trans (y/n)");
lprompt(10, 60, "Ascend order (y/n)");
for(j = 11; j < 21; j++) {
        cursor(j, 8);
        if(strlen(gets(buff))) {
                i = atoi(buff);
                putw(i, fd);
        } else {
                break;
        }
        cursor(j, 28);
        i = atoi(gets(buff));
        putw(i, fd);
        cursor(j, 50);
        putw(tolower(getchar()) == 'y', fd);
        cursor(j, 70);
        putw(tolower(getchar()) == 'y', fd);
}
```

```
        putw(-1, fd);
        fclose(fd);
        cursor(22, 0);

}

/*********************** end of function ********************************/

void lprompt(x, y, str)
int x, y;
char *str;
{

        eraeol(x, y);
        l_int();
        printf(str);
        h_int();

}

/*********************** end of function ********************************/
```

4

Code Fragments

Management of free memory is important for many C library functions. Proper management minimizes code size while maximizing the amount of data that can be manipulated by the function. This is true for `calloc()` or `malloc()`, `free()`, `fopen()`, `getc()`, and other functions in the standard library.

Many techniques and methods of memory management have been developed, and each has its advantages. Several code fragment methods, along with some useful coding techniques, are discussed in this chapter.

Given the free memory allocation scheme used in a typical standard C library, a linked list of structures is often used for data storage. Similar structures are linked together, starting with some global root, while the actual data is maintained in free memory. For example, consider the declaration in the structure in Figure 4.1.

This structure can be used to maintain a list of names in free memory. The `next` member of the structure is a pointer to the next structure in free memory. All that is needed to maintain a list of these structures is a global pointer to the first structure, as shown in Figure 4.2a.

Figure 4.1

```
struct sample {
        struct sample *next;
        char name[30];
};
```

Figure 4.2a
One-Way Linked List (Insertion)

```
struct sample {
        struct sample *next;
        char name[30];
};



struct sample *head;
extern char gname[];          /* name to be added */

struct sample *insert()
{

        struct sample *n_ptr = &head, *b;        /* 0001 */

        while (n_ptr->next) {
                if (strcmp(n_ptr->next->name, gname) >= 0)
                        break;
                n_ptr = n_ptr->next;
        }

        b = calloc(1, sizeof(struct sample));    /* 0007 */
        b->next = n_ptr->next;                   /* 0008 */
        n_ptr->next = b;                         /* 0009 */
        strcpy(b->name, gname);
        return(b);

}
```

In this figure, look at the structure declaration for `sample`. It identifies the members as (1) pointers to a structure that is identical to the one being declared (that is, a pointer to another `sample` structure), and (2) an array of up to 30 characters. You will recall that `sample` is a structure tag which can be used to reference this type of structure.

Next, the variable `head` is declared to be a pointer to a structure of type `sample`. The variable `gname[ ]` refers to a character array that exists in some other file. The attribute list for `insert()` states that it returns a "pointer to a structure of type sample."

Within the body of the `insert()` function, the first thing that happens is the declaration of two more pointers (`n_ptr` and `b`) that point to structures of type `sample`. Notice that `n_ptr` has been initialized to point to `head` as part of its declaration.

The `while` loop is controlled by `n_ptr->next`, which checks the value of `next` in the structure pointed to by `n_ptr`. If `next` contains a value of `0` (that is, if the pointer stored in `next` is `0`), the `while` loop terminates. We cannot reach the `if` statement controlled by the `while` unless `next` contains a nonzero pointer. Because it does, the pointer contained in `next` points to a "fill in" structure. In other words, `next` points to a structure that contains a `name`. The call to `strcmp()`, therefore, compares the `name` in the structure pointed to by `next` with `gname`.

This relationship is illustrated in Figure 4.2b.

The call to `strcmp()` compares the names in the list with the (global) name held in `gname`. If the comparison returns a value equal to or greater than `0`, the name is added to the list (whose names are in alphabetical order), and the `break` statement throws us out of the `while` loop. If the comparison results in a value of less than `0`, `n_ptr` is assigned the value of the pointer held in `next`. With `strcmp()`, we are simply moving down a list of structures, following the values of the `next` pointer.

The call to `calloc()` in line 0007 returns a pointer to an area with sufficient aligned free memory to hold the new structure. Space is then allocated from free memory for the new structure, and it is added to the linked list by lines 0008 and 0009. Finally, the structure is filled with the data through a call to `strcpy()`.

When using linked lists, the data item being worked with is called a node. A *node* is an arbitrary piece of memory (or even disk space) that is

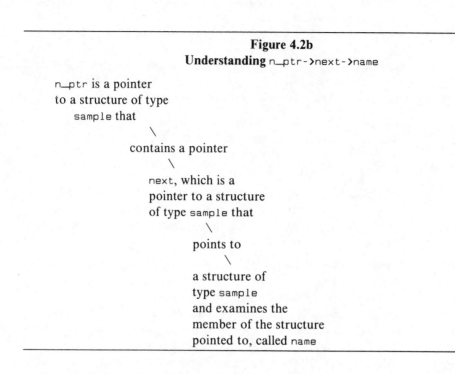

Figure 4.2b
Understanding `n_ptr->next->name`

used to store information. This term is used throughout the present and subsequent chapters to refer to whatever data item is being discussed.

Although the example in Figure 4.2a is minor, the following sequence of events, used in the example for the linked list, is typical:

1. Locate the node (data item) to be added to or deleted from the list.

2. Add (or delete) the node to (or from) the list.

3. Store the data to be associated with the node.

The primary purpose of linked lists is to store information in an orderly fashion. Code fragments give you several possible ways to accomplish this task in C.

Heads and Tails

A linked list is usually thought of as having a "head" and a "tail." Typically, the head and tail exist outside the list itself and are simply pointers that do not contain data associated with the list. The head and tail provide a means of finding the beginning and end of the list and serve as reference points when working within the list.

Figure 4.3
Example of Head and Tail

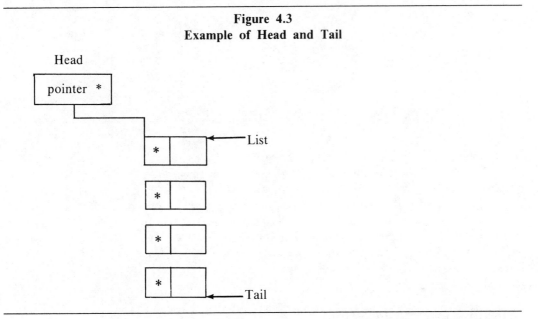

A programmer should try to use the least amount of memory possible for a linked list. This goal is influenced by the way the structure is declared. If the links are declared to be the first member of the structure, maintenance of the linked list does not require that the head be a complete structure because the head is only a pointer to the list.

The list in Figure 4.3 is a one-way, or noncircular, linked list. In this case, we take advantage of the fact that 0 is not a legal pointer value, and we use it to define the tail. In other words, if we find a pointer with a value of 0, we know that we are at the tail. The while loop in Figure 4.2a also uses this reasoning. (This construction and use for the structure have advantages for circular linked lists as well.)

One-Way Linked Lists

Figure 4.4 is a typical example of a structure that is used with a one-way linked list (hereafter called *owll*).

Figure 4.4
One-Way Linked List Structure

```
struct any {
        struct any *next;
        .
        .              /* this contains the actual data */
        .
};


struct any *any_head; /* points to the head of the list */
```

Notice that an owll needs only a single pointer in the structure to maintain the linked list. The placement of *next within the structure is not accidental. It allows movement through the linked list by treating any_head (the head of the owll) as a structure, even though any_head contains no data associated with the list. (Again, the while loop in Figure 4.2a is a direct example. Note the initialization of n_ptr.) The while loop will terminate when the value of n_ptr->next is zero. Therefore, when n_ptr->next equals 0, we are at the tail: we have reached the end of the list.

Inserting into and Deleting from a One-Way Linked List

Figure 4.5 shows the code used for inserting a new node into the linked list. This code works for both circular and noncircular linked lists. The fragment assumes that previous points to the node preceding the future location of the new node. It also assumes that new points to the new node to be added. (That is, new has been initialized to point to the structure of type any, which will now be added to the list.)

The code fragment in Figure 4.5 adjusts the pointers in the list to make new part of the list.

There will come a time when nodes in the list need to be removed. The fragment in Figure 4.6 shows how the requested node can be "unlinked" from the list. Note that you cannot simply delete the node; you must also restore the pointers to any nodes that follow it. (What would happen if this were not done?)

Figure 4.5
One-Way Linked List (Insertion)

```
struct any *previous, *new;

    .
    .
    .

new->next = previous->next;
previous->next = new;
```

Figure 4.6
One-Way Linked List (Deletion)

```
struct any *previous, *old;

    .
    .
    .

    old = previous->next;              /* 0001 */
    previous->next = old->next;        /* 0002 */
    free(old);                         /* 0003 */
```

Line 0001 initializes old to point to the node that will be deleted from the list. This initialization must be done to preserve the location of the node *following* the one to be deleted. Otherwise, the links to the rest of the list following the deleted node could not be restored.

Figure 4.6 illustrates how the pointer in node 1 (Figure 4.7) is made to point to node 3. Prior to the deletion of node 2, the pointer in node 1 points to node 2. The task is to make the pointer in node 1 point to node 3 after node 2 has been deleted. If we did not save the pointer in node 1 (previous), we would lose our link to the rest of the list (that is, from node 3 on down). Line 0002 in Figure 4.6 establishes the link between nodes 1 and 3.

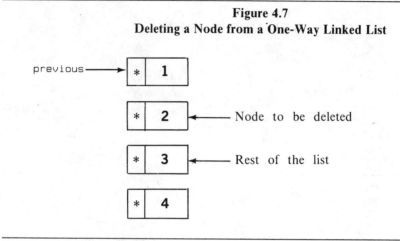

Figure 4.7
Deleting a Node from a One-Way Linked List

Circular Linked Lists

The only real difference between a circular and noncircular linked list is the way the tail is viewed. In a circular linked list, the tail points to the head. This concept is illustrated in Figure 4.8. The first task that must be accomplished for an empty list is to establish the location of its head and tail. This is done by the following code:

```
struct any *any_head = &any_head;
```

Here the line of code sets any_head to point to itself: head and tail are identical. This circumstance can occur only if there are no nodes in the list. (Refer to Figure 4.8.) The tail can be sensed only when the current node pointer is equal to the address of the head. When the node is equal, you know that you are at the end of the list. Because the code above has the head point to itself, when we test the link and find it equal to the address of the head, you know that you are at the tail. Thus, when the head points to itself, the list is empty.

Two-Way Linked Lists

The primary advantage of a two-way linked list (*twll*) is that you can scan the list from top to bottom or from bottom to top. With an owll,

Figure 4.8
Circular Linked List

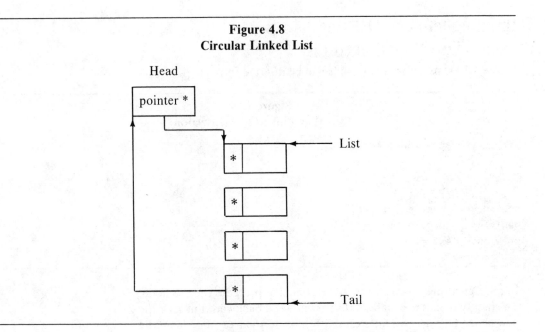

Head

pointer *

List

Tail

you can go in only one direction—from head to tail. In a twll, you can move from head to tail or from tail to head.

The basic structure for a twll is presented in Figure 4.9.

Figure 4.9
Two-Way Linked List Structure

```
struct two{
        struct two *next;
        struct two *last;
        .
        .                       /* any data in node */
        .
};
```

In this structure, `next` points from head to tail, and `last` points from tail to head. These two pointers allow you to traverse the list in either direction.

Inserting into and Deleting from a Two-Way Linked List

Figure 4.10 shows how a new node can be inserted into a twll.

Figure 4.10
Two-Way Linked List (Insertion)

```
struct two *previous, *new;
 .
 .
 .
new->next = previous->next;
new->last = previous;
previous->next = new;
new->next->last = new
```

In this figure, previous points to the node that precedes the new node. The first two lines take care of the forward and backward links for the new node. The last two lines establish links to the new node from the node below it as well as from the one above it. These relationships are illustrated in Figure 4.11.

Figure 4.11
Two-Way Linked List

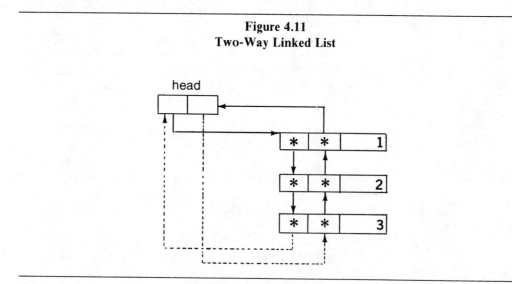

The twll is a noncircular list. We can traverse from head to tail *or* from tail to head, but the two are not connected. In this noncircular linked list, the last links in both directions have values of 0 and represent the head or tail for a given direction of search. To make a circular twll, the pointers must be established as links for the dashed lines.

The code fragment used to delete a node from a twll appears in Figure 4.12.

Figure 4.12
Two-Way Linked List (Deletion)

```
struct two *old;
   .
   .
   .
old->last->next = old->next;          /* 0001 */
old->next->last = old->last;          /* 0002 */
free(old);                            /* 0003 */
```

In this case, line 0001 causes next to point *around* old, where old points to the node to be deleted. Line 002 establishes the same bypass but in the opposite direction. In other words, the node after old points to the node before old, as shown in Figure 4.13.

Figure 4.13
Deleting Node from a Two-Way Linked List

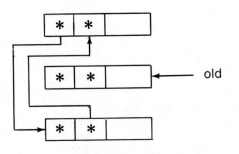

The call to free() in Figure 4.12 simply releases the memory allocated to the old node for later use, if necessary.

LIFO and FIFO with Linked Lists

Suppose that you want to simulate a stack operation. Remember that the last information placed on the stack is the first information called back from the stack. Such a stack is called a LIFO (Last In, First Out) stack. A one-way, noncircular linked list provides an easy way to simulate a LIFO stack. Think of an insert into the list as a "push" instruction and a deletion from the list as a "pop" instruction. The code used to perform a LIFO operation is presented in Figure 4.14.

Figure 4.14
LIFO Buffer (One-Way Linked List)

```
extern struct any *any_head;

void push(node)
struct any *node;
{

        node->next = any_head->next;
        any_head->next = node;

}



struct any *pop()
{

        struct any *node;

        node = any_head->next;
        if(node)
                any_head->next = node->next;
        return(node);

}
```

Note that the attribute list for pop( ) is a pointer to structure. This is what is returned from the call to pop( ). It points to the node containing the information just popped off the stack. The pop( ) function checks whether any_head contains a valid pointer. In other words, we want to make sure that there is something on the stack. If a value of zero is returned, the stack is empty, and we are at the tail. Figure 4.15 illustrates this process.

Figure 4.15
One-Way Linked List: LIFO push( ) and pop( )

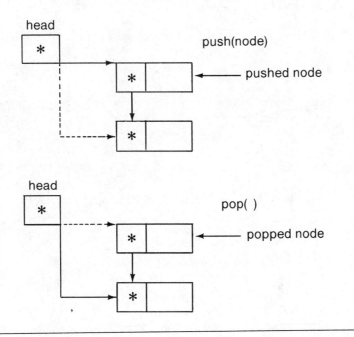

The dashed lines in Figure 4.15 represent the link from any_head to the list prior to push( ) or pop( ). The solid lines show the link after pop( ).

A FIFO (First In, First Out) buffer is used as a queue that behaves like a printer buffer or a line in a bank. If we use the bank analogy, each person (node) enters at the end of the queue and waits until the people (nodes) who entered the queue before have been processed. A FIFO can be easily implemented with a circular twll. Nodes enter the queue at the tail and move up towards the head. Figure 4.16 shows the code fragment for a FIFO buffer.

Figure 4.16
FIFO Buffer (Two-Way Circular List)

```
struct {
        struct two *next;
        struct two *last;
} two_head = {&two_head, &two_head};


void in_que(node)
struct two *node;
{
        node->last = two_head.last;
        node->next = &two_head
        two_head.last->next = node;
        two_head.last = node;

}


struct two *out_que()
{

        struct two *node = 0;

        if(two_head.next != &two_head) {
                node = two_head.next;
                two_head.next = two_head.next->next;
                two_head.next->last = &two_head
        }
        return(node);

}
```

When a new node enters the queue, the node is inserted at the tail. When a node is ready to be processed, it is extracted from the head of the queue by calling out_que( ). If the queue is empty, a 0 is returned from out_que( ). The code performs the functions of an insert and delete for a circular twll. This action is shown as Figure 4.17.

Figure 4.17
FIFO Buffer

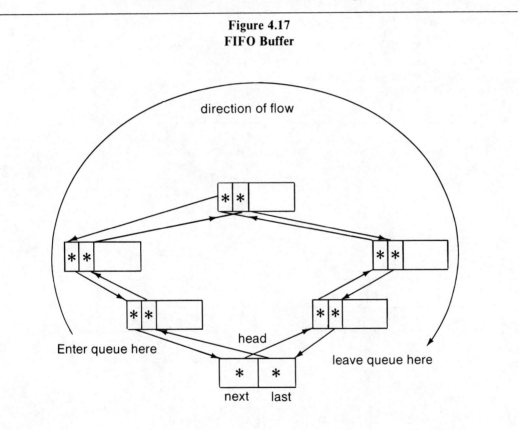

In the FIFO buffer, we can traverse the list in either direction because head and tail are in the same place (as in a circular list). In the bank analogy, however, we assume that the direction of movement for the nodes is from tail to head, taking the direction of the last pointer.

Traversing Binary Trees

A binary tree consists of a group of nodes, of which one is the root and the others are linked by branches to the left or right. In some literature, nodes that have no branches are referred to as *leaves*. In other words, leaves are the nodes that have no valid links (that is, pointers with a value of 0) in them.

In the example of a binary tree shown in Figure 4.18, node 1 is the root, and nodes 4, 5, 6, and 7 are the leaves. Branches are formed when a node contains a valid pointer to another node.

Figure 4.18
Binary Tree

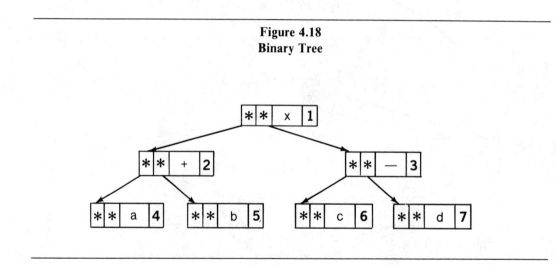

Three methods can be used to traverse a binary tree: (1) pre-order, (2) in-order, and (3) post-order. How they are different depends on when the current node is processed.

In the discussion that follows, the nodes referred to contain the information presented in Figure 4.18. In this figure, the first two members are pointers, the third member is part of an arithmetic expression, and the last member is simply a reference name for the node.

Figure 4.19 illustrates the structure for the tree.

Figure 4.19
Binary Tree Structure

```
struct tree {
        struct tree *left;
        struct tree *right;
        .
        .                     /* data in the node */
        .
};
```

Pre-Order Traversal

The algorithm for a pre-order traversal is one that processes the current node, traverses the left branch, then traverses the right branch. In Figure 4.18, traversal begins with node 1, which is the root of the binary tree. After node 1 (a multiply instruction) is processed, we then traverse to the left node (node 2) and process it (an addition instruction).

The next left traversal (node 4) provides the variable a for the addition. Because no left or right branches exist at node 4, we return to node 2 and traverse right to node 5. Now the variable b is processed as the second argument of the addition (node 4). Again, no left or right branches are encountered. We then return to node 1 from which we traverse right to node 3.

Nodes 3, 6, and 7 are processed in the same way, after which the minus (-), c, and finally d are processed. The overall processing order of nodes is 1, 2, 4, 5, 3, 6, and 7. The expression created is this:

```
* + a b - c d
```

Figure 4.20 presents the code used in processing a pre-order traversal.

The process( ) function call processes the node, and the search( ) function provides the means of moving down the branches. To simplify the code, we make this search( ) function recursive. (Consider what the code would be like if the function were nonrecursive—but only if you need a new career!) You should be able to see that we will traverse all left and right nodes and that each node is processed only once.

Figure 4.20
Binary Tree Pre-Order Search

```
void search(node)
struct tree *node;
{

        if(node) {
                process(node);          /* process node here */
                search(node->left);
                search(node->right);
        }


}
```

In-Order Traversal

With in-order traversal, we traverse the left branch, process the current node, then traverse the right branch. If the operation is performed when the two operands associated with it are processed, we get an "infix" arithmetic expression. For example, the sequence of traversing the binary tree presented in Figure 4.18 is 4, 2, 5, 1, 6, 3, and 7. Adding parentheses around expressions as they are performed yields the following arithmetic expression:

```
((a + b) * (c - d))
```

Figure 4.21 presents the code for performing an in-order traversal.

If you compare Figures 4.20 and 4.21, you will see that the only difference between them is the order in which process() is called.

Post-Order Traversal

Post-order traversal is similar to the other two types, except that both the left and right branches are traversed before the node is processed. This form of traversal yields an expression in Reverse-Polish notation (based on the tree in Figure 4.18). The following expression is the result:

```
a b + c d - *
```

Can you determine the order in which the nodes were processed? The code for the post-order traversal is presented in Figure 4.22.

Figure 4.21
In-Order Binary Tree Search

```
void search(node)
struct tree *node;
{

        if(node) {
                search(node->left);
                process(node);              /* process node here */
                search(node->right);
        }


}
```

Figure 4.22
Post-Order Binary Search

```
void search(node)
struct tree *node;
{

        if(node) {
                search(node->left);
                search(node->right);
                process(node);              /* process node here */
        }

}
```

As stated earlier, the only difference in post-order traversal is the order in which process() is called. You should keep all three methods in mind; they can be useful techniques for everything from simple numeric searches to language parsing.

Preferred Coding Techniques

The following techniques can be used in various applications. They are discussed in general terms precisely because they have such a variety of uses. (Many of these techniques are in the ISAM library, which is presented in the next chapter.)

sizeof

You already know that `sizeof` returns the machine size of a data item in C. This value is computed at compile time, not run time. Using `sizeof` [for example, `sizeof(long)` or `sizeof(char)`], rather than a constant equal to the length of a data item (such as `#define LONG 4`), promotes machine independence and enhances the portability of the code.

Using `sizeof` is the preferred method for determining data sizes. Without it, a generalized library becomes machine specific. This machine independence is the reason for `sizeof`'s extensive use throughout this book.

Finally, instead of using a constant for aggregate data types, we can use `sizeof` to eliminate the need for editing the source code that manipulates the data each time the size of a data item changes. If additional data items are added to (or deleted from) the aggregate, the source file can be recompiled, and the proper sizes will be determined automatically. The more you edit a file, the greater the chance that a "bug" will crawl into the program.

typedef

As printed out in Chapter 1, `typedef` is simply a shorthand way of representing an attribute list. No one variable is uniquely identified with `typedef`. The name associated with it is the shorthand notation that references the attribute list.

A `typedef` is needed when a library function requires a complex data type for use with the library. When this need arises, a file for inclusion in the programmer's source code (such as `#include`) should be provided with a `typedef` for the complex data attribute list. This approach minimizes the chance of programmer error. The `FILE` `typedef` in `stdio.h` is one common example.

Another use of `typedef` is for casts that are used extensively to change the attribute list of pointers. The `typedef` again minimizes the chance for introducing a "bug" into the program. The ISAM library contains numerous examples of this defensive programming techinque.

#define

Programs that use free memory [for example, calls to `calloc()` or `malloc()`], structures, and references to structure members are common. The binary tree traversals in this chapter are examples of such programs. When pointers are used to maintain links to these structures, code similar to the following

```
index->next->key
```

is often required. The macro preprocessor directive `#define` provides a convenient way to code long structure references. Figure 4.23 illustrates this technique.

Figure 4.23

```
#define KEY (index->next->key)
        .
        .
        .
        strcpy(str,KEY);                    /* 0001 */
```

If `KEY` will be referenced frequently, the `#define` macro `KEY` will prevent coding errors. Line 0001 expands to

```
strcpy(str,(index->next->key));
```

during the preprocessor pass. This macro not only prevents coding errors, but also shortens the coding process. Finally, if an error is discovered in the way the macro is used to reference `KEY`, a change at only one place in the source file is required.

Keep these ideas in mind as you read the rest of this book. Virtually everything discussed thus far is used extensively in the development of the ISAM library.

A combination of the techniques above will generalize programs, minimize the chance of proliferating bugs, and simplify coding and program development.

Editor's Note to Chapter 5

This chapter presents the functions for an index sequential access method (ISAM).

Programmers should note that the insert function, `isam1.c`, is the largest function presented in this book. Because of the variations in compiler implementations, this function may not be compilable on some CP/M 2.2 systems. In CP/M compiler testing, most compilers would compile this function with a 56K TPA. For MS-DOS compilers, the computer should have a minimum of 128K RAM.

The functions are heavily casted to ensure portability. CP/M programmers may remove some of the casts to reduce the size of the source code. However, this change would reduce the portability of the source code in 16-bit or 32-bit environments.

ISAM makes extensive use of `setjmp()` and `longjmp()`. The C compiler used must have these functions available, or the ISAM routines will not function. By definition, `setjmp()` and `longjmp()` are functions whose use depends specifically on the CPU, operating system, and especially the compiler. Modifications to the ISAM functions may be necessary to conform ISAM to your compiler and system.

UNIX programmers will need to include `setjmp.h` in their files. Also, the `typedef` for `setjmp` and `longjmp` may require modifications to the ISAM code to conform it to your compiler and system.

It is assumed that your compiler has the following functions:

```
tolower()              isalpnum()
toupper()              isdigit()
```

Most CP/M and MS-DOS compilers have these functions. The definitions for these macros/functions for UNIX are in `ctype.h`.

The definition for `tolower()` and `toupper()` varies among UNIX compilers. It is also assumed that these two functions do no conversion if the test is False. This means that `toupper('A')` should return A, not `'A' + 0x20`.

The UNIX programmer will need to modify `create()` in the ISAM functions to use `umask()` or the proper value for `pmode`.

C. D. V.

5

ISAM

The importance of data and its manipulation has been stressed throughout this text. As computers and disk technology have improved, the amount of data that users want to manipulate has increased. Unfortunately, their data requirements do not usually fit in memory. Users need an efficient way to manipulate data without the constraint of memory limitations.

This chapter presents an implementation of an Indexed Sequential Access Method (ISAM) for efficient access of data records. For example, suppose that you have a list of client numbers that your salespeople must be able to reference as quickly as possible. Assume also that you have such a large number of clients that the client file cannot fit into memory at one time. To complicate matters further, each client number is associated with additional data about the client (such as telephone number, credit limit, outstanding invoices, etc.). This associated information about each client is called a *data record*.

A number of methods can be used to find the data record for a given client. One possibility is simply to read sequentially the client file until you locate the client record. This method is extremely slow, however, especially if you have a large number of clients.

A better alternative is to create a file of client numbers and an index to the client records. You can then search the client number file, which is probably smaller than the client record file, and use the index associated with the client number to access directly the client record. But there is a "gotcha" with this method. How do you insert a client index into its proper position in the client index file without rewriting major portions of it?

You may ask, "Can't I get around the problem by not maintaining the file in sequential order?" This solution is not a good one for several reasons. First, to access the file sequentially, you must start at the front and look for the next higher index. You will spend a considerable amount of time reading the index file. Second, you have cut yourself off from more efficient searching techniques (such as binary search).

An ISAM approach to the index file solves most of the limitations mentioned above. Traditional ISAM algorithms do have some limitations, however, which we have attempted to minimize in the following sections.

A Hypothetical ISAM Example

Most ISAM implementations are composed of more than a single index. Typically, one level of the index defines a range of keys and an associated link to another index level. This second-level index contains the individual keys within the range and their associated links to the data record. A *key* is a data item that is used to find a client record. In our example, the client number is the key. Usually, keys are maintained in ascending order. Figure 5.1 shows an example of the main client index. The dashed lines indicate unused index entries.

We can assume from this example that there are six clients currently in the index file. As shown in the figure, the first entry in the main index refers to all client numbers less than or equal to 5. The level 2 index referenced by the main index contains client numbers 2, 3, and 5, with their individual links to the actual data records. Note that to find a client with a number greater than 5, you must examine the next main-index entry.

Individual index records are referred to by their level number and block number. For example, in Figure 5.1, level 2, block 5 refers to the level 2 index record containing keys 2, 3, and 5. A block is always referenced by

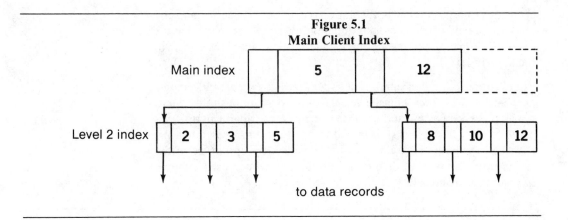

Figure 5.1
Main Client Index

the *highest* key in the index block. This can be further abbreviated as L2B5.

The problem with this simple approach is that the level 2 index record can hold only a specific number of keys (in this example, 3 keys). When a new client is added, say, with a client number of 4, *overflow* records are produced. An overflow record occurs when a new index cannot fit into the existing level 2 index. Figure 5.2 illustrates the overflow record that is generated in such a case.

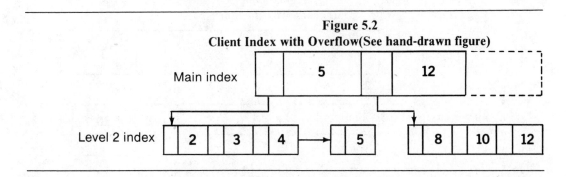

Figure 5.2
Client Index with Overflow(See hand-drawn figure)

This overflow problem may seem trivial, but numerous overflow records will cause the time spent searching a level 2 link to be almost as long as that spent reading the original data file in a simple sequential manner. Furthermore, the problem will undoubtedly get worse as the client index file grows. The only solution is to change the entire index by reading sequentially the old index and building a new one. Note that the overflow problem exists even if empty indexes are available elsewhere in the main index.

The example ISAM concept functions as expected, except that it avoids overflow records. Two things have been done to accomplish this. First, if an index becomes full and if unused entries are available in the level above it, the full index is split in half to create two indexes. Then the entries in the level above are adjusted to reflect the split. One of the empty entries above the full index is filled in. The process used is shown in Figures 5.3a and 5.3b.

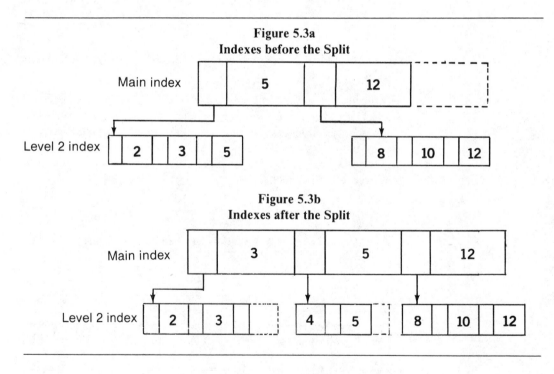

Figure 5.3a
Indexes before the Split

Figure 5.3b
Indexes after the Split

Figure 5.3b shows how the level 2 index (containing 2, 3, and 5) was split to accommodate the insertion of client number 4. This figure also shows how the main index was adjusted to make the insertion possible.

An Additional Improvement

Let's assume that we have sufficient memory for only 30 keys and their associated data. If the main-level index contains all 30 indexes, 30 is the number of records we can index. However, if we split the 30 keys into a group of 15 for the main-level index and another group of 15 for the level 2 index, we can then index 225 records with the same amount of memory. Once a size has been determined for main, you cannot split it; it is fixed.

To increase further the number of records that can be referenced with a given amount of memory, a new index level can be added between the main index and the old level 2 index. If you now divide the 30 keys between these *three* levels (that is, 10x10x10), you can access 1,000 records. This step allows splits on both index levels below the main index.

From this point on, these levels will be called main, level 2 (L2), and level 3 (L3). They are presented in Figure 5.4.

Figure 5.4
Index Levels

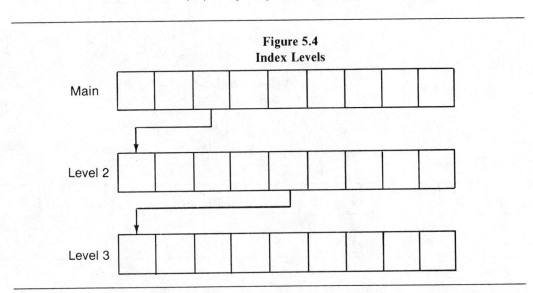

Even with the three-level approach, we can still reference only a maximum of 1,000 records. We would like to change this limit for the size of the index, even if it means sacrificing speed to increase the number of records that can be accessed.

The solution to this problem is to allow level 2 records to link on both the high and low sides of an individual level 2 record, thereby creating a new "side" link. This process should occur only when *all* level 2 records are filled. In other words, a side link is created only when a given level-block is full. You can have blocks that are not filled at this level, but you still need a side link for another block. This condition is illustrated in Figures 5.5a and 5.5b.

Figure 5.5a shows the index prior to the addition of client number 15. Figure 5.5b shows the index after client number 15 has been added into L2B18. (For simplicity, the level 3 blocks are not shown.)

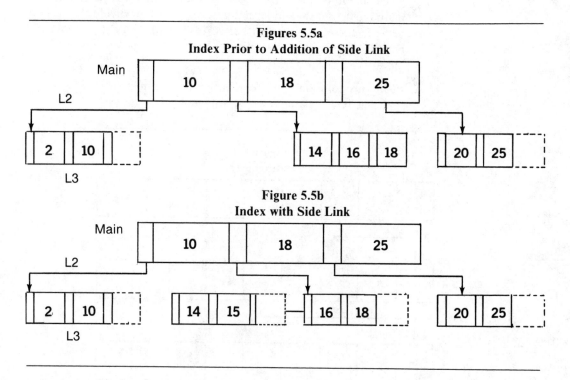

Figures 5.5a
Index Prior to Addition of Side Link

Figure 5.5b
Index with Side Link

Note that sometimes a side link must be on either the high side (based on key order) or the low side of a given L2 block. A high link refers to a side link containing keys that are greater than the highest key in the current block.

Side links are two-way linked lists. For example, the high link is used to go from L2B15 to L2B18 in Figure 5.5b. This link allows you to find L2B18. Conversely, to go from L2B18 to L2B15, you use the low link found in L2B18. Obviously, L2B18 must contain the highest key in L2B15. Otherwise, L2B18 cannot determine if the desired key is in its block or in L2B15. These links are necessary because a given main-block entry can point to only *one* L2 block. All maintenance overhead for side links, therefore, must also exist for the L2 blocks.

Memory Windows

In the previous discussion, we assumed that there was only sufficient memory to hold a maximum of 30 keys at one time. We then showed how more records can be accessed by splitting the keys into various levels. Note that the need for side links is related to the number of keys held in memory. For example, if we double the number of keys that can reside in memory (in this case, 60 keys), we can access 8,000 records and reduce the likelihood of side links.

The memory allocation for an index is fixed when the index is created. The advantage is that the programmer knows exactly how much overhead is taken by the index and can plan accordingly. Otherwise, there is a risk of not having enough memory for program execution.

In our implementation, the first word of the index file specifies the memory allocation used for that index. From that allocation, memory "windows" are reserved for main, one L2 block, one L3 block, one working area that is the larger of L2 and L3, a recovery block (used by the delete code on the disk), and other administrative requirements.

The concept of a window is illustrated in Figure 5.6. All of main, one L2 block, and one L3 block are in memory at any given time. Note that the windows are independent of each other.

Side links can exist in the block that is currently in the L2 window. Two L2 blocks with side links, including the one in the window, appear in Figure 5.6. Note that the contents of main dictate what is read into the L2 window and that L2 dictates what appears in the L3 window.

The window concept points out a potential problem. It may seem that we will be frequently using the disk to adjust what is in the L2 and L3 windows. However, a "dirty flag" is maintained on all three windows. When any data in the windowed block is altered, the dirty flag is set to

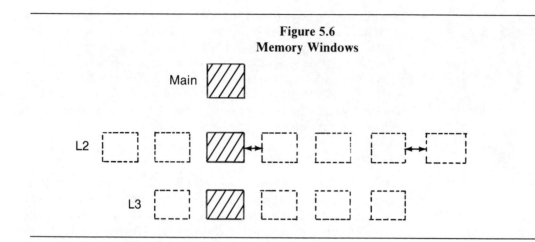

Figure 5.6
Memory Windows

TRUE. The only time this block will be rewritten to disk is when another block is needed in the window and the dirty flag is TRUE. Therefore, we will write the windowed block only if its contents have been altered, if we are finished using it, and if another block is needed in the window.

Balancing Side Links

What happens if you are adding to a file a large number of new clients who have numbers clustered around a single L2 block? For example, suppose that we added enough new clients in Figure 5.7a to fill up L2B3. As a result, side links would have to be generated off that block. Creation of these links can happen even though other L2 blocks are empty. In other words, the L2 blocks are "unbalanced."

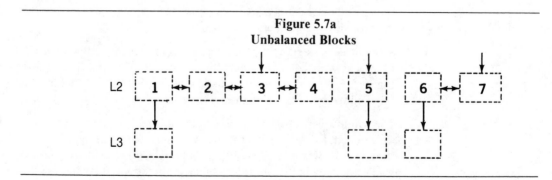

Figure 5.7a
Unbalanced Blocks

Figure 5.7b
Balanced Blocks

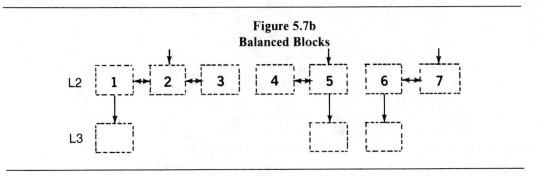

If the desired key is located in the L3 block referenced by the L2B1 block and neither block is currently in the window, the problem of unbalancing becomes apparent. Four reads (L2B3, L2B2, and L2B1, plus the associated L3 block) are required to find the key. Compare this process with finding a key associated with L2B5, which requires only two reads if it is not in the window, or with finding a key associated with L2B6, which requires three reads. Therefore, four, two, or three reads are required, depending on which key you are trying to access. The L2 blocks are not balanced.

If balancing is performed, as shown in Figure 5.7b, the number of reads required for the same keys is three, two, and three. Although the balance is not "perfect," it is better than before. Maintaining a perfect balance is not possible. [In the ISAM code, adjust() performs balancing after a key has been inserted.]

As balancing is performed by adjust(), the links from the main level to the L2 blocks are adjusted so that each L2 main link is centered on the block with the high-low links. In Figure 5.7b, the main-level links are to L2B2, L2B5, and L2B7. As you can see, if the number of L2 blocks is even, the link is made to the high side of the two blocks in the center. If the number of blocks is odd, the link is to the center block.

Balancing with the adjust() function minimizes the worst-case number of reads necessary to find a given key.

Adding Keys to an Index

The following three methods can be used to add keys to a data file and its index: (1) ascending sequential, (2) descending sequential, and (3) random. Up to this point, all discussion has focused on random additions.

When data is added to the index and data files in an ascending order, each new entry is made at the logical end-of-file (EOF). When data is added in a descending sequential order, each new entry is placed at the logical beginning-of-file (BOF). If normal splitting procedures are used in these cases, all L2 and L3 blocks will be only half-filled. The first block (in an ascending fill) and the last block (in a descending fill) are the only exceptions. Either technique uses a maximum of only 50 percent of each L2 and L3 block yielding a total utilization of only 25 percent of the index's capacity, before side links are established. This oversight is common for programmers who implement ISAM file managers.

To prevent this poor use of the L2 and L3 blocks, additions at EOF and BOF are processed differently. In either case, if the current EOF or BOF L2/L3 block is full, a split does *not* take place. An empty L2/L3 block is inserted at either EOF or BOF. This means that the previous L2/L3 block is still full. By preventing L2/L3 splits at either EOF or BOF, a sequential fill allows full usage of L2 and L3 blocks, instead of only 50 percent at each level. This process is illustrated in Figures 5.8a and 5.8b. The shaded areas represent the blocks that are currently in use.

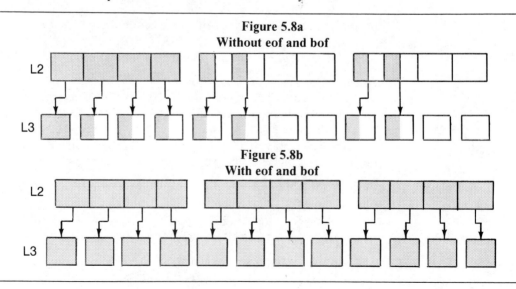

Figure 5.8a
Without eof and bof

Figure 5.8b
With eof and bof

In summary, the ISAM library passes back an offset to access a data record in an efficient manner. The programmer then uses the offset in the program itself as needed (such as for reading or writing the data record). You will find a sample program in the next chapter.

Free Memory Allocation Definitions

Two primary design considerations affect our ISAM implementation. First, the programmer should be able to work with a fixed amount of free memory that is set during the design phase. This allocation can be designed with the target machine's memory limitations in mind. Second, we want to avoid as much as possible the problems associated with traditional ISAM overflow records.

How does the ISAM library manage the allocation of free memory? Figure 5.9 shows the structure declarations and the associated macro references used by the ISAM library to map the free memory allocation.

Figure 5.9
`isamstr.h` **Structure Declaration File**

```
/*      isam structure declarations for allocated memory        */


struct  m_elem  { /* this structure defines a main element entry */

        long            offset; /* record position of "center" 12 block */
        unsigned        group;  /* # of 12 block in this main group */
        char            key[1]; /* 1st character of largest key in group */
};


struct  12_link { /* this defines an 12 block header */

        long            _lowlink;  /* rec position of next lower 12 block */
        long            _highlink; /* rec position of next higher 12 block */
        unsigned        _12_ent;          /* # of currently active 12 elements
                                    in this block */
        char            _lowkey[1]; /* 1st character of largest key in
                                    lowlink block (only valid if lowlink
                                    is not zero */
};
```

```
struct   l2_elem {  /* this defines an l2 block element */

         long            offset;  /* rec position of l3 block */
         unsigned        group;  /* # of l3 elements in referenced l3 block */
         char            key[1];  /* 1st character of largest key in l3 block */

};

struct   l3_elem {  /* this defines an l3 block element */

         long            offset;  /* rec position in data file of record
                                          with this key */
         char            l3key[1];  /* 1st character of key */

};

struct   recov   {  /* this defines a recovery block */

         long            link;      /* rec position of next recovery block */
         unsigned        rb_ent;    /* # of active free records in this block */
         long            roffset[1];  /* 1st offset of free record in this block
                                          (array length is actually r_max */

};
```

```
struct  global  {
                struct m_elem    *_bm_ptr;   /* pointer to 1st element in main
                                                    in memory */
                struct l2_elem   *_bl2_ptr;  /* ptr to 1st elem in l2 in
                                                    memory */
                struct l3_elem   *_bl3_ptr;  /* ptr to 1st elem in l3 in
                                                    memory */
                struct recov     *_br_ptr;   /* ptr to recovery block in
                                                    memory */
                struct l2_elem   *_wbl2_ptr; /* ptr to 1st elem in working l2
                                                    in memory */
                struct l3_elem   *_wbl3_ptr; /* ptr to 1st elem in working l3
                                                    in memory */
                struct l2_link   *_l2s_ptr;  /* ptr to l2 link header
                                                    in memory */
                struct l2_elem   *_cal2;     /* ptr to active l2 elem in mem */
                struct m_elem    *_cama;     /* ptr to active main elem in mem */
                struct l3_elem   *_cal3;     /* ptr to active l3 elem in mem */
                char             _m_drty;    /* main dirty flag TRUE = dirty */
                char             _l2_drty;   /* l2   dirty flag TRUE = dirty */
                char             _l3_drty;   /* l3   dirty flag TRUE = dirty */
                char             _r_drty;    /* recovery block dirty flag
                                                    TRUE = dirty */
                long             _l2_group;  /* current active l2 group record
                                                    position */
                long             _l2_cur;    /* current l2 record in memory */
                long             _l3_cur;    /* current l3 record in memory */
                long             _r_cur;     /* current recovery record in mem */
                unsigned         _l2elem;    /* sizeof an l2 element */
                unsigned         _l3elem;    /* sizeof an l3 element */
                unsigned         _l2bytes;   /* length of an l2 block */
                unsigned         _l3bytes;   /* length of an l3 block */
                unsigned         _rbytes;    /* length of a recovery block */
                int              _ifd;       /* index file descriptor */
```

```
/* main header data from disk starts here */
        unsigned        _keylen;    /* length of key */
        unsigned        _reclen;    /* length of record */
        char            _flags;     /* administrative flags */
        long            _ieof;      /* index end of file position */
        long            _deof;      /* data end of file position */
        long            _rbp;       /* first recovery block position */
        long            _l2bp;      /* first freed l2 block position */
        long            _l3bp;      /* first freed l3 block position */
        long            _frbp;      /* first freed recovery block
                                        position */
        unsigned        _m_max;     /* maximum # of main elements */
        unsigned        _l2_max;    /* maximum # of l2 elements */
        unsigned        _l3_max;    /* maximum # of l3 elements */
        unsigned        _r_max;     /* maximum # of recovery elements */
        unsigned        _cm_ent;    /* # of currently active main
                                        elements */
        char            _lp_key[1]; /* last processed key */

};
```

```
/*      these macros are used to simplify the inline code. they
        prevent having to type constructs like:
                index->_l2s_ptr->_highlink
        this would be entered as:
                highlink
*/


#define bm_ptr  (index->_bm_ptr)
#define bl2_ptr (index->_bl2_ptr)
#define bl3_ptr (index->_bl3_ptr)
#define br_ptr  (index->_br_ptr)
#define wbl2_ptr        (index->_wbl2_ptr)
#define wbl3_ptr        (index->_wbl3_ptr)
#define ws_ptr  ((struct l2_link *) wbl3_ptr)
#define l2s_ptr (index->_l2s_ptr)
#define cal2    (index->_cal2)
#define cama    (index->_cama)
#define cal3    (index->_cal3)
#define m_drty  (index->_m_drty)
#define l2_drty (index->_l2_drty)
#define l3_drty (index->_l3_drty)
#define r_drty  (index->_r_drty)
#define l2_group        (index->_l2_group)
#define l2_cur  (index->_l2_cur)
#define l3_cur  (index->_l3_cur)
#define r_cur   (index->_r_cur)
#define keylen  (index->_keylen)
#define reclen  (index->_reclen)
#define flags   (index->_flags)
#define ieof    (index->_ieof)
#define deof    (index->_deof)
#define rbp     (index->_rbp)
#define l2bp    (index->_l2bp)
#define l3bp    (index->_l3bp)
#define frbp    (index->_frbp)
#define m_max   (index->_m_max)
#define l2_max  (index->_l2_max)
#define l3_max  (index->_l3_max)
#define r_max   (index->_r_max)
```

```
#define cm_ent  (index->_cm_ent)
#define lp_key  (index->_lp_key)

#define highlink       (l2s_ptr->_highlink)
#define lowlink (l2s_ptr->_lowlink)
#define l2_ent  (l2s_ptr->_l2_ent)
#define lowkey  (l2s_ptr->_lowkey)

#define wl2_highlink   (ws_ptr->_highlink)
#define wl2_lowlink    (ws_ptr->_lowlink)
#define wl2_ent (ws_ptr->_l2_ent)
#define wl2_lowkey     (ws_ptr->_lowkey)

#define melem   (index->_l2elem)
#define l2elem  (index->_l2elem)
#define l3elem  (index->_l3elem)
#define l2bytes (index->_l2bytes)
#define l3bytes (index->_l3bytes)
#define rbytes  (index->_rbytes)
#define ifd     (index->_ifd)


/*      this macro is used for pointer arithmetic when the
        object of the pointer is a structure with a variable
        length array as the last element, such as:

        struct l2_elem {
                unsigned        count;
                long            offset;
                char            key[1];
        }       *cal2;

        calp(cal2,1) is the same as cal2++ if key was proper len

        calp expands to:

        ((char *) (cal2) + ((sizeof (*(cal2))+keylen-1)*(1)))

*/


/*
#define calp(A,B)       ((char *) (A) + ((sizeof (*(A))+keylen-1)*(B)))
*/
```

The m_elem structure declares one main-level index entry that consists of a group variable (the number of L2 blocks referenced by the main-level entry). In other words, if the link from the main level goes to three L2 side-linked blocks, the number in group would be 3.

The variable offset is the record position in the L2 index file for the center L2 block of that group. The key[ ] member of the structure is a single-character array. Because the key size is not known for any arbitrary index, the size is set when the index is created. The key size consists of the single character at key[ ], immediately followed by the rest of the key. This *must* be the last member of the structure because its size is unknown and dynamically determined. The size of a given element in the main level is sizeof(struct m_elem) + keylen - 1.

Note the flexibility of this approach. An array name is actually a reference to element zero of the array. This element is manipulated internally by the compiler as though it were an address. Declaring key[ ] as a single character array provides a way to reference the array without having to fix the size of the array itself. Because the array is the last member of the structure, we can put anything we want into it and still determine its size with the sizeof expression from the preceding paragraph.

Figure 5.10 shows one main-level element and its relationship to the L2 blocks associated with it. In the Figure, group equals 3.

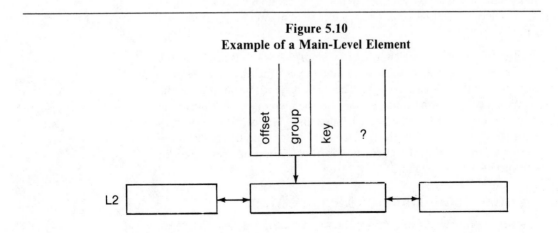

Figure 5.10
Example of a Main-Level Element

The struct l2_elem in Figure 5.9 is identical to the struct m_elem just discussed. Both group and offset refer to L3 blocks.

Each L2 block requires additional administrative information before it can accommodate side links. The struct l2_link declares this information. It consists of a low-link index (_lowlink), a high-link index (_highlink), the number of active L2 entries in the block (_l2_ent), and the highest key appearing in the low-link block (_lowkey[ ]).

The struct l3_elem declares an entry in an L3 block. In this case, offset is an index into the data file for the l3key[ ]. The number of active entries in the L3 block is maintained in the group member of the referencing L2 block (that is, struct l2_elem).

The struct recov declares a structure that is used to recover data blocks which have become empty through the deletion of one or more keys. The library example in this book allows key deletion but does not list the deletion code. (This code, however, is included on the software disk that is available separately from Que Corporation.)

The Global Structure

The ISAM library should be able to cope with multiple ISAM files, and each memory allocation should be independent of the others. When more than one index is used to reference a given data file, the key lengths are not necessarily the same. As a result, use of memory allocations will differ.

To prevent extensive recalculation of memory allocations each time the ISAM index is changed, the logical map of each memory allocation is kept within the allocation itself. The struct global contains all the administrative information necessary for the memory map. Part of the information is kept in the ISAM index file. The remaining admin-istrative information is established from the data contained in the index file. The ind_open() function builds the information required to complete the memory map.

Derived Information for Memory Map

A series of pointers are declared at the start of struct global. The first seven declarations contain pointers to the major memory blocks used by the ISAM library. Their relative positions in free memory are depicted in Figure 5.11.

Figure 5.11
Index Allocation Memory Map

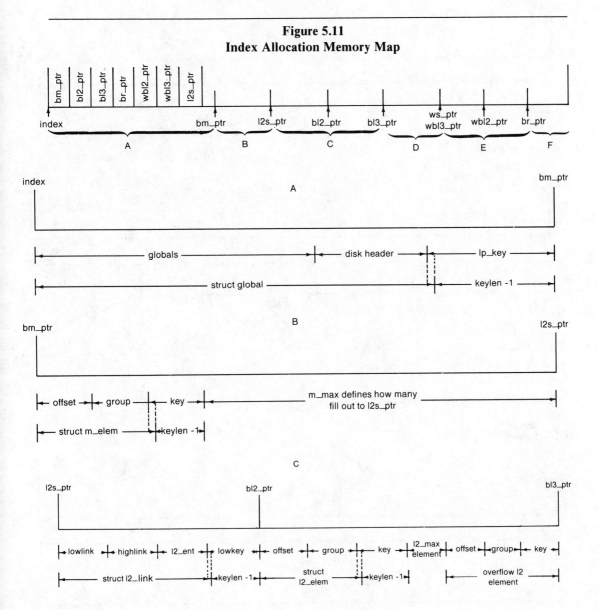

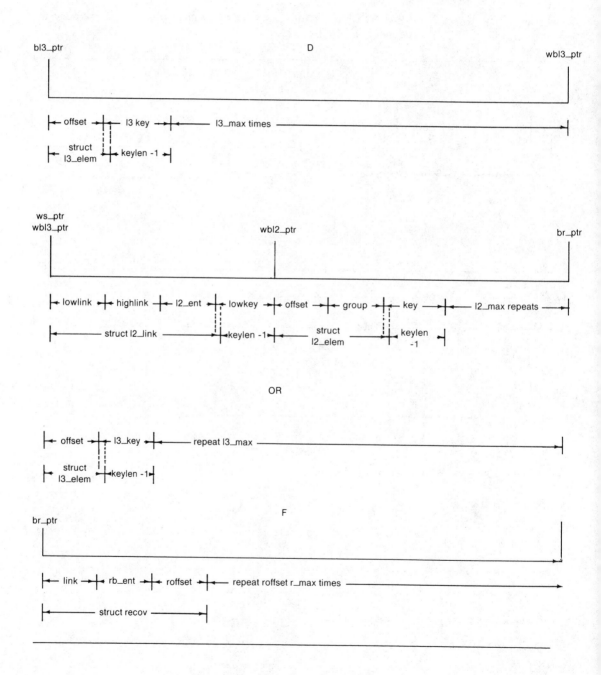

Note that _wbl3_ptr is a pointer to a union that is capable of holding either an L3 block or an L2 link and an L2 block. The pointer variable _bl2_ptr points to an area of memory that will hold an L2 block plus an l2_elem.

The next three declarations (starting with _cal2) point to their respective active elements. That is, _cal2 points to the currently active l2_elem. The other declarations are for the main-level block and the active L3 block.

The next four (char) flags indicate whether a given memory block has been altered but not yet written to disk (that is, dirty). These flags are checked by the read functions. If the flags are set to TRUE, the current block in the window is written to the disk before the requested block is read. The dirty flag is then set to FALSE.

The next four (long) declarations hold the index in memory for the currently active record. In an attempt to minimize disk access, the _l2_group variable equals the offset value from the m_elem, regardless of which L2 block is currently in the window from that group. Variable _l2_cur is the offset value of the L2 block in the window. This relationship is illustrated in Figure 5.12.

Figure 5.12
Relationship of _l2_group and _l2_cur

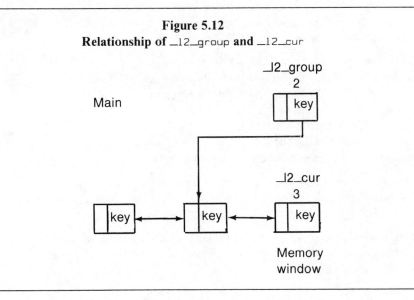

At the main-level block, the L2 grouping contains three blocks. The 2 represents the offset to the center block of the L2 grouping, followed by the key. The variable _l2_group, therefore, equals 2, and _l2_cur tells us that the currently active block is in the window and has an offset of 3. Note that if there are no side links, _l2_group and _l2_cur will always be equal. This reduces the need to start reading always from the center block of a group. The variables _l3_cur and _r_cur perform the same function as _l2_cur, but the function is performed for the L3 and recovery blocks.

The five (unsigned) variables contain information about the sizes of various data groupings. The first two variables contain the sizes of an L2 element and an L3 element, respectively. Likewise, the next three declarations contain the sizes of an L2 element, an L3 element, and recovery blocks.

The variable _ifd is the file descriptor for the index file. This variable is filled in by a normal call to open().

Data from Index Files

The other declarations in struct global are read from disk. These data items were established when the index was created, but they may have been modified by prior use of the given index. The only variables that may change during usage are the following:

_ieof	Offset to the end of the index file
_deof	Offset to the end of the data file
_rbp	Offset to the first recovery block
_l2bp	Offset to the first freed L2 block
_l3bp	Offset to the first freed L3 block
_frbp	Offset to the first freed recovery block
_cm_ent	Number of currently active m_elem

Bit position 0 of the variable _flags indicates whether duplicate keys are allowed in the index. If the bit is logic 1, no duplicates are allowed. (This is defined in file ISAM.H, discussed in a later section.)

The last variable in struct global, which is _lp_key, is not read from disk. This variable must appear at the end of global because the variable uses the technique described in the discussion on key[] to determine its length.

Macro Definitions for Structure References

Because all the free memory allocations for a given index are referenced through `index` and then subreferenced by the members of `global`, complex structure references in the code are unavoidable. These references can introduce "bugs" into the code. As you saw in Chapter 4, macro definitions substantially reduce the possibility of these errors.

All the macro definitions (that is, the `#define`'s) in the `ISAMSTR.H` file simplify structure references in the code. For example, without macro definitions, each time a reference to the memory containing the main-level index block is needed, the line

```
index->_bm_ptr
```

must be entered into the program. With macro definitions, we can simplify this to

```
bm_ptr
```

(Note that the underscore before `bm` is dropped to distinguish between the two forms and to prevent an infinitely recursive macro definition.) Although this example may seem trivial, consider the example of referencing `_lowkey`. Through the macro definitions, as defined in `ISAMSTR.H`, the code reference to

```
lowkey
```

is expanded to

```
((index->_l2s_ptr)->_lowkey)
```

Macro definitions also allow you to create a pseudovariable called `ws_ptr`, which expands to

```
((struct l2_link *) (index->_wbl3_ptr))
```

This pseudovariable references the `l2_link` associated with the `_wbl2_ptr` L2 block. A cast must be used to access the members of the `struct l2_link` because `_wbl3_ptr` points to a structure of type `l3_elem`.

Using Macros for Pointer Arithmetic

Although the parametized macro `calp` was commented out and replaced by two functions to improve code size, you need to know how calp works. If the _cal2 pointer must be incremented to point to the next l2_elem, normal pointer arithmetic will not suffice because the total key is not in the structure. (Recall that we have only the first character of the key.) The macro calp solves this problem by taking the following steps:

1. Casting the pointer (first argument) to a "pointer to char" so that the pointer has a scalar of one

2. Adding together the sizeof the structure to which the pointer points and the key length minus one

3. Multiplying the results of Step 2 by the second argument (that is, B)

4. Adding the results of Step 3 to the original pointer from Step 1. If the original pointer is not cast to a "pointer to char," the scalar used in Step 4 is the sizeof the structure to which the pointer points.

This example of a parametized macro was left in isamstr.h to illustrate the power of the #define preprocessor directive. Not all compilers will generate less code when functions are substituted for the macro. Each compiler has different code-generation techniques, and different processors also affect the efficiency with which source code is translated into machine code. The only way to determine which method works better is to try both, then compare code sizes for each method, as well as their execution speeds.

Additional Definitions

Figure 5.13 shows the isam.h file. It defines certain typedef's used for casting, error values, and external data. The typedef's allow pointer declarations to different frequently used structures and also facilitate casting. For example, the M_ELEM typedef creates an attribute list of "pointer to struct m_elem.''

The file isamd.c (Figure 5.14) actually defines all external variables used by the ISAM library. The variables _eof and _bof are used as flags to indicate that the current entry is at end-of-file or beginning-of-file, or between these two extremes. If an error condition is returned by an ISAM library function, i_errno will contain the specific type of error that occurred. (See Figure 5.13.) The variable index points to the ISAM

Figure 5.13
isam.h typedef, **Error, and External Data Definitions**

```
#define void int

#ifndef TRUE
        #define TRUE 1
        #define FALSE 0
#endif

typedef struct m_elem *M_ELEM;
typedef struct l2_elem *L2_ELEM;
typedef struct l3_elem *L3_ELEM;

#define NODUP    (flags & 1)
#define DUPKEY  1       /* Duplicate key error */
#define IRE     2       /* Index read error */
#define IWE     3       /* Index write error */
#define ICE     4       /* Index close error */
#define KNF     5       /* Key not found */
#define INV     6       /* Index not valid */
#define NEM     7       /* Not enough memory for open allocation */
#define FNF     8       /* File not found on open */
#define INE     9       /* Index is empty */
#define CCF     10      /* Cannot create file */
#ifndef EOF
#define EOF     -1
#endif

/* this file contains the global data used by isam */

extern unsigned _eof, _bof;         /* end- and start-of-file indicators */

extern int  i_errno;                /* error number */

extern struct global *index;        /* pointer to main globals from disk */

extern jmp_env _ _ienv;              /* setjmp longjmp envelope for index */

extern long _lm1;                   /* long minus 1 constant */

#define _ienv &_ _ienv
```

index file memory allocation. A long constant of value -1 is generated in variable _lm1. This variable keeps the compiler from generating many copies of the long constant -1. The last variable, _ _ienv, is declared by a typedef called jmp_env. It is used by two functions: setjmp() and longjmp(). (These two functions are described later in this chapter.)

Figure 5.14
isamd.c **File**

```
#include "stdio.h"
#include "isamstr.h"

/* this file contains the global data used by isam */

unsigned _eof, _bof;              /* end- and start-of-file indicators */

int  i_errno;                     /* error number */

struct global *index;             /* pointer to main globals from disk */

jmp_env _ _ienv;                   /* setjmp longjmp envelope for index */

long _lm1 = -1;                    /* long minus 1 constant */
```

Creating an Index

One of the first tasks involved in implementing an ISAM file is creating the index file. Two different methods can be used. The isamb.c file (Figure 5.15) contains the ind_build() function. It builds an index by computing the allocation size used by the index from the parameters passed to the function. The comment preceding the function definition defines the parameters being passed to the function.

Figure 5.15
isamb.c **File**

```c
#include "stdio.h"
#include "isamstr.h"
#include "isam.h"

char *calloc();
int creat(), write();


/**************************************************************************

        this function creates an isam file.
        filename= filename
        iflags= 1 for no dupicate keys, else 0
        max_m = # of possible main elements
        max_12 = # of possible 12 elements
        max_13 = # of possible 13 elements
        max_r = # of possible recovery block elements
        ikeylen = length of a key in bytes
        ireclen = length of a record in bytes


**************************************************************************/

int ind_build(filename, iflags, ikeylen, ireclen, max_m,
              max_12, max_13, max_r)
char *filename, iflags;
unsigned ikeylen, ireclen, max_m, max_12, max_13, max_r;
{
        unsigned temp;

        index = (struct global *)calloc(1,sizeof(struct global));
        if(!index)
                return(NEM);
        keylen = ikeylen;
        reclen = ireclen;
        flags = iflags;
        m_max = max_m;
        12_max = max_12;
        13_max = max_13;
        r_max = max_r;
```

```
l2bytes = sizeof(struct l2_link) + max_l2 * (sizeof(struct l2_elem) +
        ikeylen - 1);
l3bytes = max_l3 * (sizeof(struct l3_elem) + ikeylen - 1);

temp = sizeof(struct global) + ikeylen - 1 + max_m * (sizeof(
        struct m_elem) + ikeylen - 1) + l2bytes + l3bytes +
        (l2bytes > l3bytes ? l2bytes : l3bytes) + sizeof(
        struct recov) + (r_max - 1) * sizeof(long);

ifd = creat(filename, 2);
if(ifd < 0) {
        free(index);
        return(CCF);
}
if(write(ifd, &temp, sizeof(unsigned)) != sizeof(unsigned)) {
        free(index);
        return(IWE);
}
temp = lp_key - (char *)&keylen;
ieof = temp + sizeof(unsigned) + max_m * (sizeof(struct m_elem)
        + keylen - 1);
if(write(ifd, &keylen, temp) != temp) {
        free(index);
        return(IWE);
}
if(close(ifd)) {
        free(index);
        return(ICE);
}
free(index);
return(0);

}


/*********************** end of function **********************************/
```

It is important to understand what the code does in the lines marked with an empty comment (e.g., /**/). From this point on, lines so marked indicate programming techniques that should be studied for future use. These techniques are not fully explained. By "digging through" the code yourself, you are more likely to understand and retain the principles behind each technique and to apply them in different instances. Learning is more important (and more useful) than memorization.

Keep in mind that these lines of codes are not etched in stone—better alternatives probably exist. Study the examples and try to find other ways of writing the code. We have presented what we think is the best way to accomplish the task at hand. If you find better coding techniques, let us know about them.

In Figure 5.16, the file isamc.c presents the function ind_create(). It computes all the block variables, given a fixed memory constraint. Once the block parameters have been determined, the index is built by calling ind_build(). You should be able to see that the algorithm presented attempts to equalize the number of elements at each level and that any remaining space becomes L3 elements.

Figure 5.16
isamc.c **File**

```
#include "stdio.h"
#include "isamstr.h"
#include "isam.h"

char *calloc();
int creat(), write();

/*******************************************************************************
 *
 *      this function creates an isam file.
 *      name= filename
 *      asize= size of allocation allowed for this index
 *      ikeylen = length of a key in bytes
 *      ireclen = length of a record in bytes
 *      dupflag = true for errors on duplicate keys, else 0
 *
 ******************************************************************************/
```

```
int ind_create(name, asize, ikeylen, ireclen, dupflag)
char *name;
unsigned ikeylen, ireclen, dupflag, asize;
{

        unsigned a1, n, m , l2, l3, r, rem;
        char iflags;

        r = 30;

        n = asize - (sizeof(struct global) + ikeylen - 1);
        n -= (sizeof(struct recov) + (r - 1) * sizeof(long));

        n -= 2 * sizeof(struct l2_link) + sizeof(struct l2_elem) - 3 + 3
             * ikeylen;

        a1 = (sizeof(struct m_elem) + 2 * sizeof(struct l2_elem)
             + sizeof(struct l3_elem) - 4 + 4 * ikeylen);

        l2 = l3 = m = n / a1;
        rem = n % a1;

        while(rem > (sizeof(struct l3_elem) - 1 + ikeylen)) {
                ++l3;
                rem -= (sizeof(struct l3_elem) - 1 + ikeylen);
        }

        iflags = dupflag ? 1 : 0;

        return(ind_build(name, iflags, ikeylen, ireclen, m, l2, l3, r));

}

/*********************** end of function ********************************/
```

Primary ISAM Library Functions

The file isam3.c, presented in Figure 5.17, contains the primary ISAM library functions.

Figure 5.17
isam3.c **File**

```
#include "stdio.h"
#include "isamstr.h"
#include "isam.h"

/* these are the function return type declarations */

extern long readnext(), insert();

extern int open(), close(), read();
extern int match(), keycmp();

extern void l3write(), l2write();
extern void rwrite(), lswrite();
extern void keymove(), free();

extern char *calloc(), *calpl2(), *calpl3();
```

```
/***************************************************************************
 *
 *        index open opens an index file, allocates storage for
 *        working blocks in memory, and fills in index data locations
 *
 ***************************************************************************/

char *ind_open(filename)
char *filename;
{

        int j;
        unsigned i;

        index = (struct global *)0;
        if((j = open(filename, 2)) == EOF) {
                i_errno = FNF;
                return((char *)0);
        }


        if(read(j, &i, sizeof(i)) < sizeof(i)) {
                i_errno = INV;
                return((char *)0);
        }


        if(!(index = (struct global *)calloc(1,i))) {
                i_errno = NEM;
                return((char *)0);
        }


        i = lp_key - (char *)&keylen;
        if(read(j, &keylen, i) != i) {
                free(index);
                i_errno = INV;
                return((char *)(index = (struct global *)0));
        }
```

```
l2elem = sizeof(struct l2_elem) + keylen - 1;
l2bytes = l2_max * l2elem + sizeof(struct l2_link) + keylen - 1;
l3elem = sizeof(struct l3_elem) + keylen - 1;
l3bytes = l3_max * l3elem;
cama = bm_ptr = (M_ELEM)(lp_key + keylen);
        /* first byte after lp_key */

l2s_ptr = (struct l2_link *)calpl2(m_max, bm_ptr);
cal2 = bl2_ptr = (L2_ELEM)((char *)l2s_ptr + sizeof(struct l2_link)
        + keylen - 1);
cal3 = bl3_ptr = (L3_ELEM)((char *)l2s_ptr + l2bytes + l2elem);
wbl3_ptr = (L3_ELEM)((char *)bl3_ptr + l3bytes);
wbl2_ptr = (L2_ELEM)((char *)wbl3_ptr + sizeof(struct l2_link)
        + keylen - 1);
br_ptr = (struct recov *)((char *)wbl3_ptr + (l2bytes > l3bytes ?
        l2bytes : l3bytes));
rbytes = sizeof(struct recov) + sizeof(long) * (r_max - 1);
ifd = j;

if(cm_ent) {
        j = (unsigned)((char *)l2s_ptr - (char *)bm_ptr);
        if(read(ifd, bm_ptr, j) != j) {
                free(index);
                i_errno = INV;
                index = (struct global *)0;
        }
}
return((char *)index);

}
```

```
/**************************************************************************
 *
 *      write add writes key to index and allocates new data storage.
 *      returns offset of new storage or -1 on error
 *
 **************************************************************************/

long wa(key)
char *key;
{

        return(insert(key, _lm1));

}


/**************************************************************************
 *
 *      secondary write add writes key to index using offset and
 *      returns offset or -1 on error
 *
 **************************************************************************/

long swa(key, offset)
long offset;
char *key;
{

        return(insert(key, offset));

}
```

```
/****************************************************************************
 *
 *      read key finds first key equal to key and returns offset
 *      or -1 if not found or error
 *
 ****************************************************************************/

long rk(key)
char *key;
{

        if(i_errno = setjmp(_ienv))
                return(_lm1);

        if(match(key)) {                    /* if zero returned key match */
                i_errno = KNF;
                return(_lm1);
        }
        return(cal3->offset);


}
```

```
/****************************************************************************
 *
 *      read next key is used to find duplicate keys.
 *      returns offset of next dup key if found, else
 *      returns -1, with errno set
 *
 ****************************************************************************/


long rnk()
{

        long temp;

        if(i_errno = setjmp(_ienv))
                return(_lm1);

        if((temp = readnext()) < 0 || keycmp(lp_key, cal3->l3key)) {
                i_errno = KNF;
                temp = _lm1;
        }
        keymove(lp_key, cal3->l3key);
        return(temp);

}
```

```
/***********************************************************************
 *
 *      read next finds next sequential entry in index.
 *      if found returns offset of entry and places key
 *      at anskey, else returns -1 with errno set
 *
 ***********************************************************************/

long rn(anskey)
char *anskey;
{

        long temp;

        if(i_errno = setjmp(_ienv))
                return(_lm1);

        if((temp = readnext()) >= 0)
                keymove(anskey, cal3->l3key);
        else
                i_errno = EOF;
        keymove(lp_key, cal3->l3key);
        return(temp);

}
```

```
/*****************************************************************************
 *
 *      global read key returns offset of first key greater
 *      than or equal to key, else -1 with errno set.
 *      key found is put at anskey
 *
 *****************************************************************************/

long grk(key, anskey)
char *key, *anskey;
{

        if(i_errno = setjmp(_ienv))
                return(_lm1);
        if(match(key) < 0){
                i_errno = KNF;
                return(_lm1);
        }
        keymove(anskey, cal3->l3key);
        return(cal3->offset);


}
```

```
/**************************************************************************
 *
 *      global read next key returns offset of next key greater
 *      than or equal to last processed key (if found
 *      anskey is set equal to key found), else -1 is
 *      returned with errno set
 *
 **************************************************************************/

long grnk(anskey)
char *anskey;
{

        long temp;

        if(i_errno = setjmp(_ienv))
                return(_lm1);

        if((temp = readnext()) < 0 || keycmp(lp_key, cal3->l3key) < 0) {
                i_errno = KNF;
                temp = _lm1;
        }
        keymove(anskey, cal3->l3key);
        keymove(lp_key, cal3->l3key);
        return(temp);

}


/**************************************************************************
 *
 *      get index returns current index pointer
 *
 **************************************************************************/

char *get_ind()
{

        return((char *)index);

}
```

```
/*************************************************************************
 *
 *      set index sets current index to iptr
 *
 *************************************************************************/

void set_ind(iptr)
char *iptr;
{

        index = (struct global *)iptr;

}


/*************************************************************************
 *
 *      return last found key returns offset and key of current
 *      index position
 *
 *************************************************************************/

long rlfk(anskey)
char *anskey;
{

        if(cm_ent) {
                keymove(anskey, lp_key);
                return(cal3->offset);
        }
        i_errno = INE;
        return(_lm1);

}
```

```
/****************************************************************************
 *
 *      index close writes any dirty records back to disk,
 *      then closes file, returns -1 on error with errno set
 *
 ****************************************************************************/

int ind_close(iptr)
char *iptr;
{

        char *isav;
        unsigned i;

        isav = (char *)index;
        index = (struct global *)iptr;

        if(i_errno = setjmp(_ienv)) {
                index = (struct global *)isav;
                return(EOF);
        }


        l2write(l2_cur);
        l3write(l3_cur);
        rwrite(r_cur);
        if(m_drty) {
                lswrite((long)sizeof(unsigned), &keylen,
                                i = lp_key - (char *)&keylen);
                lswrite((long)(i + sizeof(unsigned)), bm_ptr, m_max *
                        (sizeof(struct m_elem) + keylen - 1));
        }
        if(close(ifd)) {
                i_errno = ICE;
                index = (struct global *)isav;
                return(EOF);
        }

        free(index);
        index = (struct global *)isav;
        return(0);

}
```

```
/**************************************************************************
 *
 *      Returns i_errno.
 *
 **************************************************************************/

int ind_err()
{

        return(i_errno);

}


/**************************************************************************
 *
 *      Sets to end of file.
 *
 **************************************************************************/

long ind_eof()
{

        if(i_errno = setjmp(_ienv))
                return(_lm1);

        if(cm_ent) {
                set_eof();
                keymove(lp_key, cal3->l3key);
                return(cal3->offset);
        }
        i_errno = INE;
        return(_lm1);

}
```

```
/****************************************************************************
 *
 *      Set to beginning of file.
 *
 ****************************************************************************/

long ind_bof()
{

        if(i_errno = setjmp(_ienv))
                return(_lm1);

        if(cm_ent) {
                cama = bm_ptr;
                grread(cama->offset);
                while(lowlink)
                        l2read(lowlink);
                cal2 = bl2_ptr;
                l3read(cal2->offset);
                cal3 = bl3_ptr;
                keymove(lp_key, cal3->l3key);
                return(cal3->offset);
        }
        i_errno = INE;
        return(_lm1);

}


/*********************** end of function ********************************/
```

Opening an Index

The first task in creating a new index is to open an existing one. A pointer to the file name (*filename), which is a character string, is passed to the ind_open() function. This function attempts to open the file, allocate the memory required by the index, initialize all global variables in memory, and return either a pointer to the memory allocation or a zero on error. By calling the ind_err() function, you can obtain more specific information on the error returned from a function call. This function will return the value contained in i_errno. (See Figure 5.18 for specific error values.)

Writing to an Index

When a pointer to a key is passed to the function wa() (write-add), it adds that key to the index. The offset into the data file (where the record associated with the key will be written) is returned. The swa() (secondary write-add) function is passed a pointer to the key and the data file offset for that record. This function allows a secondary key to be inserted into an index without the ISAM generating a data file offset. (A secondary key allows a second key to access the same record in the data file.)

Reading the Index

In this process, a pointer to a key is passed to the rk() function. If the key is not found or if an error occurs, the function will return a -1. Otherwise, the offset (where the data record can be found in the data file) is returned for the first sequential key that the offset matches.

The setjmp() function saves the current environment (the stack status) in __ienv and returns a 0. If the longjmp() function is called before the return from the function that called setjmp(), the environment is restored to the status it had at the time the associated setjmp() was called. Because longjmp() can be called with different __ienv's, the return is to the matching environment—call to setjmp(). This procedure gives you a way to go back effectively to the code where setjmp() was called and return the value passed to longjmp().

The environmentally paired calls setjmp() and longjmp() save code space. Without these functions, the return status would have to be checked from every (recursively called) level down to the lowest

Figure 5.18
Header File for the Program Using the ISAM Library
isamp.h Header File

```
/*  turn this define on if you want to use the error msg array */

/*
#define ERRMSG
*/

#define DUPKEY   1       /* Duplicate key error */
#define IRE      2       /* Index read error */
#define IWE      3       /* Index write error */
#define ICE      4       /* Index close error */
#define KNF      5       /* Key not found */
#define INV      6       /* Index not valid */
#define NEM      7       /* Not enough memory for open allocation */
#define FNF      8       /* File not found on open */
#define INE      9       /* Index is empty */
#define CCF      10      /* Cannot create file */
#ifndef EOF
#define EOF      -1
#endif

#ifdef  ERRMSG

/* end of file must be handled separately */

char    *isamer[]={
                "",
                "Duplicate Key Error.",
                "Index Read Error.",
                "Index Write Error.",
                "Index Close Error.",
                "Key Not Found.",
                "Index not Valid.",
                "Not Enough Memory.",
                "File Not Found.",
                "Index is Empty.",
                "Cannot Create File."
        };
#endif
```

read/write function calls. Because effective read/write functions are used frequently and must be checked for errors each time, setjmp() and longjmp() provide a direct means of error recovery.

The rnk() (read next key) function determines an offset to the next duplicate key or returns a -1 on error.

The function rn() (read next) returns the offset for the next sequential key and places the key at the location pointed to by the parameter anskey, or returns a -1 on error.

The grk() (global read key) function is passed two pointers: one to the desired key (key) and another to the location where the found key will be placed (anskey). The grk() function returns the offset of the first key found that is greater than or equal to key, or a -1 on error.

The grnk() (global read next key) function is also passed a pointer to the location where the found key will be placed. This function, however, returns an offset to the next key that is greater than or equal to the last key processed, or a -1 on error.

The function get_ind() (get index) returns the current index pointer. The set_ind() (set index) sets the current index pointer equal to the index pointer passed to the function. The rlfk() (read last found key) function copies the last found key into the memory pointed to by the passed parameter anskey. The rlfk() function returns either the offset of the data record or -1 if the index is empty.

The ind_close() (index close) function closes the index file referenced by the index pointer parameter that was passed to the function. It returns a 0 if successful, or it returns a -1 if an error occurred.

The function ind_eof() (index end-of-file) returns the offset of the last key in the index and places the current index at end-of-file, or ind_eof() returns a -1 on error. The ind_bof() (index beginning-of-file) function returns the offset of the first key in the index and places the current index at beginning-of-file, or the function returns a -1 on error.

The functions discussed above make up the basic functions used in the ISAM library. Figure 5.19 shows the contents of file isam1.c.

Figure 5.19
isam1.c **File**

```
#include "stdio.h"
#include "isamstr.h"
#include "isam.h"


/*      these are the function return type declarations */

extern long l3alloc(), l2alloc(), dalloc();
extern char *calpl2(), *calpl3();
extern int match(), keycmp();

extern void l3split(), highsplit(), adjust();
extern void grread(), maininsert(), fmove(), lmove(), l2write();
extern void l2read(), l3read(), wl2write(), wl2read();
extern void keymove();

/*************************************************************************
 *
 *      insert(key,recpos)
 *              inserts new key into index
 *              returns offset or error = -1
 *              errno elsewhere
 *
 *************************************************************************/


long insert(key, recpos)
long recpos;
char *key;
{

        int i;
        char *start, *end, *mid;
        unsigned len;

        /* set error recovery point */

        if(i_errno = setjmp(_ienv))
                return(_lm1);
```

```
/* check to see if index is empty and process as special case */

if(!cm_ent) {
        cama = bm_ptr;
        keymove(cama->key, key);
        l2_group = l2_cur = cama->offset = l2alloc();
        cama->group = 1;
        cm_ent++;
        cal2 = bl2_ptr;
        keymove(cal2->key, key);
        l3_cur = cal2->offset = l3alloc();
        l2_ent = 1;
        cal2->group = 1;
        cal3 = bl3_ptr;
        keymove(cal3->l3key, key);
        m_drty = l2_drty = l3_drty = TRUE;
        keymove(lp_key, key);
        lowlink = highlink = 0;
        return(cal3->offset = recpos == _lm1 ? dalloc() : recpos);
} /* End of if(!cm_ent) */

/* if index is not empty, locate key position in index by calling
   match(). if the exact key is found (i == 0) and no dups are
   allowed, return error code DUPKEY */

if((i = match(key)) == 0 && (NODUP)) {
        i_errno = DUPKEY;
        return(_lm1);
} /* End of if((i = match */

/* if match returns end-of-file, set _eof to TRUE and set index to
   end-of-file */

if(_eof = i < 0)
        set_eof();
```

```
/* _bof is set TRUE if at beginning-of-file */

_bof = cal3 == bl3_ptr && cal2 == bl2_ptr && cama == bm_ptr &&
        !lowlink;

/* if current l3 block is full */

if(cal2->group == l3_max) {

/* l3 block is full, check if l2 block not full */

        if(l2_ent != l2_max) {

/* l3 block full, l2 block not full, check if bottom of l3 block
   and not bottom of l2 block and next lower l3 is not full */

                if((cal3 == bl3_ptr) && (cal2 != bl2_ptr) &&
                    (((L2_ELEM)calpl2(-1, cal2))->group < l3_max)) {

/* l3 block full, l2 block not full, bottom of current l3 block and
   not at bottom of l2 block and next lower l3 not full, insert
   current key at top of next lower l3 block and adjust key in
   next lower l2 element and cal2 and cal3 */


                        cal2 = (L2_ELEM)calpl2(-1, cal2);
                        l3read(cal2->offset);
                        keymove(cal2->key, key);
                        cal3 = (L3_ELEM)calpl3(cal2->group, bl3_ptr);


                } else { /* else for if((cal3 == bl3 */
```

```
/* l3 block full, l2 block not full, but cannot insert at top of
   next lower l3 block. current l3 block is split */


                  l3split(key);   /* l2 insert */

      /* if at eof then main's key must be adjusted */

              if(_eof)
                      keymove(cama->key, key);

          } /* end of if((cal3 == bl3 */

      } else { /* else for if(l2_ent != l2_max */

/* l3 block full, l2 block full */

      /* if highlink then read highlink */

              if(highlink)
                      wl2read(highlink);

      /* check if highlink and it is not full */

              if(highlink && wl2_ent < l2_max){

/* highlink not full, split l3 block and move overflow l2
   element into lowest element of highlink. adjust cal2
   cal3 and highlink's lowkey, leaving the proper l2 and
   l3 blocks in memory */

                  l3split(key);   /* with overflow */
```

```
/* working 13 and working 12 block are a union in
   memory; therefore, a reread of highlink is needed */

        wl2read(highlink);
        l2_ent-;
        start = calpl2(wl2_ent, wbl2_ptr) - 1;
        end = start + l2elem;
        len = start + 1 - (char *)wbl2_ptr;
        lmove(start, end, len);
        fmove(calpl2(l2_max, bl2_ptr), wbl2_ptr,
                l2elem);
        wl2_ent++;
        keymove(wl2_lowkey, ((L2_ELEM)
                calpl2(l2_ent - 1, bl2_ptr))->key);
        wl2_lowlink = l2_cur;

/* determine if current added key in highlink or
   current 12 */

        if((char *)cal2 == calpl2(l2_max, bl2_ptr)) {
                l2write(l2_cur);
                l2_cur = highlink;
                fmove(ws_ptr, l2s_ptr, l2bytes);
                cal2 = bl2_ptr;

        } else { /* else for if(cal2 == calp */

                wl2write(highlink);

        } /* end of if(cal2 == calp */

} else { /* else for if(highlink && l2_ent */
```

```
/* either no highlink or highlink is full */

/* if lowlink */

        if(lowlink) {
                wl2read(lowlink);

    /* if lowlink not full */

            if(wl2_ent < l2_max) {

/* split l3 block moving lowest l2 element to
   highest lowlink element and slide current
   l2 down one element (overflow becomes highest
   current l2 element). adjust all keys and set
   cal2 and cal3 correctly */


                l3split(key);
                        /* with overflow */

        /* if at eof adjust cama->key */

                if(_eof)
                        keymove(cama->key,
                                key);
                wl2read(lowlink);
                fmove(bl2_ptr, calpl2(wl2_ent,
                        wbl2_ptr), l2elem);
                keymove(lowkey, bl2_ptr->key);
                wl2_ent++;
                l2_ent-;
                start = calpl2(1, bl2_ptr);
                end = (char *)bl2_ptr;
                len = l2_max * l2elem;
                fmove(start, end, len);
```

```
/* keep correct l2 and l3 blocks */

            if(cal2 == bl2_ptr) {
                l2write(l2_cur);
                l2_cur = lowlink;
                fmove(ws_ptr, l2s_ptr,
                      l2bytes);
                cal2 = (L2_ELEM)calpl2(
                       l2_ent - 1,
                       bl2_ptr);

            } else {  /* else if(cal2 == bl2
                */

                wl2write(lowlink);
                cal2 = (L2_ELEM)calpl2(
                       -1, cal2);
            }

        } else {  /* else for if(wl2_ent */

/* no highlink or highlink full and lowlink is full */

/* split to highlink side and do side link adjusts */

            highsplit(key);
            adjust();

        } /* end of if(wl2_ent */

    } else {   /* else of if(lowlink) */
```

```
                    /* no highlink or highlink full and no lowlink */

/* indented 5 */

                    /* if highlink is full and no lowlink */

        if(highlink) {

                    /* split 12 and adjust side links */

                    highsplit(key);
                    adjust();

        } else { /* else of if(highlink */

                    /* no highlink or lowlink */

                    /* check if main is full */

                    if(cm_ent == m_max) {

                    /* main is full with no side links on current 12 */
                    /* split 12 block with no adjust */

                            highsplit(key);

                    } else { /* else of if(cm_ent == m_max */

                    /* main not full and no side links */
```

```
/* check if at beginning-of-file or end-of-file */

if(_bof || _eof) {

        /* add a new l3 and l2 at the correct end */

        l2write(l2_cur);
        l3write(l3_cur);
        l3_cur = l3alloc();
        l2_cur = l2alloc();
        cal3 = bl3_ptr;
        cal2 = bl2_ptr;
        cal2->group = 0;
        cal2->offset = l3_cur;
        keymove(cal2->key, key);
        highlink = lowlink = 0;
        l2_ent = 1;

        /* add to end of file or beginning */

        if(_eof)
                cama = (M_ELEM)calpl2(1, cama);
        else
                maininsert();

        l2_group = cama->offset = l2_cur;
        keymove(cama->key, key);
        cama->group = 1;

} else { /* else of if(_bof || _eof */
```

```
/* main is not full and not eof or bof */
/* split l2 and l3 and insert into main */

        l3split(key);    /* with overflow */
        mid = calpl2((l2_max + 1) / 2, bl2_ptr);
        fmove(mid, wbl2_ptr,
                calpl2(l2_max + 1, bl2_ptr) - mid);
        wl2_ent = l2_ent - ((l2_max + 1) / 2);
        l2_ent = (l2_max + 1) / 2;
        wl2_highlink = wl2_lowlink = 0;
        maininsert();
        ((M_ELEM)calpl2(1, cama))->offset =
                l2alloc();
        cama->group = 1;
        cama->offset = l2_cur;
        keymove(cama->key, ((L2_ELEM)
                calpl2(l2_ent - 1, bl2_ptr))->key);
        if((char *)cal2 >= mid) {
                l2write(l2_cur);
                cama = (M_ELEM)calpl2(1, cama);
                l2_group = l2_cur = cama->offset;
                fmove(ws_ptr, l2s_ptr, l2bytes);
                cal2 = (L2_ELEM)(((char *)cal2 - mid)
                        + (char *)bl2_ptr);
        } else /* else for if(cal2 >= mid */
                wl2write(((M_ELEM)calpl2(1, cama))
                        ->offset);

    } /* end of if(_bof || _eof */

    /* increase main element entries by added entry */

    cm_ent++;

} /* end if(cm_ent == m_max */
```

```
}  /* end of if(highlink */

}  /* end of if(lowlink */

}  /* end of if(highlink && */

}  /* end of if(l_ent != l2_max */

}else  /* else if(cal2->group == l3_max (indent correct) */

        /* l3 block was not full */

        if(_eof) {

        /* if at eof then point to empty l3 pointer and adjust main
           and l2 keys */

                cal3 = (L3_ELEM)calpl3(1, cal3);
                keymove(cal2->key, key);
                keymove(cama->key, key);
        }  /* end of if(_eof) */

/* end of if(cal2->group */

/* this code is always used to insert the l3 element into the
   setup empty slot. (cal3) only an empty index or illegal dup
   condition will not reach this code */

/* check if current l3 is not empty and not at end-of-file */

if(cal2->group && !_eof) {

        /* make room for an l3 element at cal3 */

                start = calpl3(cal2->group, bl3_ptr) - 1;
                end = start + l3elem;
                len = start - (char *)cal3 + 1;
                lmove(start, end, len);

}  /* end of if(cal2->group */
```

```
        keymove(cal3->l3key, key);           /* move key to l3 */
        cal2->group++;                        /* up l3 group */
        m_drty = l2_drty = l3_drty = TRUE;    /* mark buffers dirty */
        keymove(lp_key, key);                 /* move key to lp_key */

        /* set cal3->offset and return it based on recpos. If recpos
             is equal to minus one, a new data allocation is used. otherwise
             the allocation passed is used (swa) */

        return(cal3->offset = recpos == _lm1 ? dalloc() : recpos);

}

/*********************** end of function ********************************/
```

The insert() *Function*

The insert() function implements an algorithm to insert a new key
into the index. First, insert() determines if the index is empty. If it is,
L2 and L3 blocks are created, and the key is added at the beginning-of-
file. If the index is not empty, the function match() is invoked, which
places the index at the point where the key will be added.

The rest of the code in insert() checks the status of the index and its
relation to where the key will be added. This step optimizes the index
entries. Once the relationship has been determined, one or more of the
following operations will occur:

1. An L2 block is split [l2split()].
2. An L3 block is split [l3split()].
3. A high or low link is created [highsplit()].
4. The key is inserted into an L3 block.
5. An entry is inserted into the main-level block [maininsert()].
6. The side links are adjusted [adjust()].

Notice that the typedef's L2_ELEM and M_ELEM are used extensively for casting pointers. A cast must be done whenever you want to change the context in which a pointer is used.

Most of the functions invoked by insert() are contained in Figures 5.20, 5.21, and 5.22.

The isam2.c file in Figure 5.20 contains the following functions:

match()	Finds the position of a key in an index
readnext()	Positions the index at the next key after the current key
l3split()	Splits an L3 block
highsplit()	Splits an L2 block and creates a side link

Figure 5.20
isam2.c **File**

```
#include "stdio.h"
#include "isamstr.h"
#include "isam.h"


/*      these are the function return type declarations */

extern long l3alloc(), l2alloc();
extern char *calpl2(), *calpl3();
extern int keycmp();

extern void l3split();
extern void grread(), fmove(), lmove(), l2write();
extern void l2read(), l3write(), l3read(), wl2write(), wl2read();
extern void wl3write();
extern void keymove();
extern M_ELEM mbinsh();
extern L2_ELEM l2binsh();
extern L3_ELEM l3binsh();

static int _dir;
```

```
/****************************************************************************
 *
 *      match
 *              finds first key >= current key or returns eof
 *
 *              returns:
 *                      -1 on eof (all keys less than)
 *                       0 on found equal
 *                       1 on found only greater
 *
 ****************************************************************************/

int match(key)
char *key;
{

        char *upper, *lower;

        _dir = 0;

        /* check if empty index, if so return end-of-file */

        if(!cm_ent)
                return(EOF);

        /* set upper and lower bounds for mbinsh() */

        upper = calpl2(cm_ent - 1, bm_ptr);
        lower = (char *)bm_ptr;

        /* see if at end-of-file and return EOF if true */

        if(keycmp(((M_ELEM)upper)->key, key) > 0) {
                keymove(lp_key, ((M_ELEM)upper)->key);
                return(EOF);
        }
```

```
/* position cama with mbinsh() */

cama = mbinsh(upper, lower, key);

/* group read l2 block */

l2read(l2_group = cama->offset);

/* while lowlink and key < lowkey read lowlink */

while(lowlink)
        if(keycmp(lowkey, key) <= 0) {
                l2read(lowlink);
                _dir = -1;
        } else
                break;

/* while highlink and key > highest element key read highlink */

while(highlink)
        if(keycmp(((L2_ELEM)calpl2(l2_ent - 1, bl2_ptr))->key,
                                        key) > 0) {
                l2read(highlink);
                _dir = 1;
        } else
                break;

/* set upper and lower bounds for l2binsh() */

upper = calpl2(l2_ent - 1, bl2_ptr);
lower = (char *)bl2_ptr;

/* set cal2 from l2binsh() */

cal2 = l2binsh(upper, lower, key);
```

```
        /* read l3 block */

        l3read(cal2->offset);

        /* set cal3 from l3binsh() */

        upper = calpl3(cal2->group - 1, bl3_ptr);
        cal3 = l3binsh(upper, bl3_ptr, key);

        /* move key to lp_key and return keycmp status */

        keymove(lp_key, cal3->l3key);
        return(keycmp(key, cal3->l3key));          /* must return >= 0 (not eof)*/


}


/***********************************************************************
 *
 *       read next gets next key after current position.
 *       returns -1 for eof, or next record position
 *
 ***********************************************************************/

long readnext()
{

        /* check if not at top of current l3 block */

        if((char *)cal3 < calpl3(cal2->group - 1, bl3_ptr)) {

                /* if true increment cal3 to next l3 element */

                cal3 = (L3_ELEM)calpl3(1, cal3);

        } else {
```

```
/* at top of current 13 block */

/* check if top of current 12 block */

if((char *)cal2 < calpl2(l2_ent - 1, bl2_ptr))

        /* if not increment cal2 to next 12 element */

        cal2 = (L2_ELEM)calpl2(1, cal2);

else {

        /* top of 12 and 13 blocks */

        /* check for highlink */

        if(highlink) {

                /* if highlink read it */

                l2read(highlink);

        } else {

                /* no highlink */
                /* check if top of main */

                if((char *)cama < calpl2(cm_ent - 1, bm_ptr)) {

                        /* not at top of main up cama to next
                           main element */

                        cama = (M_ELEM)calpl2(1, cama);
                        grread(cama->offset);
```

```
                                    /* go to lowest link of new l2 */

                                    while(lowlink) {
                                            l2read(lowlink);
                                    }

                        } else {

                                    /* top of main return EOF */

                                    return(EOF);
                        }
                }

                /* l2 and l3 full set cal2 to start of new block */

                cal2 = bl2_ptr;
        }

        /* l3 full, set cal3 to start of new block */

        l3read(cal2->offset);
        cal3 = bl3_ptr;
}

/* return data offset */

return(cal3->offset);

}
```

```
/***************************************************************************
 *
 *       splits an l3 block and inserts into an l2 block if necessary
 *
 ***************************************************************************/

void l3split(key)
char *key;
{

        char *start, *end, *mid;
        unsigned len;

        /* if end-of-file up cal2 to next element */

        if(_eof)
                cal2 = (L2_ELEM)calpl2(1, cal2);
        else {

        /* if not eof then one element is inserted into the l2 block with
           overflow */

                start = calpl2(l2_ent, bl2_ptr) - 1;
                end = start + l2elem;
                len = start - (char *)cal2 + 1;
                lmove(start, end, len);
        }
```

```
/* if beginning-of-file or end-of-file */

if(_bof || _eof) {

        /* write current l3 block, and generate a new empty l3 block */

        l3write(l3_cur);
        cal2->offset = l3alloc();
        cal2->group = 0;
        keymove(cal2->key, key);
        cal3 = bl3_ptr;

} else {

        /* split the l3 block and leave the correct half in
           memory with cal2 and cal3 properly adjusted */

        mid = calpl3((l3_max) / 2, bl3_ptr);
        fmove(mid, wbl3_ptr, calpl3(l3_max, bl3_ptr) - mid);
        keymove(cal2->key, ((L3_ELEM)(mid - l3elem))->l3key);
        cal2->group = (l3_max) / 2;
        ((L2_ELEM)calpl2(1, cal2))->group -= cal2->group;
        cal2->offset = ((L2_ELEM)calpl2(1, cal2))->offset;
        ((L2_ELEM)calpl2(1, cal2))->offset = l3alloc();
        if((char *)cal3 < mid)
                wl3write(((L2_ELEM)calpl2(1, cal2))->offset);
        else {
                l3_drty = TRUE;
                l3write(cal2->offset);
                cal2 = (L2_ELEM)calpl2(1, cal2);
                fmove(wbl3_ptr, bl3_ptr, cal2->group * l3elem);
                cal3 = (L3_ELEM)((char *)bl3_ptr +
                        ((char *)cal3 - mid));
        }

}
```

```
        /* adjust administrative data */

        l3_cur = cal2->offset;
        l2_ent++;
        l2_drty = TRUE;


}


/**************************************************************************
 *
 *      side splits to the high side an l2 block
 *
 **************************************************************************/

void highsplit(key)
char *key;
{

        char *start, *end;
        unsigned len;
        long l2_hold;

        /* mark l2 dirty */

        l2_drty = TRUE;

        /* if eof or bof */

        if(_eof || _bof) {

                /* check if eof */

                if(_eof) {
```

```
        /* if eof create an empty highlink */

        highlink = l2alloc();
        l2write(l2_cur);
        lowlink = l2_cur;
        l2_cur = highlink;
        highlink = 0;
        keymove(cama->key, key);
        keymove(lowkey, ((L2_ELEM)
                calpl2(l2_ent - 1, bl2_ptr))->key);
} else {

        /* if bof create an empty lowlink */

        lowlink = l2alloc();
        keymove(lowkey, key);
        l2write(l2_cur);
        highlink = l2_cur;
        l2_cur = lowlink;
        lowlink = 0;
}

/* eof or bof, adjust pointers and create a new l3 block */

cal2 = bl2_ptr;
l3write(l3_cur);
l3_cur = cal2->offset = l3alloc();
keymove(cal2->key, key);
cal2->group = 0;
l2_ent = 1;
cal3 = bl3_ptr;
l2_drty = TRUE;

} else {
```

```
/* not eof or bof */
/* split the l2 block, and keep the correct half in
   memory with all pointers adjusted */

start = calpl2(l2_max / 2, bl2_ptr);
end = (char *)wbl2_ptr;
len = ((l2_max + 1) / 2) * l2elem;
fmove(start, end, len);
l2_ent = l2_max / 2;
wl2_ent = l2_max - l2_ent;
wl2_highlink = highlink;
l2_hold = highlink = l2alloc();
wl2_lowlink = l2_cur;
keymove(wl2_lowkey, ((L2_ELEM)
        calpl2(l2_ent - 1, bl2_ptr))->key);
if((char *)cal2 >= start) {
        l2write(l2_cur);
        l2_cur = highlink;
        cal2 = (L2_ELEM)calpl2(-l2_ent, cal2);
        fmove(ws_ptr, l2s_ptr, l2bytes);
} else
        wl2write(highlink);
if(wl2_highlink)
        lswrite(wl2_highlink, &l2_hold, sizeof(long));

/* split the l3 block after room is made */

l3split(key);   /* no overflow */
}
```

```
/* these are alternate methods of doing the same test

*        if((cama->group & 1) ? !_bof : _bof) {

*        if(_bof ? !(cama->group & 1) : (cama->group & 1)) {

*/

/* adjust centering: maintain cama->group to the high side of
   center (even) or center (odd) of a group of 12 blocks */

if((_bof || (_dir < 0)) ^ (cama->group & 1)) {
        12_hold = 12_cur;
        12read(cama->offset);
        12_group = cama->offset = (_bof || (_dir < 0)) ? lowlink
                : highlink;
        12read(12_hold);
}

/* up 12 block count */

cama->group++;
}

/*********************** end of function *********************************/
```

The isam5.c file in Figure 5.21 contains the following function:

adjust()   Maintains L2 side links in a condition that
                            is as balanced as possible

Figure 5.21
isam5.c **File**

```
#include "stdio.h"
#include "isamstr.h"
#include "isam.h"


/*      these are the function return type declarations */

extern long l3alloc(), l2alloc();
extern char *calpl2(), *calpl3();
extern int keycmp();

extern void l3split();
extern void grread(), fmove(), lmove(), l2write();
extern void l2read(), l3write(), l3read(), wl2write(), wl2read();
extern void wl3write();
extern void keymove();

extern M_ELEM mbinsh();
extern M_ELEM shift();
extern L2_ELEM l2binsh();
extern L3_ELEM l3binsh();
```

```
/**************************************************************************
 *
 *      balance side links in l2 blocks for deletes
 *
 **************************************************************************/

int readjust()
{

        M_ELEM a, b;
        int i;
        int lc, uc;

        /* find first lower main element entry whose l2 group count is 2 more
           than the current group count. variable lc is the number of elements
           from cama. variable a points to lower match */

        for(lc=1, i = cama->group + 1, a = (M_ELEM)calpl2(-1, cama);
                a >= bm_ptr; lc++, a = (M_ELEM)calpl2(-1, a)) {
                if(a->group > i)
                        break;
        }

        /* find first higher main element entry whose l2 group count is 2 more
           than the current group count. variable uc is the number of elements
           from cama. variable b points to higher match */

        for(uc = 1, b = (M_ELEM)calpl2(1, cama); b < (M_ELEM)calpl2(cm_ent,
                bm_ptr); uc++, b = (M_ELEM)calpl2(1, b)) {
                if(b->group > i)
                        break;
        }

        /* if none found lower then lc set to 0 */

        if(a < bm_ptr)
                lc = 0;
```

```
/* if none found higher then set uc to 0 */

if(b >= (M_ELEM)calpl2(cm_ent, bm_ptr))
        uc = 0;

/* if higher element found */

if(uc) {

        /* if lower element found */

        if(lc)

                /* set farthest away to 0 */

                if(lc < uc)
                        uc = 0;
                else
                        lc = 0;

} else

        /* no higher found, if no lower we are balanced and return */

        if(!lc)
                return(TRUE);

l2read((a = uc ? b : a)->offset);
shift(a, cama, lc);
l2read(l2_group = cama->offset);

return(FALSE);


}
```

```
/**************************************************************************
 *
 *      shift moves one 12 link from start to end in bubble fashion.
 *      dir tells whether from higher to lower main element
 *      versus lower to higher.
 *
 **************************************************************************/

M_ELEM shift(start, end, dir)
M_ELEM start, end;
int dir;
{

        int i = 0;
        M_ELEM a = start, c = 0;
        long l_offset, 12_hold = 12_cur;
        long lowhold;

        if(dir) {

                /* shift highlink from current to lowlink of next higher
                   main element 12 group and continue until the b main
                   element is reached */

                do {
                        while(highlink)
                                12read(highlink);
                        w12read(lowlink);
                        l_offset = w12_highlink;
                        w12_highlink = 0;
                        w12write(lowlink);
                        keymove(a->key, lowkey);
                        if(a == start)
                                lowhold = lowlink;
                        lowlink = 0;
                        12_drty = TRUE;
```

```
                   if((a = (M_ELEM)((char *)a + melem))->group) {

/**/                       wl2read(highlink = a->offset);
/**/                       if((!(i++)) && l2_hold == l_offset)
                                   c = a;
                           while(wl2_lowlink)
                                   wl2read(highlink = wl2_lowlink);
                           keymove(wl2_lowkey, ((L2_ELEM)
                                   calpl2(l2_ent - 1, bl2_ptr))->key);
                           l2write(wl2_lowlink = l_offset);
                           wl2write(highlink);
                           l2read(a->offset);

                           /* adjust centering on shift throughs */

                           if(end != a)
                                   a->offset = lowlink;
                   } else {
                           a->offset = l2_cur;
                           keymove(a->key, ((L2_ELEM)calpl2(l2_ent - 1,
                                   bl2_ptr))->key);

                   }
           } while(a < end);
```

```
/* adjust centering in highest group */

if(!(a->group & 1) && a->group)
        a->offset = lowlink;

/* adjust centering of cama */

if(!(start->group & 1)) {
        if(start->group == 2) {
                l2_group = start->offset = lowhold;
                l2read(start->offset);
        } else {
                l2read(start->offset);
                l2_group = start->offset = lowlink;
        }
}

} else {
```

```
/* shift lowlinks of current to high link of next lower group
   and continue through variable a */



do {
        while(lowlink)
                l2read(lowlink);
        wl2read(highlink);
        l_offset = wl2_lowlink;
        wl2_lowlink = 0;
        wl2write(highlink);
        highlink = 0;
        l2_drty = TRUE;
        if((a = (M_ELEM)((char *)a - melem))->group) {
                wl2read(lowlink = a->offset);
                if((!(i++)) && l2_hold == l_offset)
                        c = a;
                while(wl2_highlink)
                        wl2read(lowlink = wl2_highlink);
                keymove(lowkey, ((L2_ELEM)
                        calpl2(wl2_ent - 1, wbl2_ptr))->key);
                keymove(a->key, ((L2_ELEM)
                        calpl2(l2_ent - 1, bl2_ptr))->key);
                l2write(wl2_highlink = l_offset);
                wl2write(lowlink);
                l2read(a->offset);

                /* center shift throughs */
                if(a != end)
                        a->offset = highlink;
        } else {
                a->offset = l2_cur;
                keymove(a->key, ((L2_ELEM)calpl2(l2_ent - 1,
                        bl2_ptr))->key);
        }
} while(a > end);
```

```
        /* center lowest group */

        if(a->group & 1)
                a->offset = highlink;

        /* center cama group */

        if(start->group & 1) {
                l2read(start->offset);
                l2_group = start->offset = highlink;
        }
}

/* lower count for shift out */

start->group-;

/* increase count for shift in (a and b are equal here) */

end->group++;

return(c);


}
```

```
/**************************************************************************
 *
 *        balance side links in l2 blocks for inserts
 *
 **************************************************************************/

void adjust()
{

        M_ELEM a, b;
        int i;
        int lc, uc;
        long l2_hold = l2_cur;

        /* find first lower main element entry whose l2 group count is 2 more
           than the current group count. variable lc is the number of elements
           from cama. variable a points to lower match */

        for(lc = 1, i = cama->group - 1, a = (M_ELEM)calpl2(-1, cama);
                a >= bm_ptr; lc++, a = (M_ELEM)calpl2(-1, a)) {
                if(a->group < i)
                        break;
        }

        /* find first higher main element entry whose l2 group count is 2 more
           than the current group count. variable uc is the number of elements
           from cama. variable b points to higher match */

        for(uc = 1, b = (M_ELEM)calpl2(1, cama); b < (M_ELEM)calpl2(cm_ent,
                bm_ptr); uc++, b = (M_ELEM)calpl2(1, b)) {
                if(b->group < i)
                        break;
        }

        /* if none found lower then lc set to 0 */

        if(a < bm_ptr)
                lc = 0;
```

```
        /* if none found higher then set uc to 0 */

        if(b >= (M_ELEM)calpl2(cm_ent, bm_ptr))
                uc = 0;

        /* if higher element found */

        if(uc) {

                /* if lower element found */

                if(lc)

                        /* set farthest away to 0 */

                        if(lc < uc)
                                uc = 0;
                        else
                                lc = 0;

        } else

                /* no higher found, if no lower we are balanced and return */

                if(!lc)
                        return;

        if(a = shift(cama, uc ? b : a, uc))
                l2_group = (cama = a)->offset;

        l2read(l2_hold);


}

/********************* end of function ********************************/
```

Figure 5.22 contains the isam.c file, which includes the rest of the functions you will need for the library.

The three binary-search functions—mbinsh( ), l2binsh( ), and l3binsh( )—have been written to converge on the *first sequential key* of a group of duplicate keys (if allowed). The grread( ) function reads the designated group into the L2 block window if a member of that group is not already active in the window.

If a new element will be inserted in the main-level block, then maininsert( ) is used to create the necessary space. The functions lmove( ) and fmove( ) move data in memory from top to bottom [that is, lmove( ) last to first] and bottom to top [fmove( ) first to last].

Several functions are defined to read and write blocks into or from specific windows. These functions are l2write( ), l2read( ), l3write( ), l3read( ), wl2write( ), wl2read( ), wl3write( ), wl3read( ), rread( ), and rwrite( ).

The functions responsible for allocating disk space are l2alloc( ) (allocates an L2 block on disk), l3alloc( ) (allocates an L3 block on disk), ralloc( ) (allocates a recovery block on disk), and dalloc( ) (allocates a data block on disk).

The functions lsread( ) and lswrite( ) perform the actual reading and writing of blocks to and from the disk. These functions invoke lseek( ) to establish the proper offset in the disk file and to read or write the appropriate record. If an error is detected in either function, a longjmp( ) is performed with the appropriate error value. The longjmp( ) function allows immediate error processing by the highest-level function within the current library (invoked by the user program). By doing a longjmp( ), you eliminate error-recovery checks at all intermediate levels (back to the major level).

The keycmp( ) and keymove( ) functions compare and move keys. The calpl2( ) and calpl3( ) functions are used, instead of the parametized macro calp, to minimize the amount of code space needed by the library. The functions calpl2( ) and calpl3( ) also do pointer arithmetic on the L2 and L3 element pointers.

Figure 5.22
isam.c **File**

```
#include "stdio.h"
#include "isamstr.h"
#include "isam.h"

/*      these are the function return type declarations */

extern long lseek();
extern char *calpl2(), *calpl3();
extern int read(), write();


/************** this shows a recursive-call binary search ***************

M_ELEM mbinsh(upper, lower, key)
M_ELEM upper, lower;
char *key;
{

        M_ELEM mid;

        if(upper == lower)
                return (upper);

        mid = calpl2(((((char *)upper - (char *)lower) / (2*melem)), lower);
        keycmp(key, mid->key) < 0 ? (lower = calpl2(1, mid)) : (upper = mid);
        return(mbinsh(upper, lower, key));

}


***********************************************************************/
```

```
/*************************************************************************
 *
 *       main binary search routine
 *               searches lower bound to upper bound recursively
 *               eof must be checked prior to call
 *
 *               returns pointer to element >= last processed key (lp_key)
 *
 *************************************************************************/

M_ELEM mbinsh(upper, lower, key)
M_ELEM upper, lower;
char *key;
{

        M_ELEM mid;

        while(upper != lower) {

                mid = (M_ELEM)calpl2((((char *)upper - (char *)lower) /
                        (2 * melem)), lower);
                keycmp(key, mid->key) < 0 ? (lower = (M_ELEM)calpl2(1, mid))
                        : (upper = mid);
        }
        return(upper);


}
```

```
/****************************************************************************
 *
 *      L2 binary search routine
 *              searches lower bound to upper bound recursively
 *              eof must be checked prior to call
 *
 *              returns pointer to element >= last processed key (lp_key)
 *
 ****************************************************************************/

L2_ELEM l2binsh(upper, lower, key)
L2_ELEM upper, lower;
char *key;
{

        L2_ELEM mid;

        while(upper != lower) {
                mid = (L2_ELEM)calpl2(((((char *)upper - (char *)lower) /
                        (2 * l2elem)), lower);
                keycmp(key, mid->key) < 0 ? (lower = (L2_ELEM)calpl2(1, mid))
                        : (upper = mid);
        }
        return(upper);

}
```

```
/**************************************************************************
 *
 *      L3 binary search routine
 *              searches lower bound to upper bound recursively
 *              eof must be checked prior to call
 *
 *              returns pointer to element >= last processed key (lp_key)
 *
 **************************************************************************/

L3_ELEM l3binsh(upper, lower, key)
L3_ELEM upper, lower;
char *key;
{

        L3_ELEM mid;

        while(upper != lower) {
                mid = (L3_ELEM)calpl3(((((char *)upper - (char *)lower) /
                        (2 * l3elem)), lower);
                keycmp(key, mid->l3key) < 0 ? (lower = (L3_ELEM)calpl3(1, mid))
                        : (upper = mid);
        }
        return(upper);

}
```

```
/***************************************************************************
 *
 *      group read
 *              checks to see if currently active l2 group is same
 *              as calling group. if not read new group
 *
 ***************************************************************************/

void grread(cgroup)
long cgroup;
{

        if(l2_group == cgroup)
                return;

        l2read(cgroup);

        l2_group = cgroup;

}


/***************************************************************************
 *
 *      makes room for new entry in main at cama
 *
 ***************************************************************************/

void maininsert()
{

        char *start;

        start = calpl2(cm_ent, bm_ptr) - 1;
        lmove(start, start + melem, start - ((char *)cama) + 1);

}
```

```
/*************************************************************************
 *
 *       moves from last to first for len bytes
 *
 *************************************************************************/

void lmove(start, end, len)
char *start, *end;
unsigned len;
{

        while(len-)
                *end- = *start-;


}


/*************************************************************************
 *
 *       moves from first to last for len bytes
 *
 *************************************************************************

void fmove(start, end, len)
char *start, *end;
unsigned len;
{

        while(len-)
                *end++ = *start++;


}
```

```
/*****************************************************************************
 *
 *       if current l2 block is dirty, writes to offset disk address
 *
 *****************************************************************************/

void l2write(offset)
long offset;
{

        if(l2_drty) {
                lswrite(offset, l2s_ptr, l2bytes);
                l2_drty = FALSE;
        }


}


/*****************************************************************************
 *
 *       first writes current l2 block to disk if dirty,
 *               then reads l2 block from offset
 *
 *****************************************************************************/

void l2read(offset)
long offset;
{

        if(offset != l2_cur) {
                l2write(l2_cur);
                lsread(offset, l2s_ptr, l2bytes);
                l2_cur = offset;
        }


}
```

```
/***************************************************************************
 *
 *      if current l3 block is dirty, writes to offset disk address
 *
 ***************************************************************************/

void l3write(offset)
long offset;
{

        if(l3_drty) {
                lswrite(offset, bl3_ptr, l3bytes);
                l3_drty = FALSE;
        }


}


/***************************************************************************
 *
 *      first writes current l3 block to disk if dirty,
 *            then reads l3 block from offset
 *
 ***************************************************************************/

void l3read(offset)
long offset;
{

        if(offset != l3_cur) {
                l3write(l3_cur);
                lsread(offset, bl3_ptr, l3bytes);
                l3_cur = offset;
        }


}
```

```
/***********************************************************************
 *
 *      writes 12 block at work 12 to disk at offset
 *
 ***********************************************************************/

void wl2write(offset)
long offset;
{

        lswrite(offset, ws_ptr, l2bytes);

}


/***********************************************************************
 *
 *      reads 12 block from disk at offset to work 12
 *
 ***********************************************************************/

void wl2read(offset)
long offset;
{

        lsread(offset, ws_ptr, l2bytes);

}
```

```
/***********************************************************************
 *
 *      writes 13 block at work 13 to disk at offset
 *
 ***********************************************************************/

void w13write(offset)
long offset;
{

        lswrite(offset, wb13_ptr, 13bytes);


}


/***********************************************************************
 *
 *      reads recovery block from disk at offset, only used with delete code
 *
 ***********************************************************************/

void rread(offset)
long offset;
{

        if(offset != r_cur) {
                rwrite(r_cur);
                lsread(offset, br_ptr, rbytes);
                r_cur = offset;
        }

}
```

```
/***************************************************************************
 *
 *      writes recovery block to disk at offset, only used with delete code
 *
 ***************************************************************************/

void rwrite(offset)
long offset;
{

        if(r_drty) {
                lswrite(offset, br_ptr, rbytes);
        }

}


/***************************************************************************
 *
 *      gets allocation on disk for l2 block, returns disk offset
 *
 ***************************************************************************/

long l2alloc()
{

        long i;

        if(i = l2bp) {
                lsread(i, &l2bp, sizeof(long));
        } else {
                i = ieof;
                ieof += l2bytes;
        }
        return(i);

}
```

```
/*************************************************************************
 *
 *      gets allocation on disk for l3 block, returns disk offset
 *
 *************************************************************************/

long l3alloc()
{

        long i;

        if(i = l3bp) {
                lsread(i, &l3bp, sizeof(long));
        } else {
                i = ieof;
                ieof += l3bytes;
        }
        return(i);

}
```

```
/*************************************************************************
 *
 *      gets allocation on disk for recovery block, returns disk offset.
 *              only used with delete
 *
 *************************************************************************/

long ralloc()
{

        long i;

        if(i = frbp) {
                lsread(i, &frbp, sizeof(long));
        } else {
                i = ieof;
                ieof += rbytes;
        }
        return(i);


}
```

```
/***************************************************************************
 *
 *      gets data allocation for disk. returns disk offset
 *
 ***************************************************************************/

long dalloc()
{

        long i, j;

        if(rbp) {
                rread(rbp);
                i = br_ptr->roffset[-(br_ptr->rb_ent)];
                if(!br_ptr->rb_ent) {
                        j = frbp;
                        frbp = rbp;
                        rbp = br_ptr->link;
                        br_ptr->link = j;
                }
                r_drty = TRUE;
        } else {
                i = deof;
                deof += reclen;
        }
        return(i);

}
```

```
/************************************************************************
 *
 *      performs all actual disk reads by isam. on error, executes a longjmp
 *              with IRE as error code. seeks to offset, reads len bytes
 *              to ptr
 *
 *   ,
 ************************************************************************/

void lsread(offset, ptr, len)
long offset;
char *ptr;
unsigned len;
{

        lseek(ifd, offset, 0);
        if(len != (read(ifd, ptr, len))) {
                longjmp(_ienv, IRE);    /* index read error */
        }


}
```

```
/*******************************************************************
 *
 *      performs all actual disk writes by isam. on error, executes a longjmp
 *              with IWE as error code. seeks to offset, writes len bytes
 *              from ptr
 *
 *******************************************************************/

void lswrite(offset, ptr, len)
long offset;
char *ptr;
unsigned len;
{

        lseek(ifd, offset, 0);
        if(len != write(ifd, ptr, len))
                longjmp(_ienv, IWE);     /* index write error */


}


/*******************************************************************
 *
 *      this compares k2 to k1 and returns >0 if k2>k1,
 *              0 if k2==k1. or <0 if k2<k1
 *
 *******************************************************************/

int keycmp(k1, k2)
char *k1, *k2;
{

        int i;

        for(i = keylen; *k2 == *k1 && -i; k1++, k2++)
                ;
        return(*k2 - *k1);

}
```

```
/***************************************************************************
 *
 *       this moves a key for keylen from k2 to k1
 *
 ***************************************************************************/

void keymove(k1, k2)
char *k1, *k2;
{

        unsigned i = keylen;

        while(i-)
                *k1++ = *k2++;

}


/***************************************************************************
 *
 *       sets current index pointers to end-of-file
 *
 ***************************************************************************/

void set_eof()
{

        cama = (M_ELEM)calpl2(cm_ent - 1, bm_ptr);
        grread(cama->offset);
        while(highlink)
                l2read(highlink);
        cal2 = (L2_ELEM)calpl2(l2_ent - 1, bl2_ptr);
        l3read(cal2->offset);
        cal3 = (L3_ELEM)calpl3(cal2->group - 1, bl3_ptr);
```

```
/****************************************************************************
 *
 *      does pointer arithmetic on main elements and l2 elements.
 *              adds inc * (length of l2 element in bytes) to ptr
 *
 ****************************************************************************/

char *calpl2(inc, ptr)
char *ptr;
int inc;
{

        return(ptr + inc * l2elem);

}


/****************************************************************************
 *
 *      does pointer arithmetic on l3 elements.
 *              adds inc * (length of l3 element in bytes) to ptr
 *
 ****************************************************************************/

char *calpl3(inc, ptr)
char *ptr;
int inc;
{

        return(ptr + inc * l3elem);

}

/********************** end of function *******************************/
```

Editor's Note to Chapter 6

This chapter presents a book cataloger based on the ISAM functions presented in the previous chapter. For successful use of the book cataloger, all ISAM functions must function properly.

The book cataloger is a large program that may not be executable in CP/M systems with less than a 56K TPA. MS-DOS systems should have a minimum of 128K of RAM to compile, link, and execute this program.

The book cataloger uses the terminal-handling functions presented in Chapter 3. All editor's notes applicable to terminal handlers apply also to Chapter 6.

UNIX programmers should use `termcap` and `curses` in place of the terminal handlers. Raw mode should be set with `ioctl()` or `raw()` so that unbuffered single character reads from the console are immediately passed to the program.

The UNIX programmer is also responsible for trapping Del and interrupts (such as Ctrl-C), using the `signal()` system call to ensure that ISAM operation is terminated gracefully.

Additionally, the editor's note in Chapter 5 concerning `setjmp`, `longjmp`, `creat()`, and `ctype.h` is applicable to the book cataloger program regardless of the operating system environment.

C. D. V.

6

A Book Catalog Program

The book catalog program in this chapter can be used to catalog a home library. This program uses the C libraries from Chapters 3 and 5, as well as techniques discussed in Chapter 4. The program adds books to the catalog and randomly retrieves book information by multiple methods. Editing and deleting of the information in the catalog, however, are not supported.

This program can store book titles of up to 60 characters; the author's last name (up to 20 characters); the author's first and middle initials; the book ISBN; a general description of the book (limited only by free memory) and a series of keywords (each of which may have up to 20 characters). The number of keywords is limited only by the amount of free memory. Random retrieval is allowed by title, author name, ISBN, or keyword. If you are looking for more than one book by the same author, a continued search can make available additional titles.

Nine files maintain the catalog: six index files and three data files. The data files are book.dat, whose record is shown in Figure 6.1; gencom.dat, shown in Figure 6.2; and keyword.dat, shown in Figure 6.3.

291

Figure 6.1
book.dat **Record**

Field width	Data item
00-60	Book title
61-81	Author last name
82	Author first initial
83	Author middle initial
84	Last character of ISBN
85-88	First 9 characters of ISBN stored as a long
89-92	Offset in gencom.dat of general comment

Figure 6.2
gencom.dat **Record**

Field width	Data item
00-03	Offset end-of-file for gencom.dat
04-nn	General comment NULL terminated

Figure 6.3
keyword.dat **Record**

Field width	Data item
00-19	Keyword

The index file (book.ism) holds an index of the books by a hash on the title. The book title is hashed into a long, which becomes the key for the book data in the book.dat file. The author's last name has an identical hash scheme that uses the resulting long as the key for the author.ism index file. The isbn.ism index file has a five-byte key that consists of the long ISBN number and the ISBN's last character. The keyword.ism index has an offset into the keyword.dat file and a long key, which is a hash of the keyword.

The last two index files cross-link the keywords and the book. The `bookkey.ism` index file contains a key that is the `offset` of the book data in the `book.dat` file. The index file also has an associated offset into the `keyword.dat` file. The key in the `keybook.ism` index file is the keyword's offset. The index in that file is the book's offset. Figure 6.4 illustrates the relationship between these files.

Figure 6.4
File Links

book.dat	B1		*G1		B2				*G2
gencom.dat	G1				G2				
keyword.dat	K1		K2		K3				

book.ism	hash	*B1	hash	*B2
	key		key	

author.ism	hash	*B1	hash	*B2
	key		key	

isbn.ism	isbn	*B1	isbn	*B2
	key		key	

keyword.ism	K1	*K1	K2	*K2	K3	*K3
	key		key			

keybook.ism	*K1	*B2	*K2	*B2	*K1	*B1	*K3	*B1
	key		key		key		key	

bookkey.ism	*B2	*K1	*B2	*K2	*B1	*K1	*B1	*K3
	key		key		key		key	

In this figure, all fields with the word "key" under them represent keys in an index file. The letter-number combinations in the figure represent a data record (that is, B1 means Book 1 data record, Gx is General comment record for record x, and Kx is Keyword x). All fields that have references preceded by an *, represent an offset to the record following the *. In the `book.ism` index file, for example, *B1 represents the offset of the B1 data record in the `book.dat` file.

Creating Index and Data Files

The library program catalogs the books, maintains all catalog files that use the ISAM library, and interacts with the operator through the terminal library. Before the catalog can be used, however, data and index files must be created. The bookcr.c program in Figure 6.5 accomplishes this task.

Figure 6.5
bookcr.c **Program**

```
#include "stdio.h"
#include "bookstr.h"


extern int ind_create();


/***************************************************************************
 *
 * this program creates all the index and data files needed for the
 * book catalog program. the algorithm used to determine the size of
 * each of the index files is
 *
 *              noe=number of entries to handle comfortably
 *              scale = cuberoot( 2 * noe)
 *
 *                  # bytes
 *                     6              main element overhead
 *                     4              main element key
 *                     6              12 element overhead
 *                     4              12 element key
 *                     6              w12 element overhead
 *                     4              w12 element key
 *                     4              13 element overhead
 *                     4              13 element key
 *                    ----
 * (keysize * 4 + 22)  38            size per element (spe)
 *
```

```
*
*                          10              12 overhead
*                           4              12 overhead key
*                           6              12 overflow overhead
*                           4              12 overflow key
*                          10              w12 overhead
*                           4              w12 overhead key
*                       30*4+6            recovery block overhead (126)
*                         101              struct global
*                           4              lp_key
*                         ---
* (keysize * 4 + 253)     269             overhead size (os)
*
*             book.ism = spe * scale + os     (keysize 4 noe 500) (649)
*             author.ism                      (keysize 4 noe 500) (649)
*             isbn.ism                        (keysize 5 noe 500) (693)
*             keyword.ism                     (keysize 20 noe 1000) (1659)
*             bookkey.ism                     (keysize 4 noe 3000) (991)
*             keybook.ism                     (keysize 4 noe 3000) (991)
*
*************************************************************************/

void main()
{

        long geof = 0 + sizeof(long);
        int gfd;

        printf("\nCreating book.ism\n");
        if(ind_create("book.ism", 650, 4, sizeof(struct books), FALSE) != 0) {
                printf("\nCannot create BOOK.ISM.\n");
                exit();
        }


        printf("Creating author.ism\n");
        if(ind_create("author.ism", 650, 4, 0, FALSE) != 0) {
                printf("\nCannot create AUTHOR.ISM.\n");
                exit();
        }
```

```
printf("Creating isbn.ism\n");
if(ind_create("isbn.ism", 700, 5, 0, TRUE) != 0) {
        printf("\nCannot create ISBN.ISM.\n");
        exit();
}

printf("Creating keyword.ism\n");
if(ind_create("keyword.ism", 1660, 20, 20, TRUE) != 0) {
        printf("\nCannot create KEYWORD.ISM.\n");
        exit();
}

printf("Creating bookkey.ism\n");
if(ind_create("bookkey.ism", 1000, 4, 0, FALSE) != 0) {
        printf("\nCannot create BOOKKEY.ISM.\n");
        exit();
}

printf("Creating keybook.ism\n");
if(ind_create("keybook.ism", 1000, 4, 0, FALSE) != 0) {
        printf("\nCannot create KEYBOOK.ISM.\n");
        exit();
}

printf("Creating book.dat\n");
if(creat("book.dat", 2) < 0) {
        printf("\nCannot create BOOK.DAT\n");
        exit();
}

printf("Creating gencom.dat\n");
if((gfd = creat("gencom.dat", 2)) < 0) {
        printf("\nCannot create GENCOM.DAT\n");
        exit();
}
```

```
lseek(gfd, 0, 0);
printf("Initializing gencom.dat.\n");
if(write(gfd, &geof, sizeof(long)) < sizeof(long)) {
        printf("\nCannot initialize GENCOM.DAT\n");
        exit();
}

printf("Closing gencom.dat\n");
if(close(gfd) < 0) {
        printf("\nCannot close GENCOM.DAT\n");
        exit();
}

printf("Creating keyword.dat\n");
if(creat("keyword.dat", 2) < 0) {
        printf("\nCannot create KEYWORD.DAT\n");
        exit();
}

}

/********************* end of function *********************/
```

The structure-description file (bookstr.h) is shown in Figure 6.6.

The comment at the beginning of the bookcr.c file explains how the memory allocations are determined for each index file. The formulas assume that the index structures do not require alignment bytes (for example, a long requires double-word address alignment). If the hardware environment under which the catalog is implemented requires alignment, the constants must be adjusted. We chose the variables in the example catalog as representative numbers for a typical home library.

The ind_build() function from the ISAM library creates and initializes each index file. The three data files are then created and initialized. After this program terminates successfully, the catalog files are ready for data input.

Figure 6.6
bookstr.h **Structure File**

```
struct books{
        char name[61];
        char last[21];
        char finit;
        char minit;
        char isbnp;
        long isbn;
        long goff;        /* general comment file offset */
};

struct genc{
        struct genc *link;
        char string[1];
};

struct keyw{
        struct keyw *link;
        char keyword[21];
};

#define benv &env

#ifndef void
#define void int
#endif
#ifndef TRUE
#define TRUE 1
#define FALSE 0
#endif

#define OOM    11        /* out of memory error */
#define BFWE   12        /* book file write error */
#define GFWE   13        /* general comment file write error */
#define KFWE   14        /* keyword file write error */
#define BFRE   15        /* book file read error */
#define GFRE   16        /* general comment file read error */
#define KFRE   17        /* keyword file read error */
```

The Catalog Program Control Module

The catalog program's `bookm.c` module (Figure 6.7) contains the main entry point for the program and implements the general program control algorithm.

This module defines all global variables used by the catalog program and includes fatal error messages. First, a `setjmp()` established a fatal-error processing point. Any fatal errors that occur during the cataloging session will be processed at the point established by the `setjmp()`. The screen is then cleared, and the program prints sign-on and operation messages while the files open. Next, a menu of the catalog program's available procedure options is displayed, and the user selection is obtained. The appropriate function executes based on the user's selection.

The `edit()` function is used to obtain from the user all textual information except the ISBN number. We chose this function, rather than `gets()`, to illustrate how a simple line editor works. The ISBN number is in the form of *n-nnn-nnnnn-a,* where *n* is a number and *a* is an alphanumeric character. Each book has a unique ISBN number, which is the standard identifier in the publishing industry.

Figure 6.7
`bookm.c` **Module**

```
#include "stdio.h"
#include "bookstr.h"
#include "isamp.h"


char *bookidx, *authidx, *isbnidx, *bkidx, *kbidx, *kwidx;
struct books book;
struct genc *ghdr;
struct keyw *khdr;
char *edit();


int bfd, gfd, kfd;
long geof;                    /* gencom file end of file pointer */
char null[1] = '\0';


jmp_env env;
```

```
char *booker[] = {
                "",
                "Duplicate Key Error.",
                "Index Read Error.",
                "Index Write Error.",
                "Index Close Error.",
                "Key Not Found.",
                "Index not Valid.",
                "Not Enough Memory.",
                "File Not Found.",
                "Index is Empty.",
                "Cannot Create File.",
                "Out of Memory.",
                "Book File Write Error.",
                "Gencom File Write Error.",
                "Keyword File Write Error.",
                "Book File Read Error.",
                "Gencom File Read Error.",
                "Keyword File Read Error."
};
```

```
/***********************************************************************
 *
 *      main level function that opens and closes the data base and
 *      handles the menu selection
 *
 ***********************************************************************/

void main()
{

        int berr, i;
        char buff[2];

        if(berr = setjmp(benv)) {
                eraeol(22, 0);
                printf("Catalog error: %s\n",berr == EOF ? "End of File" :
                        booker[berr]);
                exit();
        }
        clrscr();
        lprompt(0, 0, "Book Catalog Program Version 1.0");
        cursor(0, 50);
        printf("Opening Files");

/*      opens indices    */

        if((berr = open_book()) < 0) {
                eraeol(22, 0);
                printf("Cannot open book files. %s\n", booker[ind_err()]);
                exit();
        }

        lprompt(0, 50, "Mode: ");
```

```
while(TRUE) {
        eraeol(0, 56);
        printf("Menu");
        for(i = 1;i < 22; i++)
                eraeol(i, 0);
        cursor(6, 0);
        printf("1. Add books.\n2. Find book by title.\n");
        printf("3. Find book by ISBN.\n");
        printf("4. Scan books by author\n");
        printf("5. Scan books by keyword\n6. Quit.");
        eraeol(22, 0);
        printf("Select function from menu. Enter number: ");
        switch(i = atoi(edit(22, 41, 2, buff))) {
                case 1:
                        badd();
                        eraeop(22, 0);
                        continue;

                case 2:
                        bget();
                        continue;

                case 3:
                        iget();
                        continue;

                case 4:
                        sauth();
                        continue;

                case 5:
                        skeyw();
                        continue;

                case 6:
                        break;
```

```
        default:
                eraeol(23, 0);
                printf("Invalid entry please try again.");
                continue;
        }

        break;
}

eraeol(22, 0);
printf("Closing book files\n");
if(clos_book() < 0) {
        eraeol(22, 0);
        printf("Cannot close book files\n");
        exit();
}

}

/*********************** end of function ********************************/
```

Because this program uses the terminal library described in Chapter 3, the data module scrdat.c from that library must be compiled and linked with the catalog modules.

The Primary Functions of a Catalog Program

The bookn.c module (in Figure 6.8) contains the control code for each primary cataloging function (for example, add a book, search by title, etc.).

The display of general comments and messages lets you easily follow the flow of bookn.c. The techniques used were all discussed earlier in this text.

Figure 6.8
bookn.c **Module**

```
#include "stdio.h"
#include "bookstr.h"
#include "isamp.h"

extern struct books book;
extern long look_auth(), look_book(), look_isbn(), look_key();
extern long getn_auth(), get_key(), gn_key();
char *edit();


/*****************************************************************************
 *
 *      this function calls the functions to get book information and
 *      then causes it to be added to the data base
 *
 *****************************************************************************/

void badd()
{

        while(TRUE) {
                eraeop(0, 56);
                printf("Add book");
                gbook();          /* get book name from user */
                gauthor();        /* get author name from user */
                gisbn();          /* get isbn from user */
                ggdes();          /* get general description from user */
                eraeop(12, 0);
                dgdes();          /* display general description */
                gkeys();          /* get keys from user */
                if(yesno(22, 0, "Is this data correct? ")) {
                        eraeol(22, 0);
                        printf("Putting data to disk\n");
                        put_book();    /* put book in file */

                }
```

```
            clr_book();       /* clear book storage */
            if(!yesno(22, 0, "Do you have more books to add? "))
                    break;
    }

}

/*************************************************************************
 *
 *      searches for a book by title and displays it if found
 *
 *************************************************************************/

void bget()
{

    long boff;

    while(TRUE) {
            eraeop(0, 56);
            printf("Find book");
            gbook();                            /* get title */
            if((boff = look_book()) < 0) {
                    eraeol(23, 0);
                    printf("Cannot find this book");
            } else {
                    get_book(boff);             /* read book */
                    pr_book();                  /* display book */
            }
            if(!yesno(22, 0, "Would you like to find another book? "))
                    break;
    }
    eraeol(23, 0);

}
```

```
/*************************************************************************
 *
 *      locate a book by ISBN
 *
 *************************************************************************/

void iget()
{

        long boff;

        while(TRUE) {
                eraeop(0, 56);
                printf("Find ISBN");
                gisbn();                        /* get isbn from user */
                if((boff = look_isbn()) < 0) {
                        eraeol(23, 0);
                        printf("Cannot find this ISBN");
                } else {
                        get_book(boff);         /* read book */
                        pr_book();              /* display book */
                }
                if(!yesno(22, 0, "Would you like to find another ISBN ? "))
                        break;
        }
        eraeol(23, 0);

}
```

```
/************************************************************************
 *
 *      locate all books by author
 *
 ************************************************************************/

void sauth()
{

        long boff;
        char author[21];
        int mi, fi;


        while(TRUE) {
                eraeop(0, 56);
                printf("Scan author");
                gauthor();              /* get author name from user */
                strcpy(author, book.last);
                mi = book.minit;
                fi = book.finit;
                boff = look_auth();     /* search for first author book */
                while(TRUE) {
                        if(boff < 0) {
                                eraeol(23, 0);
                                printf("Cannot find this author");
                                break;
                        } else {
                                eraeop(1, 0);
                                get_book(boff); /* read book */
                                pr_book();      /* display book */
                        }

                        if(!yesno(22, 0,
                                "Would you like to continue this author? "))
                                break;
                        strcpy(book.last, author);
                        book.minit = mi;
                        book.finit = fi;
                        boff = getn_auth();             /* search for next */
                }
```

```
                        if(!yesno(22, 0, "Would you like to scan another author? "))
                                break;
                }
                eraeol(23, 0);

        }


        /*************************************************************************
         *
         *       searches books by keyword
         *
         *************************************************************************/

        void skeyw()
        {

                int ans;
                long boff, koff;
                char buff[41];

                eraeop(0, 56);
                printf("Scan keyword");

                while(TRUE) {
                        eraeol(22, 0);
                        printf("Enter keyword? ");
                        if(!gkeyw(22, 15, buff))             /* get keyword from user */
                                break;
                        if((koff = look_key(buff)) < 0) { /* search for key */
                                eraeol(23, 0);
                                printf("Cannot find keyword.");
                                continue;
                        }
```

```
eraeol(23, 0);
boff = get_key(koff);            /* finds first book for key */
while(TRUE) {
        if(boff < 0) {
                eraeol(23, 0);
                printf("Cannot find this keyword");
                break;
        } else {
                eraeop(1, 0);
                get_book(boff); /* read book */
                pr_book();      /* display book */
        }

        if(!yesno(22, 0,
                "Would you like to continue this keyword? "))
                break;
        boff = gn_key();         /* finds next book for key */
}
ans = yesno(22, 0, "Would you like to scan another keyword? ");
eraeol(23, 0);
if(!ans)
        break;
}

}
```

```
/*************************************************************************
 *
 *      displays current book on the screen
 *
 *************************************************************************/

void pr_book()
{

        prtitle();
        prauthor();
        prisbn();
        while(TRUE) {
                dgdes();
                if(!yesno(22, 0, "Would you like to see keywords? "))
                        break;

                dkeys();
                if(!yesno(22, 0,
                        "Would you like to see general description? "))
                        break;
        }
        clr_book();

}
```

```
/****************************************************************************
 *
 *      prompts and gets a yes/no answer. returns TRUE for yes.
 *      x is row coordinate for prompt, y is column, prompt
 *      points to prompt string
 *
 ***************************************************************************/

int yesno(x, y, prompt)
int x, y;
char *prompt;
{

        int ans;

        do {
                eraeol(x, y);
                printf(prompt);
        } while((ans = tolower(getchar())) != 'y' && ans != 'n');
        return(ans == 'y');

}

/*********************** end of function *********************************/
```

Catalog Program User Input/Output Support Functions

The booki.c module (Figure 6.9) contains the hashing algorithm that converts an ASCII character string into a long hash total. This module also contains all of the routines that cope with user input and output of data items (for example, book title, ISBN, etc.) for the catalog program. The textual line editor function [edit()] is also used.

The code in Figure 6.9 is consistent with techniques presented earlier in this book. You should pay particular attention, however, to how the hash(), gisbn(), prisbn(), and edit() functions work. The ggdes(), dgdes(), gkeys(), and dkeys() functions manage one-way linked lists (as discussed in Chapter 4) of general descriptions and keywords.

Figure 6.9
booki.c **Module**

```
#include "stdio.h"
#include "bookstr.h"

extern struct books book;
extern struct genc *ghdr;
extern struct keyw *khdr;
extern char *calloc(), *edit();
extern jmp_env env;
```

```
/****************************************************************************
 *
 *      hash will return a long hash value from the uppercase
 *      equivalent of a character string
 *
 ****************************************************************************/

long hash(ptr)
char ptr[];
{

        long a = 0, b = 0;
        int i = strlen(ptr), j = 0, k;

        while(j < i) {
                for(k = 1; k <= sizeof(long) && j < i; k++, j++)
                   b += (long)(toupper(ptr[j]) & 0xff) <<
                        (sizeof(long) - k) * 8;
                a += b;
        }
        return(a);

}
```

```
/****************************************************************************
 *
 *      gets book title from the user and puts it in book.name
 *
 ****************************************************************************/

void gbook()
{

        while(TRUE) {
                lprompt(2, 0, "Book Name: ");
                edit(2, 11, 61, book.name);
                if(strlen(book.name)) {
                        break;
                }
        }
        eraeol(22, 0);
        prtitle();

}


/****************************************************************************
 *
 *      displays a book title on the screen
 *
 ****************************************************************************/

void prtitle()
{

        lprompt(2, 0, "Book Name: ");
        printf(book.name);

}
```

```
/***************************************************************************
 *
 *       gets an author name from the user and puts it in book.last,
 *       book.finit, and book.minit
 *
 ***************************************************************************/

void gauthor()
{

        while(TRUE) {
                lprompt(4, 0, "Last Name: ");
                edit(4, 11, 21, book.last);
                if(strlen(book.last)) {
                        break;
                }
        }
        eraeol(22, 0);
        lprompt(4, 40, "First Initial: ");
        book.finit = toupper(getchar());
        lprompt(4, 58, "Middle Initial: ");
        book.minit = toupper(getchar());
        prauthor();

}
```

```
/****************************************************************************
 *
 *      displays author information
 *
 ****************************************************************************/

void prauthor()
{

        lprompt(4, 0, "Last Name: ");
        printf(book.last);
        lprompt(4, 40, "First Initial: ");
        putchar(book.finit);
        lprompt(4, 58, "Middle Initial: ");
        putchar(book.minit);

}


/****************************************************************************
 *
 *      gets ISBN from user and puts first 9 digits converted to long
 *      in book.isbn. the last character may be alphanumeric and is
 *      placed in book.isbnp
 *
 ****************************************************************************/

void gisbn()
{

        char j[11];
        int k = 16, l = 0;
        int i;

        lprompt(6, 10, "ISBN: ");
```

```
while(TRUE) {
        i = getchar();
        if(i == 0x7f || i == 0x08) {
                if(l) {
                        if(atdash(l)) {
                                k-;
                        }
                        k-;
                        l-;
                        eraeol(6, k);
                }
                continue;
        }
        if(l == 10 && i == '\n')
                break;
        if((l == 9 && isalnum(i)) || (l < 9 && isdigit(i))) {
                j[l++] = i;
                if(atdash(l)) {
                        putchar('-');
                        k++;
                }
                k++;
        } else {
                eraeol(6, k);
        }
}
book.isbnp = j[9];
for(book.isbn = 0, i = 0; i < 9; i++)
        book.isbn = book.isbn * 101 + (j[i] - '0');
                                                /* () allows for
                                                 * j[i]-'0' to be
                                                 * done in int math
                                                 * instead of long
                                                 */

prisbn();

}
```

```
/***************************************************************************
 *
 *       returns TRUE if ISBN position is at a dash
 *
 ***************************************************************************/

int atdash(l)
{

        return(l == 1 || l == 4 || l == 9);

}


/***************************************************************************
 *
 *       displays ISBN
 *
 ***************************************************************************/

void prisbn()
{

        lprompt(6, 10, "ISBN: ");
        printf("%01ld-", book.isbn / 100000000);
        printf("%03ld-", book.isbn / 100000 % 1000);
        printf("%05ld-", book.isbn % 100000);
        putchar(book.isbnp);

}
```

```
/***************************************************************************
 *
 *      prints a prompt at position x,y in low intensity after clearing to eol
 *
 ***************************************************************************/

void lprompt(x, y, pmt)
int x, y;
char *pmt;
{

        eraeol(x, y);
        l_int();
        printf(pmt);
        h_int();

}
```

```
/*****************************************************************************
 *
 *      gets general description from user
 *
 *****************************************************************************/

void ggdes()
{

        char buff[81];
        int i;
        int x = 12;
        struct genc *p = &ghdr;

        eraeop(10, 0);
        lprompt(10, 30, "General Description");
        while((i = strlen(strcat(edit(x, 0, 80, buff), "\n"))) > 1) {
                if(p->link = (struct genc *)calloc(1,
                        sizeof(struct genc) + i)) {

                        strcpy(p->link->string, buff);
                        p = p->link;
                        if(++x > 20) {
                                x = 12;
                        }
                } else
                        longjmp(benv, OOM);
        }
        p->link = 0;

}
```

```
/**************************************************************************
 *
 *      this function displays the general description
 *
 **************************************************************************/

void dgdes()
{

        struct genc *p = &ghdr;
        char *str;
        int x = 12;
        int i;

        eraeop(10, 0);
        lprompt(10, 30, "General Description");
        while(p->link) {
                cursor(x, 0);
/**/            str = (p = p->link)->string;
                while(*str) {
                        putchar(*str);
                        if(*str++ == '\n') {
                                if(++x > 20 && (p->link || *str)) {
                                        if(yesno(22, 0, "Next Page? ")) {
                                                eraeop(x = 12, 0);
                                        } else
                                                return;
                                }
                        }
                }
        }

}
```

```
/**************************************************************************
 *
 *        gets keywords from user
 *
 **************************************************************************/

void gkeys()
{

        char buff[41];
        struct keyw *p = &khdr;
        int x = 12, y = 7, i;

        eraeop(10, 0);
        lprompt(10, 35, "Keywords");
        while(TRUE) {
                eraeol(x, y);
                i = gkeyw(x, y, buff);
                if(i) {
                        if(p->link = (struct keyw *)calloc(1,
                                sizeof(struct keyw))) {

                                strncpy(p->link->keyword, buff, 21);
                                p = p->link;
                                lprompt(x, y, p->keyword);
                                if((y += 22) > 65)
                                        x++, y = 7;
                                if(x > 21)
                                        eraeop(x = 12, y = 7);
                        } else {
                                longjmp(benv, OOM);
                        }
                } else {
                        break;
                }
        }
        p->link = 0;

}
```

```
/**************************************************************************
 *
 *      really gets the keyword from user
 *
 **************************************************************************/

int gkeyw(x, y, buff)
int x, y;
char *buff;
{

        int i;

        eraeol(x, y);
        i = strlen(edit(x, y, 21, buff));
        if(i) {
                strcat(buff, "                     ");
                buff[20] = NULL;
                makupper(buff);
        }
        return(i);

}


/**************************************************************************
 *
 *      makes a string uppercase
 *
 **************************************************************************/

void makupper(buff)
char *buff;
{

        for(; *buff; buff++)
                *buff = toupper(*buff);

}
```

```
/***************************************************************************
 *
 *      displays keywords to user
 *
 ***************************************************************************/

void dkeys()
{

        struct keyw *p = &khdr;
        int x = 12, y = 7, i;

        eraeop(10, 0);
        lprompt(10, 35, "Keywords");
        while(TRUE) {
                if(p->link) {
                        p = p->link;
                        cursor(x, y);
                        printf("%s", p->keyword);
                        if((y += 22) > 65)
                                x++, y = 7;
                        if(x > 20 && p->link){
                                if(!yesno(22, 0, "Next page? "))
                                        break;
                                eraeop(x = 12, y = 7);
                        }
                } else {
                        break;
                }
        }

}
```

```
/*************************************************************************
 *
 *      edit() gets an input a x,y for length n into buffer
 *
 *************************************************************************/

char *edit(x, y, n, buff)
int x, y, n;
char buff[];
{

        int k = y;
        int i, l = 0;

        eraeol(x, y);
        while(TRUE) {
                cursor(x, k);
                i = getchar();
                if(i == 0x7f || i == 0x08){
                        if(l) {
                                k-;
                                l-;
                                eraeol(x, k);
                        }
                        continue;
                }
                if(i == '\n') {
                        buff[l] = NULL;
                        break;
                }
```

```
            if(l < n-1) {
                    if(isprint(i)) {
                            eraeol(23, 0);
                            buff[l++] = i;
                            k++;
                    } else {
                            eraeol(23, 0);
                            printf("Invalid character entered.");
                            eraeol(x, k);
                    }
            } else {
                    eraeol(23, 0);
                    printf("Input too long, last character ignored.");
                    eraeol(x, k);
            }
    }
    eraeol(23, 0);
    return(buff);

}

/********************** end of function **********************************/
```

The ISAM Interface Module

The bookf.c module (Figure 6.10) contains the functions that interface
directly with the ISAM library functions discussed in Chapter 5.

Figure 6.10
bookf.c **Module**

```
/*      file-handling routines for book program */


#include "stdio.h"
#include "isamp.h"
#include "bookstr.h"

extern struct books book;
extern struct genc *ghdr;
extern struct keyw *khdr;
extern long swa(), wa(), rk(), rnk(), hash(), lseek(), geof;
extern char *ind_open(), *calloc(), *bookidx, *authidx, *isbnidx;
extern char *bkidx, *kbidx, *kwidx;
extern void set_ind(), longjmp();
extern jmp_env env;
extern int bfd, gfd, kfd, ind_err();
extern char null[];

/**************************************************************************
 *
 *      opens all index files
 *
 **************************************************************************/

int open_book()
{

        if(!(bookidx = ind_open("book.ism")))
                return(-1);

        if(!(authidx = ind_open("author.ism")))
                return(-1);

        if(!(isbnidx = ind_open("isbn.ism")))
                return(-1);
```

```
        if(!(bkidx = ind_open("bookkey.ism")))
                return(-1);

        if(!(kbidx = ind_open("keybook.ism")))
                return(-1);

        if(!(kwidx = ind_open("keyword.ism")))
                return(-1);

        if((bfd = open("book.dat",2)) == EOF)
                return(-1);

        if((gfd = open("gencom.dat",2)) == EOF)
                return(-1);

        if(read(gfd, &geof, sizeof(geof)) < sizeof(geof))
                return(-1);

        if((kfd = open("keyword.dat", 2)) == EOF)
                return(-1);

        return(0);

}


/***************************************************************************
 *
 *      closes index files
 *
 ***************************************************************************/

int clos_book()
{

        if(ind_close(bookidx) < 0)
                return(-1);
```

```
        if(ind_close(authidx) < 0)
              return(-1);

        if(ind_close(isbnidx) < 0)
              return(-1);

        if(ind_close(bkidx) < 0)
              return(-1);

        if(ind_close(kbidx) < 0)
              return(-1);

        if(ind_close(kwidx) < 0)
              return(-1);

        if(close(bfd) == EOF)
              return(-1);

        lseek(gfd, 0l, 0);
        if(write(gfd, &geof, sizeof(geof)) < sizeof(geof))
              return(-1);

        if(close(gfd) == EOF)
              return(-1);

        if(close(kfd) == EOF)
              return(-1);

        return(0);

}
```

```
/**************************************************************************
 *
 *      updates index and data files for a book
 *
 **************************************************************************/

void put_book()
{

        long boff, goff, koff, lkey;
        struct genc *gptr;
        struct keyw *kptr;
        int i;

        set_ind(isbnidx);
        if(rk(&book.isbnp) >= 0) {                                /*1*/
                eraeol(23, 0);
                printf("Duplicate ISBN.");
                return;
        }

        set_ind(bookidx);                                         /*2*/
        lkey = hash(book.name);
        if((boff = wa(&lkey)) < 0)
                longjmp(benv, ind_err());

        set_ind(authidx);                                         /*3*/
        lkey = hash(book.last);
        if(swa(&lkey, boff) < 0)
                longjmp(benv, ind_err());

        set_ind(isbnidx);                                         /*4*/
        if(swa(&book.isbnp, boff) < 0)
                longjmp(benv, ind_err());
```

```
if(ghdr)                                                /*5*/
        book.goff = geof;
else
        book.goff = 0l;

lseek(bfd, boff, 0);
if(write(bfd, &book.name[0], sizeof(struct books)) <
        sizeof(struct books))

        longjmp(benv, BFWE);

lseek(gfd, geof, 0);
for(gptr = ghdr; gptr; gptr = gptr->link) {
        i = strlen(gptr->string);
        if(write(gfd, gptr->string, i) != i)
                longjmp(benv, GFWE);
        geof += i;                                      /*6*/
}
if(write(gfd, null, 1) != 1)
        longjmp(benv, GFWE);
geof++;                                                 /*6*/
lseek(gfd, 0l, 0);
if(write(gfd, &geof, sizeof(long)) < sizeof(long))
        longjmp(benv, GFWE);

/*      keywords         */
```

```
        for(kptr = khdr; kptr; kptr = kptr->link) {
                set_ind(kwidx);
                if((koff = rk(kptr->keyword)) < 0)              /*7*/
                        if((koff = wa(kptr->keyword)) < 0)
                                longjmp(benv, ind_err());
                        else {
                                lseek(kfd, koff, 0);
                                if(write(kfd, kptr->keyword, 20) < 20)
                                        longjmp(benv, KFWE);
                        }
                set_ind(bkidx);
                if(swa(&boff, koff) < 0)
                        longjmp(benv, ind_err());

                set_ind(kbidx);
                if(swa(&koff, boff) < 0)
                        longjmp(benv, ind_err());

        }
}


/****************************************************************************
 *
 *      reads a book from the index and data files
 *
 ****************************************************************************/

void get_book(boff)
long boff;
{

        struct genc *gptr;
        struct keyw *kptr;
        long koff;
        int i;

        lseek(bfd, boff, 0);
        if(read(bfd, &book, sizeof(struct books)) != sizeof(struct books))
                longjmp(benv, BFRE);
```

```
gptr = &ghdr;
if(book.goff) {
        lseek(gfd, book.goff, 0);
        do {
                gptr->link = (struct genc *)calloc(1,80 +
                        sizeof(struct genc));
                gptr = gptr->link;
                if(!gptr)
                        longjmp(benv, OOM);
                if((i = read(gfd, gptr->string, 80)) != 80) {
                        if(i < 0)
                                longjmp(benv, GFRE);
                        gptr->string[i] = NULL;
                        break;
                }
                gptr->string[i] = NULL;
                if(i > strlen(gptr->string))
                        break;
        } while(TRUE);
}
gptr->link = 0;

kptr = &khdr;
set_ind(bkidx);
if((koff = rk(&boff)) >= 0) {
        do {
                kptr->link = (struct keyw *)calloc(1,
                        sizeof(struct keyw));
                kptr = kptr->link;
                if(!kptr)
                        longjmp(benv, OOM);
                lseek(kfd, koff, 0);
                if(read(kfd, kptr->keyword, 20) != 20)
                        longjmp(benv, KFRE);
                kptr->keyword[20] = NULL;
        } while((koff = rnk()) >= 0);
}
```

```
        if(koff < 0)
                if(ind_err() != KNF)
                        longjmp(benv, ind_err());
        kptr->link = 0;

}


/*********************************************************************
 *
 *      searches for a book by title
 *
 *********************************************************************/

long look_book()
{

        long boff, lkey;
        char title[61];

        lkey = hash(book.name);
        set_ind(bookidx);
        if((boff = rk(&lkey)) < 0)
                if(ind_err() != KNF)
                        longjmp(benv, ind_err());
        while(boff >= 0) {
                lseek(bfd, boff, 0);
                if(read(bfd, title, 61) != 61)
                        longjmp(benv, BFRE);
/**/    if(makupper(title), makupper(book.name), strcmp(title, book.name) == 0)
                        break;
                if((boff = rnk()) < 0)
                        if(ind_err() != KNF)
                                longjmp(benv, ind_err());
        }
        return(boff);

}
```

```
/*************************************************************************
 *
 *      finds the first entry for an author
 *
 *************************************************************************/

long look_auth()
{

        long boff, lkey;
        char author[sizeof(book.last) + sizeof(book.finit) +
                sizeof(book.minit)];

        lkey = hash(book.last);
        set_ind(authidx);
        if((boff = rk(&lkey)) < 0)
                if(ind_err() != KNF)
                        longjmp(benv, ind_err());
        while(boff >= 0) {
                lseek(bfd, boff + ((char *)book.last - (char *)&book), 0);
                if(read(bfd, author, sizeof(book.last) + sizeof(book.finit) +
                        sizeof(book.minit)) != sizeof(book.last) +
                        sizeof(book.finit) + sizeof(book.minit))
                        longjmp(benv, BFRE);
/**/    if(makupper(author), makupper(book.last),
                strcmp(author, book.last) == 0) {
                        if(isalnum(book.finit)) {
                                if(book.finit == author[sizeof(book.last)])
                                        if(isalnum(book.minit)) {
                                                if(book.minit == author[
                                                        sizeof(book.last)
                                                        + sizeof(book.finit)])

                                                        break;
                                        } else
                                                break;
                        } else
                                break;

        }
```

```
            if((boff = rnk()) < 0)
                    if(ind_err() != KNF)
                            longjmp(benv, ind_err());
        }

        return(boff);

}


/****************************************************************************
 *
 *      finds an entry that matches ISBN
 *
 ****************************************************************************/

long look_isbn()
{

        long boff;

        set_ind(isbnidx);
        if((boff = rk(&book.isbnp)) < 0)
                if(ind_err() != KNF)
                        longjmp(benv, ind_err());

        return(boff);

}
```

```
/***************************************************************************
 *
 *        finds the next book for author or -1 if not found
 *
 ***************************************************************************/

long getn_auth()
{

        long boff;
        char author[21];

        set_ind(authidx);
        do {
                if((boff = rnk()) < 0)
                        if(ind_err() != KNF)
                                longjmp(benv, ind_err());
                        else
                                break;
                lseek(bfd, boff + ((char *)book.last - (char *)&book),
                        0);                                             /*8*/

                if(read(bfd, author, sizeof(book.last)) != sizeof(book.last))
                        longjmp(benv, BFRE);
        } while(makupper(author), makupper(book.last),
                strcmp(author, book.last));                            /*9*/
        return(boff);

}
```

```
/*****************************************************************************
 *
 *          finds an entry based on keyword
 *
 *****************************************************************************/

long look_key(keywd)
char *keywd;
{

        long koff;

        set_ind(kwidx);
        if((koff = rk(keywd)) < 0)
                if(ind_err() != KNF)
                        longjmp(benv, ind_err());

        return(koff);

}
```

```
/************************************************************************
 *
 *         reads a key from keybook index
 *
 ************************************************************************/

long get_key(koff)
long koff;
{

        long boff;

        set_ind(kbidx);
        if((boff = rk(&koff)) < 0)
                if(ind_err() != KNF)
                        longjmp(benv, ind_err());
        return(boff);

}


/************************************************************************
 *
 *         finds next key from keybook index
 *
 ************************************************************************/

long gn_key()
{

        long boff;

        set_ind(kbidx);
        if((boff = rnk()) < 0)
                if(ind_err() != KNF)
                        longjmp(benv, ind_err());
        return(boff);

}
```

```
/***************************************************************************
 *
 *      clears a book from memory
 *
 ***************************************************************************/

void clr_book()
{

        struct genc *gptr;
        struct keyw *kptr;

        book.name[0] = NULL;
        book.last[0] = NULL;

        gptr = ghdr;
        while(gptr) {
                free(gptr);
                gptr = gptr->link;
        }
        ghdr = 0;

        kptr = khdr;
        while(kptr) {
                free(kptr);
                kptr = kptr->link;
        }
        khdr = 0;

}

/********************** end of function ********************************/
```

The open_book( ) and clos_book( ) functions open and close all files in the catalog program. The put_book( ) function sets the current ISAM index to the ISBN index pointer [set_ind( )]. A read key [rk( ) at /*1*/] executes to determine whether the ISBN is in the index, and an error is processed if there is a match.

The current index is set to the book index (/*2*/); a hash value on the book title (book.name) is obtained; and a write-add [wa( )] is attempted, using the hash value as a key. The wa( ) function returns an offset into the book.dat data file. This offset is then stored in boff.

Next, the current index is set to the author index (/*3*/). A hash value is obtained on the author's last name (book.last), and a secondary write-add [swa( )] is performed, using the hash value of the author's last name and the offset obtained from the write-add on the book title. The ISBN index file is updated in the same manner (/*4*/).

The swa( ) function is used because the offset for the book data record was established by the write-add on the book title (in /*2*/). If a write-add were used to enter the author's name, the ISAM library would assign an offset where the library thought the book's data record was located. This value might not agree with the offset obtained when the book was added by its title. Searching for a book by author and obtaining an offset to a different book than the one actually sought is therefore a possibility.

Setting the offset into the general description data file (book.goff at /*5*/) completes the book data record. Then the book record writes to the book.dat data file at the offset obtained from the write-add on the book title (/*2*/). The general description writes to the gencom.dat data file, using the offset stored in geof. This offset is then updated to reflect the new end-of-file (/*6*/). The value of geof is rewritten at the beginning of the general description file.

Every keyword in the keyword index file (keyword.ism) is searched to determine whether the keyword already exists (/*7*/). If it does not exist, a write-add [wa( )] adds the keyword to the index and data files. Secondary write-adds, using the offset obtained from the book title write-add and the rk( ) or wa( ) functions that processed the keyword, are then performed on the bookkey and keybook index files.

The get_book( ) function simply reads a book at offset boff from the data file into memory. Note, however, that more than one file must be read. ISAM searches on the bookkey index file locate all keywords associated with the book.

The `look_book()`, `look_auth()`, `look_isbn()`, and `look_key()` functions search for the book by title, author, ISBN, and keyword, respectively. The `getn_auth()` and `gn_key()` functions locate the next match on the author or keyword. Note how the `lseek()` function uses `boff` and pointer arithmetic on the structure `book` to seek to the last name of the author associated with that book (/*8*/). The casts ensure a scalar of 1.

It is important that you understand how the expression in the `do-while` statement works (/*9*/). This expression consists of three sub-expressions: `makupper(author)`, `makupper(book.last)`, and `strcmp-(author, book.last)`. These subexpressions are evaluated from left to right, with the last subexpression establishing the value of the (total) expression.

Why did we use a complex expression? The two calls to `makupper()` convert the ASCII strings to uppercase for the compare subexpression; they have no other purpose. If a `continue` were used within the `do-while`, the `while` test would still execute correctly. If the two calls to `makupper()` were included at the end of the compound statement enclosed by the `do-while`, however, they would execute only if the `continue` had been encountered earlier.

The `clr_book()` function clears all variables and frees all memory associated with a book record.

Concluding Thoughts

As an exercise, study carefully the code in this chapter, drawing on information presented earlier. For example, if you have difficulty understanding what a particular variable does or how it functions, try constructing an attribute list for it. That should help you understand what is being done.

The best way to learn and retain coding techniques is to wade through someone else's code, then immediately use it in code of your own. Do *not* assume that the code presented here is the best code possible. Try to find other ways of accomplishing the tasks presented and share your alternatives with us.

Appendix A

ISAM Library

This minimanual describes the user functions in the ISAM library.

A. `int ind_build(filename, iflags, ikeylen, ireclen, max_m,`
    `        max_l2, max_l3, max_r);`
    `char *filename, iflags;`
    `unsigned ikeylen, ireclen, max_m, max_l2, max_l3, max_r;`

This function builds an ISAM index based on the passed parameters, where

filename	points to the ASCII filename of the index
iflags	equals True for no duplicate keys; otherwise, is False
ikeylen	is length of a key in bytes
ireclen	is length of a data record in bytes
max_m	is number of elements in a main-level block
max_l2	is number of elements in an l2 block
max_l3	is number of elements in an l3 block
max_r	is number of elements in a recovery block

Notes: `ireclen` may be 0 if only secondary write-adds to an index will be performed.

The function returns 0 if successful. If unsuccessful, the function returns one of the following error codes: `NEM`, `CCF`, `IWE`, or `ICE`.

B. `int ind_create(name, asize, ikeylen, ireclen, dupflag)`
    `char *name;`
    `unsigned asize, ikeylen, ireclen, dupflag;`

This function builds an ISAM index based on the passed parameters, where

`name`	points to the ASCII file name
`asize`	is size of memory allocation for index
`ikeylen`	is key length in bytes
`ireclen`	is data record length in bytes
`dupflag`	is True for no duplicates; otherwise, is False

Notes: `ireclen` may be 0 if only secondary write-adds to an index will be performed.

The function returns 0 if successful. If unsuccessful, the function returns one of the following error codes: `NEM`, `CCF`, `IWE`, or `ICE`.

The function allocates an equal number of entries to all levels of elements. Any remaining memory is added to 13 blocks. Recovery blocks are fixed at 30 elements.

C. `char *ind_open(filename)`
    `char *filename;`

This function opens an index file, allocates storage in memory for working blocks, and fills in index data locations. A pointer to the index memory allocation is returned if the operation is successful; otherwise, a 0 is returned. The function `ind_err()` can determine the specific type of error: `FNF`, `INV`, or `NEM`.

D. `int ind_close(iptr)`
    `char *iptr;`

This function flushes the index referenced by `iptr` and then closes the file. The function returns 0 if the operation is valid or -1 if an error occurs. `ind_err()` returns the error code `IWE` or `ICE`.

E. `void set_ind(iptr)`
    `char *iptr;`

This function sets the current index to `iptr`.

F. `char *get_ind()`

This function returns the current index pointer.

G. `int ind_err()`

This function returns the specific error and is valid only if the
last ISAM function returned an error indication. The following
is a list of error codes:

Value	Mnemonic	Meaning
-1	EOF	End-of-file
1	DUPKEY	Illegal duplicate key
2	IRE	Index read error
3	IWE	Index write error
4	ICE	Index close error
5	KNF	Key not found
6	INV	Index not valid
7	NEM	Not enough memory
8	FNF	File not found
9	INE	Index is empty
10	CCF	Cannot create file

H. `long wa(key)`
    `char *key;`

This function attempts to insert key into the index and to
allocate a record data block. The function returns either the
offset to the data record or -1 on error DUPKEY, IRE, or IWE.

I. `long swa(key,offset)`
    `char *key;`
    `long offset;`

This function attempts to insert key into the index by using the
offset furnished as the record data block offset. The function
returns either the offset furnished or -1 on error DUPKEY, IRE, or
IWE.

J. `long rk(key)`
    `char *key;`

This function searches the index for key. The function returns
either the offset of the first matching key or -1 if an error
occurred (IRE or IWE) or key was not found (KNF).

K. `rnk()`

This function reads the index's next key and compares it to the last processed key. The function returns either the new key's offset if the key matches or -1 for error or no match (IRE, IWE, or KNF).

Note: This function can locate duplicate keys if allowed during `ind_build` or `ind_create`.

L. `long rn(anskey)`
`char *anskey;`

This function reads the next sequential key in the index. If found, the key is placed at `anskey`. The function returns either the entry's offset or -1 on error IRE, IWE, or EOF.

M. `long grk(key,anskey)`
`char *key,*anskey;`

This function searches the index and locates the first `key` equal to or greater than `key`. The function places the located key in `anskey` and returns either the located key's offset or -1 on error IRE, IWE, or KNF.

N. `long grnk(anskey)`
`char *anskey;`

This function locates the next key equal to or greater than the last processed key, places the key in `anskey`, and returns either the key's offset or -1 on error IRE, IWE, or KNF.

O. `long rlfk(anskey)`
`char *anskey;`

This function sets `anskey` to the last processed key and returns either the key's offset or -1 for empty index (INE).

P. `long ind_eof()`

This function places the index at end-of-file and returns either the offset of the last entry or -1 on error IRE, IWE, or INE.

Q. `long ind_bof()`

This function places the index at beginning-of-file and returns the first entry's offset or -1 if error IRE, IWE, or INE has occurred.

Appendix B

Terminal Library

This minimanual describes the user functions in the terminal library.

A. The file `scrdat.c` contains the global variables used by the terminal library. The file must be included in any program that uses this library. If this data can be linked in at a fixed location relative to the base of the program, the install program can directly modify this data on the disk. If a fixed location cannot be determined, then the install program can write a data file to the disk, and the user program can use the function `r_cur()` to read this data into `scrdat.c` variables. Because the data in `scrdat.c` is global, the user program can access these variables to determine the terminal configuration (for example, find the number of lines on a screen.)

B. `int r_cur(name)`
   `char *name;`

   This function opens the data file specified by `name` and reads in the terminal information from that file. The function returns 0 if successful or -1 on error.

C. `int cursor(row,col)`
   `int row,col;`

   This function places the cursor at `row`, `column`, if possible. The function returns either 0 if successful or -1 if the address is not legal. The upper left corner of the terminal is address 0,0.

347

D.   void clrscr()

This function clears the screen and homes the cursor.

E.   void home()

This function homes the cursor to the upper left character position on the screen.

F.   int eraeop(row,col)
     int row,col;

This function erases to end-of-page from row, column and leaves the cursor at row, column. The function returns either 0 if the position is legal or -1 if the position is illegal.

G.   int eraeol(row,col)
     int row,col;

This function erases to end-of-line from row, column and leaves the cursor at row, column. The function returns either 0 if the position is legal or -1 if it is illegal.

H.   int h_int()

This function sets the screen attribute to high intensity at the current cursor position and returns either 0 if the high intensity feature is supported or -1 if it is not supported.

I.   int l_int()

This function sets the screen attribute to low intensity at the current cursor position. If the low intensity feature is supported, a 0 is returned. If it is not supported, a -1 is returned.

Appendix C

Book Catalog Program

The book catalog program is terminal oriented and must be installed by the install program listed in Chapter 3.

This book catalog program catalogs and randomly retrieves books. The version presented in the text does not allow for editing or deleting of data once it has been added to the catalog. The menu-driven catalog program provides the following functions: (1) adding a book to the catalog, (2) retrieving a book by title, (3) retrieving a book by ISBN, (4) retrieving books by author, and (5) retrieving books by keyword.

The data maintained by the catalog includes: (1) title of book (up to 60 characters); (2) author's last name (up to 20 characters); (3) author's first initial; (4) author's middle initial; (5) ISBN (up to 10 characters); (6) a general description (limited only by memory) of the book; and (7) a list (limited only by memory) of keywords, each of which may have up to 20 characters.

In a title search, all alphabetical characters are converted to uppercase prior to comparison. In an author-name search, the last name is converted to uppercase. If the first initial is entered, the first initial must match. If both initials are entered, both must match, or a match on only the last name is performed. Keywords are stored and compared in uppercase.

Appendix D

Linking Order for the Libraries and Programs

Following is the order in which the functions or program modules should be linked to form libraries or executable programs.

The Disk Sort Program (Chapter 2)

`disksort, bsort, ssort, qsort`

(Note that `bsort`, `ssort`, and `qsort` may be added to the library in any order.)

The Terminal Library (Chapter 3)

`rcur, clrscr, eraeop, eraeol, home, hint, lint, cursor, send`

The Installation Program (Chapter 3)

`install, install1, install2, msgins,` and the cursor library

The ISAM Library (Chapter 5)

`isamc, isamb, isam3, isam1, isam2, isam4, isam5, isam, isamd`

The Book Cataloger (Chapter 6)

`scrdat, bookm, bookn, booki, bookf,` the ISAM library, and the cursor library

350

Using the Code in
the UNIX Environment

The following changes should be made to the functions and programs presented in this book to use them effectively in a UNIX environment.

A. `creat( )`

All calls to `creat( )` should be modified to include the appropriate call to `umask( )` or the appropriate value for `pmode`.

B. Terminal Handler and Installation Program

The entire code presented in the terminal handler and installation program in Chapter 3 is inapplicable to UNIX.

C. `ctype.h`

The `ctype.h` header file should be included in the book cataloger files for the definitions of `isalphnum( )`, `isdigit( )`, `tolower( )`, and `toupper( )`.

The definitions of these macros/functions may vary between compilers. The functions and programs presume that `tolower( )` and `toupper( )` check if a conversion is necessary. This means that the function and program calls to `tolower( )` and `toupper( )` assume that the original character is returned if no conversion is needed [that is, `toupper('A')` returns A].

D. Interrupts

The book cataloger and ISAM functions require that Del and other interrupts, such as Ctrl-C, should be trapped by using the `signal()` system call. Without this trapping, the index created by ISAM will be corrupted if the functions are abruptly aborted.

E. `setjmp()` and `longjmp()`

UNIX programmers should include the `setjmp.h` file in the ISAM function files and book catalog program files. In addition, the actual calls for the `setjmp()` and `longjmp()` in the function and program files may require editing to conform to the specifications for your operating system and host CPU.

F. Terminal I/O handling

The libraries `curses` and `termcap` should be used in place of the terminal handlers presented in Chapter 3. Either the `raw()` or `getch()` functions of `curses` or the `ioctl()` function for raw mode should be used for unbuffered input from the terminal.

Using the Code in the CP/M and MS-DOS Environments

Results of Compiler Testing

The functions and programs presented in this book were tested on eight different C compilers (including the Eco-C Compiler) used in the CP/M and MS-DOS worlds. Test results varied widely. The following compilers were tested:

Aztec CII, CP/M and MS-DOS
C-Systems C, CP/M
Computer Innovations C86, MS-DOS
Lattice™ C, MS-DOS
SuperSoft™ C, CP/M
Whitesmith™ C, MS-DOS

Two additional non-CP/M, non-MS-DOS compilers were tested:

Aztec CII, 6502/Apple DOS 3.3
Quantum C, QNX

Aztec CII (Version 1.05g), CP/M, MS-DOS, and 6502®/Apple DOS

Test results were uniform for all three versions.

353

`stdio.h` required minor modification.

`disksort.c` (Chapter 2), the terminal and cursor handlers and install program (Chapter 3), and the book cataloger (Chapter 6) required a different version of `getchar()`. Aztec's `getchar()` is buffered; the programs and functions required nonbuffered input from the console. A direct BIOS call to the terminal for input should be implemented.

The compiler encountered a problem in `install.c` where a pointer value is assigned to the `long offset` variable. A cast to `long` is necessary.

`install.c` (Chapter 3) also required an ASCII-to-long [`atol()`] and is-control [`iscntrl()`] functions not provided with the compiler.

The ISAM functions (Chapter 5) and the book cataloger (Chapter 6) could not be linked and executed because of the lack of `setjmp()` and `longjmp()` functions. These functions will be implemented in Version 1.06 of the compilers, but this version was not available for testing.

C-Systems C, Version 1.18

`msgins.c` (Chapter 3) was too large to compile because of string space restrictions. The file was split into two files, appropriate `extern` declarations were made, and the file was successfully compiled.

`install2.c` involves the subtraction of `BASE` (defined as `0x100`) and a constant. The line

```
    static long offs = 0x103 - BASE;
```

should be broken into a declaration (`static long offs;`) and an assignment [`offs = (long)0x103 - BASE;`].

The function `iscntrl()` must be added.

`getchar()` does buffered input from the terminal. The programs must be modified so that single-character unbuffered I/O from the terminal is possible.

The ISAM functions (Chapter 5) and book cataloger (Chapter 6) could not be linked and executed because of the absence of `setjmp()` and `longjmp()` functions.

Computer Innovations C86, Version 1.32d

All main modules required the inclusion of `stdio.h`.

getchar() does buffered input from the terminal. The programs must be modified so that single-character unbuffered I/O from the terminal is possible.

install.c (Chapter 3) requires an ASCII-to-long [atol()] function that is not provided with the compiler.

The ISAM functions (Chapter 5) and book cataloger (Chapter 6) could not be linked and executed because of the absence of setjmp() and longjmp() functions. These functions are available in the Version 2 of the compiler, but this version was not available for testing.

Lattice C, Version 1.04a

The read/write modes for open() and creat() should be modified to conform to the compiler's specifications.

The atoi(), atol(), iscntrl(), toupper(), and tolower() functions must be added to the library.

The ISAM functions (Chapter 5) and book cataloger (Chapter 6) could not be linked and executed without the setjmp() and longjmp() functions. These functions are available in Version 2 of the compiler, but this version was not available for testing.

Whitesmith's C

Whitesmith's is advertised as a Version 6-compatible compiler. Some modification will be necessary to use the functions and programs in this book.

qsort.c would not compile properly because the compiler does not recognize a static function definition.

All files require that std.h be included before stdio.h to use Kernighan and Ritchie's style of function names.

install.c required _recsize to be defined in the fopen() call.

install.c was not successfully compiled because the preprocessor was unable to handle the macro expansions.

The ISAM functions (Chapter 5) and book cataloger (Chapter 6) could not be linked and executed without the setjmp() and longjmp() functions.

SuperSoft C, Version 1.2.3
Quantum C, QNX

Testing on these programs was incomplete because of compiler difficulties (SuperSoft) and differences in disk format (QNX), neither of which could be investigated before going to press. Consultation with these publishers is recommended to discover what changes must be made to the functions and programs in this book.

Notes for Using Functions and Programs under CP/M and MS-DOS

The main problems noted during the testing of the compilers involved buffered input from the terminal [through the function getchar()], the lack of setjmp() and longjmp() for the ISAM functions, function/program size, and missing or different "standard" functions.

The programmer should test getchar() to ensure that single-character unbuffered input from the terminal is possible. If getchar() is buffered, another function that performs unbuffered input should be written, and the functions and programs in this book modified accordingly.

setjmp() is the function that sets the pointer for an interfunction jump. longjmp() is the function that clears the stack and performs inter-function jump. The ISAM functions can be written without setjmp() and longjmp(), but the resulting code may be too large to compile and execute.

These two functions are CPU, operating system, and compiler specific. If your C compiler has setjmp() and longjmp(), check the compiler's documentation for any modifications that must be made to the functions and programs in this book to make them conform to your compiler.

Most functions and programs in this book will compile, link, and execute on CP/M computers with a 56K TPA. A CP/M 3.0 (CP/M Plus) system with bank switching is preferred to a CP/M 2.2 system because of the extra 2K to 5K RAM space available through bank switching. Generally, MS-DOS computers required 128K of RAM for compilation, linkage, and execution.

To ensure portable code, the ISAM functions in this book make extensive use of casts. This casting increases the size of the source code and may exceed the internal limitations of some compilers. To alleviate some of these problems, you may safely remove many of these casts *if* portability is not necessary and if the compiler properly handles pointer arithmetic and scalar conversions on the data types (K & R specifications).

Many MS-DOS compilers produce a relocatable executable file (.EXE) as their final output. To use the terminal installation program presented in Chapter 3, you must successfully convert these files to binary image files through the use of the EXE2BIN utility provided with MS-DOS.

We assume that your compiler does not convert uppercase letters to lowercase letters in the source code. If the compiler ignores character case, multiply defined labels or names will result.

Miscellaneous Functions

Because of the variations in libraries with C compilers, certain "standard" functions may not be provided or may act differently from compiler to compiler. The following is a list of some of the potential "offenders." All functions assume the ASCII character set.

A. `atol()`

The function commonly missing from most compilers was `atol()`.
The complete source to an `atol()` is presented here.

```
long atol(s)
char *s;
{

                long value;
                int minus;

                while(isspace(*s))
                        s++;
                if(*s == '-') {
                        s++;
                        minus = 1;
                   } else
                        minus = 0;
                value = 0;
                while(isdigit(*s))
                        value = value * 10 + *s++ - '0';
                return(minus ? -value : value);

}
```

B. `int isalpnum(i)`
    `int i;`

This function returns nonzero if `i` is an alphanumeric character;
otherwise, the function returns a zero.

C. `int isctrl(i)`
    `int i;`

This function returns nonzero if `i` is Del (0x7f) or less than Space
(0x20); otherwise, a zero is returned.

D. `int tolower(i)`
    `int i;`

If `i` is an uppercase letter, `tolower()` returns the corresponding
lowercase letter. If `i` is not uppercase, `tolower()` returns `i`.

E. `int toupper(i)`
    `int i;`

If `i` is a lowercase letter, `toupper()` returns the corresponding uppercase letter. If `i` is not lowercase, `toupper()` returns `i`.

F. `char *calloc(nelem, elsize)`
    `unsigned nelem, elsize;`

`calloc()` is the dynamic memory allocator function. `calloc()` returns a character pointer to a block of memory large enough to hold `nelem` number of items of size `elsize`.

`calloc()` was chosen for this book because it exists in most compilers' libraries and because it performs the proper internal alignment on computer systems that require this alignment.

If your compiler does not have `calloc()` but does have `alloc()` [or the UNIX `malloc()` function], `calloc()` can be written to `alloc()` by multiplying the number of elements (`nelem`) by the element size (`elsize`) and using the resulting `unsigned int` in the call to `alloc()`.

G. `void free(ptr)`
    `char *ptr;`

`free()` is the complement to `calloc()` and frees the memory that was pointed to by the call to `calloc()`. `free()` must be able to free in any order the memory returned by `calloc()`. This means that you must be able to `free()` memory in a different order than that in which you `calloc()` memory.

H. `int creat(filename, mode)`
    `char *filename;`
    `int mode;`

    `int open(filename, mode)`
    `char *filename;`
    `int mode;`

The functions `creat()` and `open()` follow this convention for `mode`:

    0 = read only
    1 = write only
    2 = read/write

Bibliography

Bell Telephone Laboratories, Inc. *UNIX*™ Time-Sharing System. Vol. 1, *UNIX Programmer's Manual*. Revised and Expanded Version. New York: Holt, Rinehart and Winston, 1983.

Burge, W. H. *Recursive Programming Techniques*. Reading, Massachusetts: Addison-Wesley, 1975.

Kernighan, Brian W., and Dennis M. Ritchie. *The C Programming Language*. Englewood Cliffs, New Jersey: Prentice-Hall, Inc., 1978.

Knuth, Donald E. *The Art of Computer Programming*. Vol. 3, *Sorting and Searching*. Reading, Massachusetts: Addison-Wesley, 1973.

Purdum, Jack J. *C Programming Guide*. Indianapolis, Indiana: Que Corporation, 1983.

Index

361

MORE COMPUTER KNOWLEDGE FROM QUE

C Programmer's Library Software
by Jack Purdum, PhD., Tim Leslie, and Alan Stegemoller

These software diskettes contain all the programs found in the book, *C Programmer's Library*. In addition, there is a special bonus program, the Delete Function for ISAM. By using these diskettes, you can save hours of time and effort and be sure the code is accurate.

$124.95
IBM PC format, order #270
8-inch SSSD format, order #271

Other formats available. Call Que for information.

C Programming Guide
by Jack Purdum, Ph.D.

This popular and easy-to-read tutorial provides a thorough foundation in C programming. Example programs illustrate each aspect of the C language, while parallel programs in BASIC allow readers familiar with the BASIC language to grasp quickly the fundamentals of C.

"I recommend this book to anyone interested in learning more about the C language. Read it *before* trying to tackle Kernighan and Ritchie."
—Jerry Pournelle, BYTE Magazine

$17.95
Order #16

Understanding UNIX: A Conceptual Guide
by Paul N. Weinberg and James R. Groff

For business managers, educators, and DP professionals, this book offers a superb introduction to the UNIX operating system. It discusses where UNIX fits in the world of computing, describes the major UNIX features and benefits, and explains the structure of UNIX. The book also includes an explanation of the file system, multiuser capability, and specific uses of UNIX, such as software development, communications, and office support. Not a technical rehash of programmers' manuals, *Understanding UNIX* offers a fresh, comprehensive view of the advantages and limitations of UNIX. Read it and learn why UNIX is becoming the most popular operating system for today's small computers.

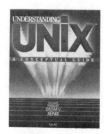

$17.95
Order #120

ORDER TODAY!
Use this order form or call Que at
1-800-428-5331

Please send me the following items:

Item	Title	Price	Quantity	Total
270	C Programmer's Library Software, IBM PC format	$124.95		
271	C Programmer's Library Software, 8-inch SSSD format	$124.95		
272	C Programmer's Library Software, special format*	$129.95		
16	C Programming Guide	$ 17.95		
120	Understanding UNIX: A Conceptual Guide	$ 17.95		
	SUBTOTAL			
	SHIPPING & HANDLING ($1.50 per item)			
	INDIANA RESIDENTS ADD 5% SALES TAX			
	GRAND TOTAL			

METHOD OF PAYMENT:

☐ Check   Charge My: ☐ VISA   ☐ MasterCard   ☐ AMEX

Cardholder's Name_____

Card Number_____

Exp. Date _____

SHIP TO_____

ADDRESS _____

CITY _____ STATE_____ZIP_____

*Special format software: call Que for information and write requested format here:

_____

Que Corporation
7999 Knue Road
Suite 202
Indianapolis, IN 46250

FOLD HERE

REGISTER YOUR COPY OF
C PROGRAMMER'S LIBRARY

If you would like to receive additional information about the *C Programmer's Library* and information about new products relating to the C programming language and the UNIX operating system, complete this registration card and return it to Que Corporation.

Name _____

Address _____

City_____ State_____ Zip_____

Where did you buy your copy of *C Programmer's Library?*

_____

How do you plan to use the programs in this book?

_____

_____

_____

What other kinds of publications about C and UNIX would you be interested in?

_____

_____

Which C compiler do you use?_____

Version Number_____

Which operating system do you use? _____

THANK YOU!

FOLD HERE

_____

_____

_____

C Programmer's Library Registration
Que Corporation
7999 Knue Road
Suite 202
Indianapolis, IN 46250